IET COMPUTING SERIES 30

Trustworthy Autonomic Computing

Other volumes in this series:

Volume 1	**Knowledge Discovery and Data Mining** M.A. Bramer (Editor)
Volume 3	**Troubled IT Projects: Prevention and turnaround** J.M. Smith
Volume 4	**UML for Systems Engineering: Watching the wheels, 2nd Edition** J. Holt
Volume 5	**Intelligent Distributed Video Surveillance Systems** S.A. Velastin and P. Remagnino (Editors)
Volume 6	**Trusted Computing** C. Mitchell (Editor)
Volume 7	**SysML for Systems Engineering** J. Holt and S. Perry
Volume 8	**Modelling Enterprise Architectures** J. Holt and S. Perry
Volume 9	**Model-Based Requirements Engineering** J. Holt, S. Perry and M. Bownsword
Volume 13	**Trusted Platform Modules: Why, when and how to use them** A. Segall
Volume 14	**Foundations for Model-based Systems Engineering: From Patterns to Models** J. Holt, S. Perry and M. Bownsword
Volume 15	**Big Data and Software Defined Networks** J.Taheri (Editor)
Volume 18	**Modeling and Simulation of Complex Communication** M. A. Niazi (Editor)
Volume 20	**SysML for Systems Engineering: A Model-Based Approach, 3rd Edition** J.Holt and S. Perry
Volume 22	**Virtual Reality and Light Field Immersive Video Technologies for Real-World Applications** G. Lafruit and M. Tehrani
Volume 23	**Data as Infrastructure for Smart Cities** L. Suzuki and A. Finkelstein
Volume 24	**Ultrascale Computing Systems** J. Carretero, E. Jeannot and A. Zomaya
Volume 25	**Big Data-Enabled Internet of Things** M. Khan, S. Khan, A. Zomaya (Editors)
Volume 26	**Handbook of Mathematical Models for Languages and Computation** A. Meduna, P. Horáček, M. Tomko
Volume 29	**Blockchains for Network Security: Principles, technologies and applications** H. Huang, L. Wang, Y. Wu, K. R. Choo (Editors)
Volume 32	**Network Classification for Traffic Management: Anomaly detection, feature selection, clustering and classification** Z. Tari, A. Fahad, A. Almalawi and X. Yi
Volume 33	**Edge Computing: Models, technologies and applications** J.Taheri and S. Deng (Editors)
Volume 34	**AI for Emerging Verticals: Human-robot computing, sensing and networking** M. Z. Shakir and N. Ramzan (Editors)
Volume 35	**Big Data Recommender Systems Vol 1 & 2** O. Khalid, S. U. Khan, A. Y. Zomaya (Editors)
Volume 37	**Handbook of Big Data Analytics Vol 1 & 2** V. Ravi and A. K. Cherukuri (Editors)
Volume 39	**ReRAM-based Machine Learning** H. Y, L. Ni and S. M. P. Dinakarrao
Volume 40	**E-learning Methodologies: Fundamentals, technologies and applications** M. Goyal, R. Krishnamurthi and D. Yadav (Editors)
Volume 44	**Streaming Analytics: Concepts, architectures, platforms, use cases and applications** P. Raj, C. Surianarayanan, K. Seerangan and G. Ghinea (Editors)
Volume 44	**Streaming Analytics: Concepts, architectures, platforms, use cases and applications** P. Raj, A. Kumar, V. García Díaz and N. Muthuraman (Editors)
Volume 54	**Intelligent Network Design Driven by Big Data Analytics, IoT, AI and Cloud Computing** S. Kumar, G. Mapp and K. Cergiz (Editors)
Volume 115	**Ground Penetrating Radar: Improving sensing and imaging through numerical modelling** X. L. Travassos, M. F. Pantoja and N. Ida

Trustworthy Autonomic Computing

Thaddeus Eze

The Institution of Engineering and Technology

Published by The Institution of Engineering and Technology, London, United Kingdom

The Institution of Engineering and Technology is registered as a Charity in England & Wales (no. 211014) and Scotland (no. SC038698).

First published 2022

The Institution of Engineering and Technology
Futures Place
Kings Way, Stevenage
Herts, SG1 2UA, United Kingdom

www.theiet.org

British Library Cataloguing in Publication Data
A catalogue record for this product is available from the British Library

ISBN 978-1-78561-883-3 (hardback)
ISBN 978-1-78561-884-0 (PDF)

Typeset in India by Exeter Premedia Services Private Limited
Printed in the UK by CPI Group (UK) Ltd, Croydon
Cover Image: MF3d / E+ via Getty Images

Dedication

To the memories of mum and dad. To my siblings. To my lovely wife, Ezinne, and our three boys.

Contents

About the Author

Thaddeus Eze is a cybersecurity senior lecturer and researcher at the Computer Science Department, University of Chester, UK. He is the programme leader for MSc Cybersecurity (Conversion) and the postgraduate assessment officer for the Computer Science department. His research interests include cybersecurity awareness and training, trustworthy autonomic computing, ethical hacking, cryptography, and digital forensics. He is a member of CIISec and was the Vice Chair of the IEEE Young Professionals, UK & Ireland Section from 2014 to 2022. He's the Convener and organiser of the IEEE UK & Ireland YP Postgraduate STEM Research Symposium (three successful editions already organised). He was actively involved in organising the first ever UK Pitch Bootcamp and the IEEE Professional Development Networking Workshop 2017. He is a 2004 graduate of Anambra State University, Nigeria, with BSc (Upper 2nd Class) in Computer Science. He holds an MSc (with Distinction, 2010) in Mobile Computing and Communications and a PhD in Trustworthy Autonomics from the University of Greenwich, London, UK.

Preface

Computing systems are growing exponentially in terms of increasing heterogeneity, scale, and ubiquity, and are becoming exceedingly complex for human management. These systems are getting more pervasive, being embedded in everyday objects, and are exposed to environments where system working conditions are dynamic, uncertain and sometimes, unpredictable. IBM [1] introduced the Autonomic Computing concept in 2001 as a solution for managing such heterogeneously knitted and pervasively ubiquitous systems. The autonomic computing concept seeks to reduce the complexity of system management and maintenance by shifting the responsibility for low-level tasks from humans to the system while allowing humans to concentrate on high-level tasks. This is achieved by building self-managing systems that are generally capable of self-configuring, self-healing, self-optimising, and self-protecting (self-CHOP). These self-CHOP capabilities are commonly considered the foundational autonomic functionalities of an autonomic computing system. Autonomic computing systems or autonomic systems are also known as self-managing systems

The autonomic computing concept is now well understood. However, there has been limited progress towards trustworthy autonomic computing. This book seeks to bring focus on the issues of autonomics trustworthiness – *trustworthiness* is defined in this book to mean *a quality that enables the user to be confident that an autonomic system will remain correct in the face of any possible contexts and environmental inputs and sequences of these*. In other words, it enables users to be confident that an autonomic system will do what it is expected to do over short- and longer-term time frames. This book makes the case for autonomic system trustworthiness, exposes the issues therein and offers ways (methods and techniques) of achieving trustworthy autonomic systems. Case example scenarios are used to demonstrate these methods and techniques. I believe that the ultimate goal of autonomic computing should transcend the achievement of self-management to include the achievement of consistency and reliability of results through self-management.

> ***[trustworthiness* is defined in this book to mean *a quality that enables the user to be confident that an autonomic system will remain correct in the face of any possible contexts and environmental inputs and sequences of these]***

Despite the progress in autonomic computing research, there are still significant challenges in the area of trustworthiness. These include the lack of support for inbuilt mechanisms for trustworthiness in the design methods used for the technology, the limitations regarding the way autonomic systems are validated, and the lack of self-monitoring support that is capable of achieving stability over longer term time frames. Without addressing trustworthiness, there is the possibility of overall inconsistency in the autonomic system despite autonomic control decisions being validated within the internally defined logical boundary. There are also the issues of autonomic interoperability of co-existing autonomic elements in multi-element systems. Autonomic systems, designed in isolation, should be able to cooperatively work together towards a common goal, and efficiently too, in a mutli-system environment.

An analysis-by-problem approach, introduced in Chapter 2, has been used to show the pattern of how the trustworthy autonomic challenge is being tackled by the autonomic computing research community. This shows that only a few studies have identified trustworthiness as a challenge and fewer have proposed actual methodologies relating to validation, trustworthiness and certification – of which the majority are application-dependent.

The coverage of this book includes foundations of autonomic computing and trustworthy autonomics, speaking autonomics [definition of autonomics terminology], level of autonomics, autonomic architecture, trustworthy autonomics, runtime self-validation and conformance testing, autonomics enabled techniques, logic and functions, and interoperability. The breakdown of the different chapters is as follows:

- Chapter 1: Trustworthy Autonomics Primer
  This chapter gives a low-level overview of the autonomic computing concept and leads a general introductory discussion on trustworthy autonomic computing. Focus includes making the case for trustworthy autonomic computing, the state-of-the-art in research, relevant tools, and terminologies.

- Chapter 2: Evolution of Autonomic Computing
  This chapter takes a holistic view of the entire field of autonomic computing research in order to gain a clearer picture of the need for and lack of effort towards trustworthy autonomic computing. It also establishes an understanding of the level of work that has already gone into the autonomic computing research, how that can be harnessed, and where the work needs to be concentrated in order to achieve trustworthiness.

- Chapter 3: Autonomic Enabling Techniques
  Autonomic enabling techniques are tools for designing and delivering desired autonomic functionalities. This chapter presents some of these techniques and shows examples of how they can be used to achieve relevant autonomic computing features.

- Chapter 4: Trustworthy Autonomic Computing
  For complete reliance on autonomic computing systems, the human user will need a level of *trust* and confidence that these systems will satisfy specified

requirements and will not fail. This chapter looks at the differences between Trustworthy Autonomic Computing and Trusted (or Trustworthy) Computing and then presents a framework for a trustworthy autonomic architecture which forms the basis for several implementations in this book.

- Chapter 5: TrAArch Implementations
  This chapter provides an implementation and empirical analysis of a new trustworthy autonomic architecture (TrAArch) framework. This framework has inbuilt mechanisms and instrumentation to support trustworthiness. Two experimental demonstrations – an easy-to-understand autonomic marketing scenario and a more complex self-adapting datacentre resource request and allocation management case scenario are used.

- Chapter 6: Multi-agent Interoperability
  The deployment of autonomic systems has grown over time, both in scale and ubiquity, leading to situations where more autonomic managers (agents) could be integrated to achieve a common goal. This chapter provides an overview of interoperability solutions and makes case for a proposed solution that is suitable for trustworthy autonomic computing. An implementation and empirical analysis of the proposed solution is presented.

- Chapter 7: Level of Autonomicity
  Level of autonomicity is one of the pillars of trustworthy autonomic computing as it ensures that autonomic systems are defined in a universal language. This chapter introduces the concept of measuring the level of autonomicity (*LoA*) for autonomic systems, reviews some of the existing approaches for measuring level of autonomicity, and presents a quantitative technique for measuring *LoA*.

Why the Book

I decided to write this book because it was the type of book I wished I had had when I started my research in trustworthy autonomics. One of my early studies [2], during my PhD, revealed that the early stage research in autonomic computing focused mainly on stating the problem and challenges of an ever-growing system complexity, the need for solution and justifying autonomicity as that solution, developing and applying autonomic techniques, and identifying and solving specific problems in isolation. There were limited published information, especially books, on autonomic computing and absolutely no book on trustworthy autonomics when I first started my research. Though there are now more books, especially journal compilations, and informative websites on self-managing systems and autonomic computing, there is still a very limited number of books on trustworthy autonomic computing. I still find it difficult to find books aimed at beginners and newcomers in trustworthy autonomic computing. Beginners still struggle with understanding where to start, what to read first and where to get the expected prerequisite skills.

This book does not have abbreviations, making it easy to read and work with. It is intended to be an ideal guide for independent study. It includes sample program codes for the relevant in-text activities, simulations and use-case/case study demonstrations. These easy-to-understand sample codes will help readers easily walk through the examples as well as design their own experiments.

This book uses simple examples and well-documented diagrams and images to explain techniques and processes. The examples used in this book are clearly presented and easy to understand, making them accessible to all. Each chapter begins with an introduction and explains how it fits into and supports the beginner's understanding of trustworthy autonomics.

This book has been planned to have a very wide appeal and is targeted at:

- Early researchers in autonomic and trustworthy autonomic computing. This offers a go-to book for foundational knowledge, proof of concepts and novel trustworthy autonomic techniques and approaches.
- Teachers and students of autonomic computing and multi-agent systems who need an easy-to-use text with sample codes, exercises, use-case demonstrations; it is also suitable for self-teaching.
- Early programmers who require accessible pseudocode and code examples for application demonstrations.
- Others studying or researching other areas of computer science and engineering requiring a basic grounding in the techniques presented in the book.

Another interesting aspect of this book is that some of the techniques explained here are generic and can be used in other fields. For example, Chapter 3 presents autonomic enabling techniques most of which are relevant concepts in different fields of study. These concepts are presented, with simple examples, in ways that clearly show how they work and how they can be implemented. This can help in developing understanding of these concepts and ideas of how they can be adapted in other application domains.

Case studies and simulations are presented in a way that makes them easy to be replicated. For simulations and some example demonstrations, enough details are provided that will allow users to replicate the experiments and compare results. To support this, this book comes with the simulator (TrAArch Simulator) that was used for the experiments in this book. The simulator is well-documented and supports the creation of a wide range of experimental scenarios. The documentation helps in understanding the design of the simulator (in case if someone wants to design theirs) and how to use it for different experiments.

This book draws from my PhD research, to build on identified gaps in relevant autonomic and trustworthy autonomic computing topic areas and establish grounded understanding in these areas.

Acknowledgments

I would like to thank the IET for the invitation to write this book and their patience despite the numerous missed deadlines. The making of this book was fraught with many challenges – no thanks to the Covid-19 pandemic. Glad that we are here at last.

Many thanks to my lovely family for their immeasurable support and understanding throughout this project and beyond. To my wife, Ezinne, who makes me look like a superdad. Throughout my countless busy times she maintains sanity at home and makes raising a family look easy. To our first son, my pride, Chisom (10), who asked all the questions and always wanted to help. Special thanks to him for making the objects used in this book's chapter photos. To our special and smart boy, Chidia (7) the handsome one, and to the 'Chairman' of the house, Chidera (1), for the joy you boys bring. The joy of meeting you at the door is always a natural therapy for a stressful day. Thank you, and thank you again!

I would also like to thank Dr Richard Anthony for encouraging me to take on this project. As my PhD supervisor, you introduced me to the autonomic computing research. Your support was top-notch that I came from knowing nothing about autonomic computing to being invited to write a book on the topic.

Above all, many thanks to God!

Downloadable material

As a supporting material for this book, a simulator is provided and can be downloaded from https://drive.google.com/file/d/1uOKVKkB8lFG8h4MhsjOmPFwFjDWP0vLd/view?usp=share_link (https://bit.ly/3hzGFqI). Note that this is an executable file and so your computer might flag it as a security threat. The TrAArch simulator is an application developed in C# for simulating autonomic managers for datacentres. This is a direct demonstration of the TrAArch presented in Chapter 4. The simulator can be used to evaluate the performance of three autonomic managers. For help or information regarding the simulator, please contact thaddeusonyinyeeze@gmail.com.

Chapter 1

Trustworthy autonomics primer

This chapter will give a low-level overview of the autonomic computing concept and lead a general introductory discussion on trustworthy autonomic computing. Focus will include making the case for trustworthy autonomic computing, the state-of-the-art in research, relevant tools and terminologies.

There are a wide range of views on meaning, architecture, methodology and implementations in trustworthy autonomic computing which will be addressed. These will be covered under two core areas of *introduction to autonomic computing* and *foundations of trustworthy autonomics*.

To help the reader's appreciation of trustworthy autonomic computing, it is important to first understand the meaning of autonomic computing and what makes a system autonomic. In this chapter you will learn:

- The general functionalities of an autonomic system
- The building blocks and internal structure of autonomic elements
- Why trustworthy autonomic computing is necessary
- The meaning of key autonomic terminologies

1.1 Introduction to autonomic computing

This section gives a general overview of autonomic computing and what it means to say that a system is *autonomic*. To start with, the differences between the keywords of *automation, autonomy* (*autonomous*) and *autonomic* (*autonomicity*) are discussed in order to provide relevant working definitions. These definitions establish how these terms are used in this book.

1.1.1 Autonomic computing definitions

Because terms do have a wide range of definitions, it is important to clearly differentiate these to help the understanding of the reader of this book. The terms **automation**, **autonomy** and **autonomic** all refer to processes that may be completed, to various extents, without human intervention. Each of these seeks to remove human intervention as much as possible – and this has been achieved in different degrees.

Automation deals with replacing repetitive manual processes with technology. This technology, e.g., a software, hardware, systems or a combination of all, follows a well-defined sequence of steps to complete the same task. In automation, the processes are well-known and perfected. Some level of human participation is still required. However, automation makes processes faster, efficient and reduces the possibility of error. For example, most car factories have replaced the manual assembly of car parts by humans with robotic arms. Figure 1.1, a MeArm robot arm that I assembled as part of a study, illustrates a robot arm that can be assembled to automate a particular task.

Let's assume that the task here is to grab an object and move it from position A to position B, defined by the simple algorithm:

```
Check ObjectPosition
Condition: ObjectInPositionA
if Condition = True
    RobotArm: GrabObject
    RobotAction: MoveObject-To-PositionB
else
    RobotAction: NoAction
```

Algorithm 1.1

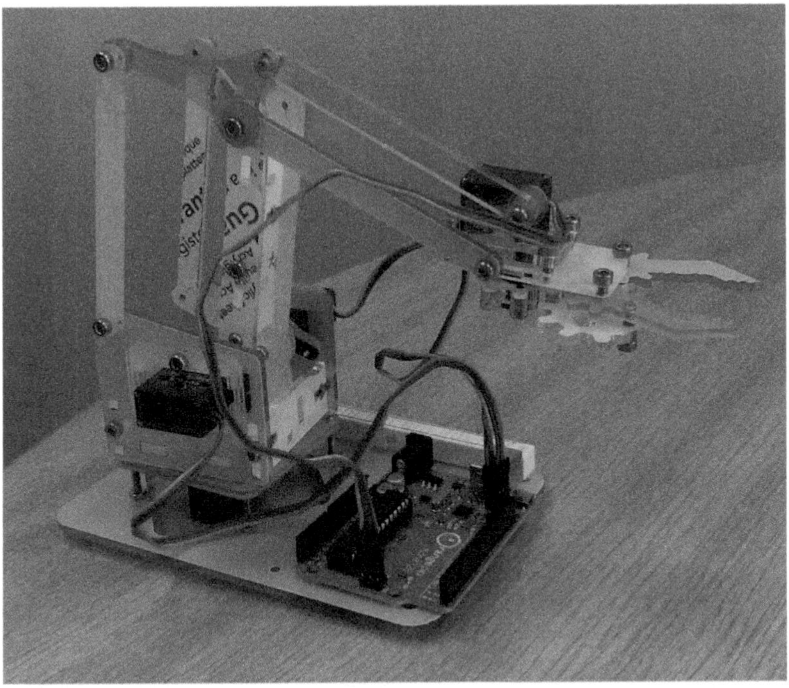

(a)

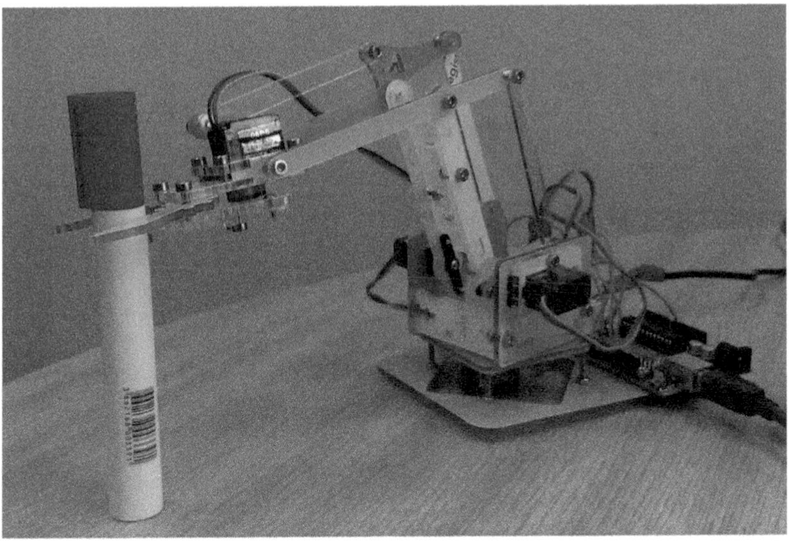

(b)

Figure 1.1 *MeArm robot arm. This is an open-source robot arm design that could be built from a small number of components. Its movement is controlled by four small motors.*

Instead of having a human to regularly monitor and move any object found in position A to position B, this task can be automated using a robotic arm configured with Algorithm 1.1. As long as there is no obstacle in its path, the robot arm will always move any object in position A to position B.

Autonomy goes beyond automation to include some level of independent decision-making. It focuses on a particular task and *guides itself* (self-direction) towards achieving that task. It involves independent decision-making based on coded logic (e.g., Algorithm 1.1 with some additional tweaks) and real-time events. Using the robot arm example, if there is an obstacle in its path, the robot arm automatically decides how best to achieve the task of moving the object from position A to position B regardless of the obstacle. The robot arm decides how to navigate around the obstacle (e.g., move further left, raise the arm higher, alert human administrator, remove the obstacle) for the success of the task. Autonomous systems are *context-aware* systems.

Autonomic adds another layer of human independence to autonomous. It involves context-aware decision-making processes for the success of a particular task and the successful operation of the system. The robot arm in Figure 1.1 is operated by four different motors. If, e.g., one of the motors stops working or malfunctions, meaning that the robot could not turn left, the robot could still achieve the task by turning right (assuming there is 360° turning capability) all the way to the desired position – this is known as *fault tolerance*. Given a particular goal, whereas the system may have the self-governance/self-direction (autonomy) to decide between relevant parameters for achieving that goal, autonomic capability ensures that the system continues to operate under uncertain conditions and to cope with dynamic changes in the environment [3]. Autonomic systems are *self-managing* systems. The measure (or classification) of autonomic systems, according to the degree of autonomicity achieved, is covered in Chapter 7.

The idea of autonomic computing is to reduce the complexity of system management and maintenance by shifting the responsibility for low-level tasks from the user to the system while allowing the user to concentrate on high-level tasks. This is achieved by building self-managing systems that are capable of self-configuring, self-healing, self-optimising and self-protecting – these are known as the autonomic functionalities and are discussed in section 1.1.2. With such capabilities, self-managing (autonomic) systems are able to automatically manage mundane tasks in the background while still focusing on achieving the goal of the system. Examples of such tasks include addressing runtime behavioural, structural or code errors as well as unplanned configuration tasks and spontaneous trend shifts. These are dynamic, unpredictable events and should be handled in the background. This approach is similar to the biological nervous system where, e.g., breathing rate, heartbeat, sweating, are regulated without the consciousness of the mind [4] so that activities like deciding where to go and how to get there can gain more focus.

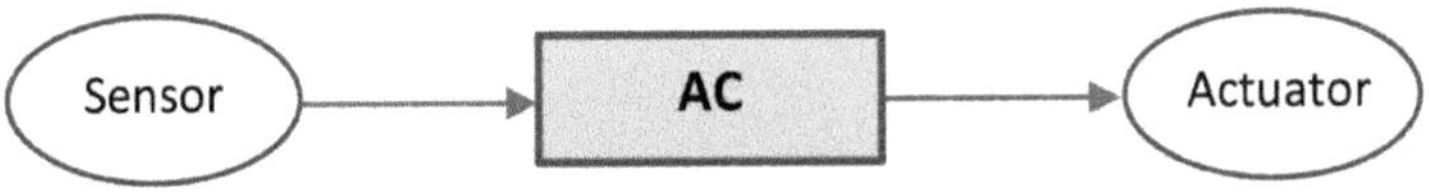

Figure 1.2 *High-level autonomic system structure. The sensor receives inputs (context information) into the system, and the AC analyses these inputs and based on the outcome of the analysis decides on an adaptation action that is then executed by the actuator.*

The high-level design of the internal structure of an autonomic system is shown in Figure 1.2. The sensor represents the source of contextual information (e.g., unforeseen events and changes in the system's environment). These received information are analysed by the autonomic controller (AC) and based on the analysis, actions are decided that are executed by the actuator. In the end, instead of directly controlling the system, the human operator defines general rules and policies, for the AC, to guide the self-management process of the system. Autonomics technology is suitable for large scale and heterogeneous systems with dynamic processes of sometimes unknown and unpredictable outcomes.

Many techniques, e.g., machine learning, policy autonomics, fuzzy logic and utility functions have been used to build autonomic systems – some of these are covered in Chapter 3. There are also various autonomic architecture designs incorporating dynamic adaptation solutions, building on the traditional MAPE (monitor, analyse, plan and execute) control loop. The MAPE control (Figure 1.3), originally described in Reference [1], gives the basic view of the design and mechanisms of autonomic systems. The monitor component receives status updates of the managed system, filters and then passes data received to the analyse function. The data are analysed and the suggested decision (course of action) is passed to the plan function. The plan function maps out how the decision will be implemented and then passes it to the execute function for execution.

Autonomic system can also be seen as a **multi-agent system**, comprising of different *agents* known as ***autonomic elements***, working together to achieve a particular goal – the intended or original goal of the system. 'Multi-agent systems' is a generic term referring to systems consisting of different sub-systems (agents) that cooperate (interact) with each other in order to achieve a common goal. The idea of a system with several components working together towards a common goal has been applied to an increasing number of domains including distributed systems, autonomic systems, supply chains, networks of networks and so on.

1.1.2 Autonomic functionalities

Autonomic functionalities are the building blocks of autonomic systems. These are the characteristics or functional areas that define the capabilities of autonomic systems. Autonomic functionalities can be emergent, and these vary (or are

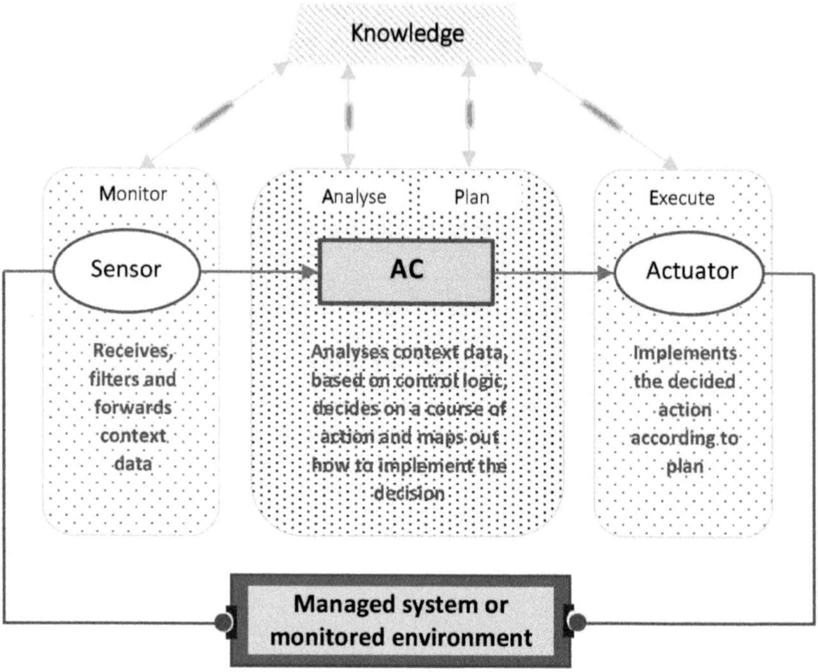

Figure 1.3 MAPE autonomic architecture. This is based on the monitor, analyse, plan and execute (MAPE) control loop.

defined) according to application instances. Although there is an ongoing debate on the composition of autonomic functionalities, and the list is substantially growing [3, 5], the self-CHOP (self-Configuring, self-Healing, self-Optimising and self-Protecting) functionalities remain the original/core and most widely accepted four functionalities. There are other more generic, or evolving, functionalities (e.g., self-stabilising, self-aware, self-regulating) and these are denoted as self-* functionalities.

To provide a working knowledge, we will focus on the self-CHOP functionalities in this section. This is because a computing system is said to be autonomic if it is capable of demonstrating at least one of these four functionalities/attributes.

1.1.2.1 Self-configuration

A system is self-configuring when it is able to automate its own installation and setup according to high-level goals. This means that the system is capable of carrying out automatic configuration of components. For example, when a new component is introduced into an autonomic system or a multi-system environment, it registers itself so that other components can easily interact with it.

Corporate systems, like data centres and networks, are examples of large-scale system environments with heterogeneity of devices, services, platforms and vendors where new installations and upgrades could lead to complex compatibility issues. An autonomic system would rely on high-level policies, representing business-level objectives, to configure its components and sub-systems to automatically and seamlessly adjust to new environmental conditions.

Examples
Most times, when a new compatible component is attached to a network, it gets automatically configured and deployed. The work of the Dynamic Host Configuration Protocol (DHCP) is an example of self-configuration. The DHCP automatically assigns IP addresses and other network configuration parameters to each network device on the network. This prepares these devices and makes them able to communicate with other devices on the network, without the help of the human user. Another example is the auto configuration capability of operating systems. When a new device, say a printer, is attached to a computer, some operating systems are able to automatically find and install the printer's driver and get it ready for use. Self-configuration is usually behind the general '*plug and play*' concept.

1.1.2.2 Self-healing

A system is self-healing when it is able to detect errors or symptoms of potential errors by monitoring its own platform and automatically initiating remediation. Fault tolerance is a typical example of self-healing. It allows the system to continue its operation possibly at a reduced level instead of stopping completely as a result of a part failure. Fault-tolerant solutions may require a level of redundancy that allows the system some options to switch to when necessary.

In the early years of technological innovation, systems were designed to display error messages and hang up if problems occur. Modern systems, with fault tolerance capabilities, are able to overcome, repair or isolate errors and continue.

Examples
Self-healing capabilities have evolved over the centuries – for example, from the ancient Romans who used self-healing concrete that allowed crystals to grow into cracks to repair them to modern unmanned spacecraft that are capable of repairing themselves to continue their mission. Some modern cars have a safety feature that allows the car to be driven, at a reduced restricted speed when a major component fails, as it may be dangerous for the car to come to a sudden halt, say in a motorway. This attribute enables an autonomic system to focus on achieving its original goal, set out at the beginning, regardless of unexpected contextual problems.

1.1.2.3 Self-optimisation

A system is self-optimising when it is capable of adapting to meet current requirements and also of taking necessary actions to self-adjust (adjustment to preferences) to better its performance. Resource management (e.g., load balancing) is a typical example of self-optimisation. A component of a system may be overloaded to the point that it introduces delay and bottleneck that ultimately affects the goal of the system. A self-optimising system has the capability of maximising its resources in a way that avoids overloading of its components so that it concentrates on achieving its original goal.

Example
A self-optimising autonomic system would self-adjust its behaviour, without affecting its intended goal, in the face of uncertain events – for example, changing workloads, components, demands and external conditions. The system does not always succeed but the idea here is to attempt to stay on achieving the intended goal, regardless of unplanned performance challenges.

1.1.2.4 Self-protection

A system is self-protecting when it is able to detect and protect itself from attacks by automatically configuring and tuning itself to achieve security and data protection goals. It may also be capable of proactively preventing a security breach through its knowledge based on previous occurrences. While self-healing is reactive, self-protecting is proactive. Autonomic systems are capable of *learning* from past events and be able to proactively defend themselves against malicious and non-malicious attacks/problems unresolved by the self-healing component.

Example
With self-protection, the system is able to detect and stop threats that are capable of *harming* its operations. An intrusion prevention system (IPS) is a typical example. The idea here is the ability of the system to continuously monitor its operating environment, identify possible threats that may mitigate against its goal, gather information about the threats (that will be useful in subsequent similar situations) and stop them from preventing the system from achieving its goal.

Note that while *self-CHOP* and *self-** may be used interchangeably in different texts, self-CHOP refers to the traditional four autonomic functionalities (the self-Configuring, self-Healing, self-Optimising and self-Protecting functionalities) and self-* refers to generic autonomic functionalities that comprise of both the self-CHOP functionalities and any other possible or application-dependent functionalities (e.g., self-stabilising, self-aware, self-regulating, etc.). For more on the above definitions, see References 6–8.

1.1.3 The autonomic computing system

For a generalised context, it is important to introduce some useful terminologies that may be easily misunderstood. Some of these have been used interchangeably in other texts and this can be confusing. Let us follow on from section 1.1.1, referring to Figure 1.3, Figure 1.4 gives us a clearer definition of an autonomic system.

An autonomic element (Figure 1.4) will consist of at least one managed system and one autonomic manager who controls, manages and represents the managed system(s). An autonomic manager (Figure 1.4b) will comprise of relevant resources and tools required to autonomically control a non-autonomic system. The managed system could be a CPU, a printer, a database, a window blind, a car, a heating system, a data centre, a business process, etc. An autonomic system could also be an interactive collection of autonomic elements that interact with each other, including the environment, via their autonomic managers. This '*environment*' may also include a touch-point through which the system programmer could interact with the system. Self-management of the autonomic elements' internal behaviour and relationships with others will be based on the policies established by the human (e.g., the user, programmer) or other elements from the internal self-management of the individual autonomic elements – just as the social intelligence of an ant colony arises largely from the interactions among individual ants. A distributed, service-oriented infrastructure will support autonomic elements and their interactions.

The autonomic manager is powered by the *manager logic*. This is a term used in this book to describe the actual individual control logic employed by autonomic managers in order to achieve stated system performance goals. It explains the inbuilt functions and logic of autonomic managers. This is not a formal autonomic terminology but is specifically used in this book to explain the technology and algorithms behind the workings of autonomic managers.

1.2 Foundations of trustworthy autonomics

This section will lead a general introductory discussion on trustworthy autonomic computing, why it is important and the state of the art in research. The autonomic computing concept has received strong interest amongst the academic and industrial research communities since its introduction in 2001. It is now well-understood and established across an ever-widening spectrum of application domains. However, there has been limited progress towards trustworthy autonomic computing – a quality that enables the confidence of the user in the ability of the autonomic system to remain correct in the face of any possible contexts and environmental inputs and sequences of these.

The main idea put forward in this book is that trustworthiness (and any other desired autonomic capability) should be conceived at the design stage. This means that the architecture should be flexible (and yet robust) enough to provide instrumentations that allow designers to specify processes to achieve desired goals. It then follows that we need to rethink the autonomic architecture. This is the basis of the trustworthy autonomics solution presented in Chapters 4 and 5. This section discusses a general review of early research effort towards trustworthy autonomics – that

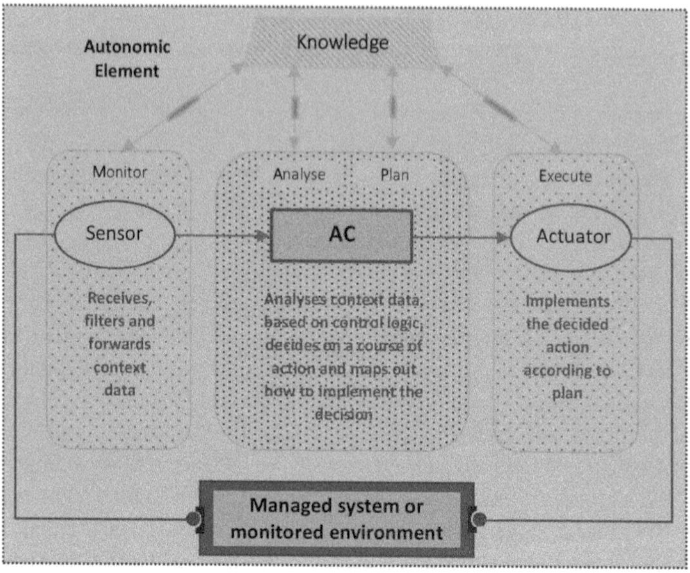

(a)

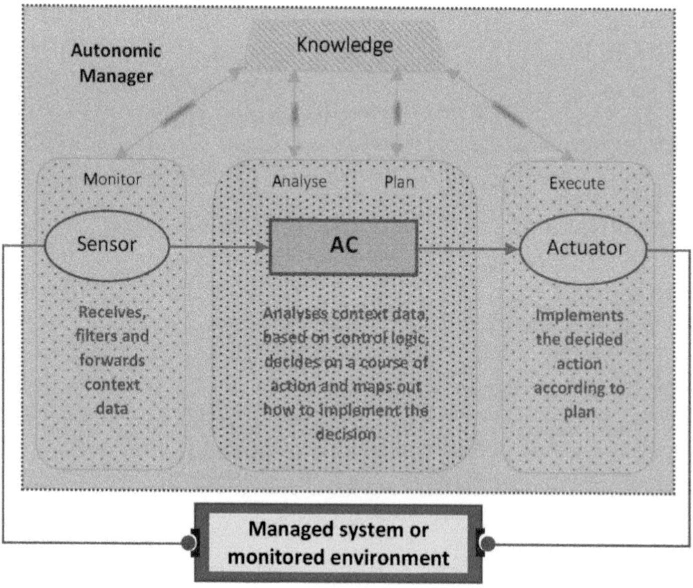

(b)

Figure 1.4 *(a) Autonomic element – comprising the entire system, including the managed or monitored target (b) Autonomic manager – excludes the managed or monitored target*

includes validation, trustworthiness and certification and then presents the pillars of trustworthy autonomic systems.

1.2.1 Towards trustworthy autonomics

Let us start with a general overview of early research towards trustworthy autonomics, covering validation, trustworthiness (sometimes referred to as reliability or dependability in other works) and certification.

Chan *et al.* [9] ask the critical question of '*How can we trust an autonomic system to make the best decision*?' and propose a '*trust*' architecture to win the trust of autonomic system users. The proposal is to introduce *trust* into the system by assigning an 'instantaneous trust index' (ITI) to each execution of a system's autonomic manager – where ITI could be computed, e.g., by examining what fraction of the actions, suggested by the autonomic manager, the user accepts unchanged, or by examining how extensive the changes that the user makes to the suggested actions are. The overall trust index, which reflects the system user's level of trust in the autonomic manager, is computed as the function $f(ITIi)$ where $i = 1, 2, 3, \ldots$ and *ITIi* are the individual ITIs for each autonomic manager execution. This kind of solution is favoured in this book as it considers trust as architecture-based and also defines trust in the language of the user – it is the user who needs to be satisfied that the autonomic system is making and executing the best (beneficial) decisions. However, this method will be overly complex (and may be out of control) in large systems with multiple autonomic managers if the user is required to moderate every single autonomic manager-suggested action. In such systems, some of the autonomic manager's decisions are not transparent to the human user.

Another effort that supports the idea that dependability should be architecture-based, i.e., conceived at design time and not retrofitted to systems, is the work in Reference [10]. Hall and Rapanotti [10] in proposing an Assurance-Driven Design posit that engineering design should include the detailing of a design for a solution that guarantees satisfaction of set requirements and the construction of arguments to assure users that the solution will provide the needed functionality and qualities. The key point here is that trustworthiness is all about securing the confidence of the user (that the system will do what it says) and the way to achieve this is by getting the design (architecture) right. This is also the main thrust of this book. Shuaib *et al.* [11] propose a framework that will allow for proper certification of autonomic systems. Central to this framework is an alternative autonomic architecture based on Intelligent Machine Design (IMD) which draws from the human autonomic nervous system.

Shinji *et al.* [12] propose a policy verification and validation framework that is based on model checking to verify the validity of administrator's specified policies in a policy-based system because a known performing policy may lead to erroneous behaviour if the system, in any aspect, is changed slightly. The framework is based on checking the consistency of the policy and the system's defined model or characteristics. This is another important aspect of the proposed solution in this book – validation is done with reference to the system's defined goal. A trustworthy autonomic grid computing architecture is presented in Reference 13. This is to be enabled through a proposed fifth self-* functionality, self-regulating. Self-regulating capability is able to derive policies from high-level policies and requirements at runtime to regulate self-managing behaviours. One concern here is that proposing a fifth autonomic functionality to regulate the self-Configuring (self-CHOP), Healing, Optimising, and Protecting functionalities as a solution to autonomic system trustworthiness assumes that trustworthiness can be achieved when all four functionalities perform 'optimally'.

> ***[One concern here is that proposing a fifth autonomic functionality to regulate the self-Configuring (self-CHOP), Healing, Optimising, and Protecting functionalities as a solution to autonomic system trustworthiness assumes that trustworthiness can be achieved when all four functionalities perform 'optimally']***

This assumption is not entirely correct. The self-CHOP functionalities alone do not guarantee trustworthiness in autonomic systems. For example, the self-CHOP functionalities do not address validation that is a key factor in autonomic system trustworthiness.

Another idea is that trustworthiness is achieved when a system is able to provide accounts of its behaviour to the extent that the user can understand and trust. But these accounts must, amongst other things, satisfy three requirements: provide a representation of the policy guiding the accounting, provide some mechanism for validation and provide accounting for system's behaviour in response to user demands [14]. The system's actions are transparent to the user and also allow the user, if required, the privilege of authorising or not authorising a particular process. This is a positive step (at least it provides the user a level of confidence and trust) but also important is a mechanism that ensures that any 'authorised' process does not lead to undependable or misleading results.

> ***[This is a positive step (at least it provides the user a level of confidence and trust) but also important is a mechanism that ensures that any 'authorised' process does not lead to undependable or misleading results]***

This is one aspect not considered by many research efforts. There are possibilities of erratic behaviour, which is not healthy for the system, despite the autonomic manager's decisions being approved. This aspect is addressed in the solution proposed in this book.

Heo and Abdelzaher [15] presented '*AdaptGuard*', a software designed to guard adaptive systems from instability resulting from system disruptions. The software is able to infer and detect instability and then intervenes (to restore the system) without actually understanding the root cause of the problem – root-cause-agnostic recovery.

Instability is another aspect addressed in the solution proposed in this book. Because autonomic manager control brevity could lead to instability despite process correctness, it is important to also consider this scenario. Hawthorne *et al.* [16] demonstrate Teleo-Reactive (T-R) programming approach to autonomic software systems and show how T-R technique can be used to detect validation issues at design time and thus reduce the cost of validation issues. T-R programming is similar to Reflective Programming as both techniques allow the development of codes that can modify themselves, i.e., adaptive programs. However, based on conditions and priorities, the code in T-R dynamically adapts without needing to rewrite itself as in Reflection [17]. Also, with Reflection it is possible to modify a code directly while it is running while with T-R, it is impossible to predict what bit of code is running at any given time.

Validation is central to achieving trustworthy autonomics, and this has to meet runtime requirements. A generic self-test approach is presented in Reference [18]. The authors of [18] extended the Monitor Analyse Plan and Execute (MAPE) control loop to include a new function called *Test* (Figure 1.5). By this, they define a new control loop comprising **M**onitor, **A**nalyse, **D**ecision, **T**est and **E**xecute – MADTE activities.

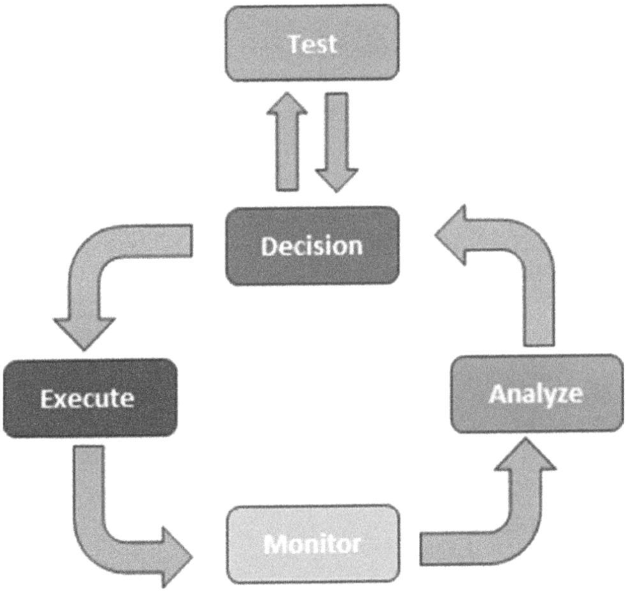

Figure 1.5 *MAPE based autonomic control loop with a self-test component [18]. The self-test component ensures that adaptation decisions are tested or validated before they are executed.*

The MADTE loop works like the MAPE loop only that the *Decision* activity calls the *Test* activity to validate a chosen action should it determine to adapt a suggested behaviour. The *Test* activity carries out a test on the action and returns its result to the *Decision* activity that then decides whether to implement, skip or choose another action. An adaptation is favoured if the *Test* indicates that it will lead to a component's better performance in terms of characteristics such as optimisation, robustness or security. The process is repeated if the latter is the case. When an action is decided on, the *Decision* activity passes it to the *Execute* activity for implementation. This is vital to runtime self-validation and is consistent with the solution in this book in terms of designing validation into the system's architecture.

A feedback-based validation that relies on a kind of secondary (mostly external) expertise feedback to validate the output of a system is presented in Reference 19. This is reactionary and makes no contribution to the result of the system in the first place. Though this may suffice for some specific system's needs, what is generally required for autonomic system validation is runtime validation of decisions (or processes) that lead to system outputs.

> ***[It should be noted that autonomic system trustworthiness goes beyond secure computing. It is result oriented; not focusing on how a goal is achieved but on the dependability of the output achieved]***

It should be noted that autonomic system trustworthiness goes beyond secure computing. It is result oriented; not focusing on how a goal is achieved but on the dependability of the output achieved. All systems, no matter how simple, are designed to meet a particular need, but not all systems have security concerns. So, trustworthiness is not all about security and validation. On the other hand, it is not about showing that a system or process works but also making sure that it does exactly what it is meant to do, in a way that ensures a dependable outcome. This aspect is addressed in the proposed trustworthy autonomic architecture, in Chapter 4, by a component that carries out a longer-term assessment of the system's actions. These have been the evolving challenges and where work must be concentrated if we are to achieve certifiable autonomic systems.

This section has presented a broad and general background study that analysed early research towards trustworthy autonomic computing. More recent studies have leveraged existing achievements but do not differ significantly in what has been achieved. There is, however, increased awareness of the need and effort towards trustworthy autonomics. This is covered in section 2.3.

1.2.2 Pillars of trustworthy autonomic systems

One significant realisation from the analysis so far is the possibility of an autonomic manager's adaptive smartness to introduce a kind of noise in terms of, e.g., instability into the system over time. In this case, the system may not have breached any adaptation rules but may be pushing out results that ultimately may not be reliable or may lead to spikes or instability in the control behaviour. For results to be fit-for-purpose, there needs to be a rolling evaluation of the impact of the autonomic manager's actions on the system.

So, the pillars of trustworthiness would ensure, amongst other things:

- continuous evaluation of control actions – validation of adaptive decisions and behaviour;
- fit-for-purpose results – dependable and reliable outcomes;
- and support for the definition of systems in a universal language – this needs to be at both system design (for understanding of the system and the trust and validation requirements) and post system design (for system classification and evaluation). See *Level of Autonomicity* in Chapter 7. For a robust solution then, trustworthiness support needs to be conceived during system design and so should be integrated into the autonomic architecture.

So, the identified pillars of trustworthy autonomic systems are validation, dependability and architecture considerations.

1.2.2.1 Self-validation

Robust self-management in autonomic computing systems resulting in dynamic changes and reconfigurations requires that autonomic systems should be able to continuously perform self-validation of their own behaviour and configuration, against their high-level behavioural goals and be able to reflect on the quality of their own adaptation behaviour. It is important to note that there is a significant difference between trustworthy autonomic computing and trusted (or secure) computing – this is explained in section 4.2. For complete reliance on autonomic systems, the human user will need a level of trust and confidence that these systems will satisfy specified requirements, will remain correct in the face of any possible environmental dynamism and will not fail.

> [***It is also not enough that systems are safe, secure and performing within the boundaries of specified rules; outputs must also be seen to be reliable, not misleading, and hence dependable.***]

Trustworthiness is sometimes referred to as reliability and dependability in other works. Trustworthiness, or the lack of it, may explain the level of the public's acceptance of autonomic systems. A primary feature of a trustworthy autonomic system is self-validation. Figure 1.6 is a revision of the autonomic architecture (Figure 1.2) to include self-validation (represented by the VC component) capability.

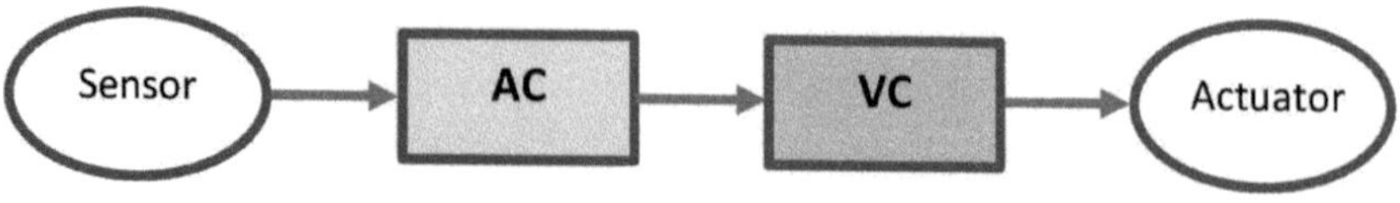

Figure 1.6 *Self-validating autonomic architecture. The sensor receives inputs (context information) into the system, the autonomic controller (AC) analyses these inputs and based on the outcome of the analysis decides an adaptation action, the validation check (VC) validates the decided action before it is then executed by the actuator.*

The autonomic decisions, made by the autonomic controller (AC) for actuation based on context information, are passed to the validation controller (VC) for validation against high-level policies, representing business-level objectives before those decisions are executed. The dynamic nature of autonomic systems makes it close to impossible to comprehensively predict possible outcomes at design time. So, it becomes highly complex to predetermine whether the AC's decision(s) are in the overall interest and good of the system. There is a vital need therefore to dynamically validate the runtime decisions of the system.

So, runtime validation is a continuous and dynamic self-validation of own behaviour. That is to say that the autonomic system is able to continuously check its own actions to ensure that those actions satisfy the goal of the system. Validation in trustworthy autonomic computing will need to meet runtime specifications. Design-time validation, on the other hand, does not suffice for autonomic system trustworthiness as it depends on (or is limited to) the designer's knowledge of the system's environment and operations.

1.2.2.2 Dependability

An autonomic system is dependable to the extent that its results (outputs) are consistent and with minimum fluctuation from the desired goal. A good way of ensuring dependability is by dynamically monitoring the impact of the autonomic manager's intervention over time. This may mean looking at the system's state after a particular number of autonomic decision-making cycles and deciding whether to allow the autonomic manager to carry on or enforce some retuning. Another aspect of dependability is self-stabilisation [20].

> ***Self-stabilisation mechanisms reduce the reliance of autonomic systems on external supervision and extend their behavioural scope and trustability. It helps a system track its goal in a gradual manner to avoid over-compensation when a system is already close to its goal or under-compensation that could lead to erratic behaviour or misleading results.***

Take an autonomic resource allocation system for example. The system allocates resources according to requests. A robust system would be able to track known working state and revert to such state in the case of detected disruption. System state could be tracked as a one-off (e.g., the initial state or a state at time *T*) or as several over a period of time. Now, reverting to a known working state could bring destabilisation if one of the systems requesting resources is no longer operating at the level of the known state. At this point, resetting the system to the initial state or time *T* would destabilise the system rather than help. A solution could be tracking and resetting to the nearest known working state, but the nearest known working state may not be a safe state if the lag between disruption and identification of the disruption is not considered. To obtain a safe state we can measure the lag (how long it takes the system) to identify disruption and then plug that value as a tolerance-range-check.

The tolerance-range-check guides the resetting process outside a crisis state to a safe state. For example, if a disruption occurs at time t_1 and the system identifies it at time t_2, it will only be safe to reset the system to t_1 or below but not far from t_1. Between t_1 and t_2 is crisis state and further down from t_1 to t_0 may cause destabilisation as serviced systems may not be operating at those levels. For some systems, it may be possible to calculate average latency (or lag) say t_{avg} (with some safety margins) and always reset to $(t_2 - t_{avg})$. Another solution might be to reset the system to the latest resource allocation time. The DYCASS project [21] provides a lead in this methodology.

1.2.2.3 Architecture

Trustworthiness requires a holistic approach. It requires a long-term focus as against the near-term needs that merely address methods for securing (or building trust in) existing systems. This means that trustworthiness needs to be designed into systems as integral properties. In real life when buildings are constructed, required specifications (e.g., floor space, pillar strength, anti-vibration measures, drainage) are usually specified and catered for in the building design produced by the architect. This enables the builders to make provisions for all requirements from foundations up. A building that is structurally adjusted to accommodate some fittings cannot be said to be of the same standing as one that catered for those fittings in the first instance from scratch. In the same way, it is best to cater for relevant autonomic capability requirements in the design stage of autonomic systems. This is why this book advocates for architecture-based solutions. So, architecture plays a very significant role in building trustworthy autonomic systems.

The evolution of autonomic architecture is presented in Chapter 2, while a trustworthy autonomic architecture, capable of meeting the identified requirements, is presented in Chapter 4.

1.3 Conclusion

This chapter has introduced the autonomic computing concept as a solution to dealing with the problem of increasing cost of ownership and complex management of computing systems, while also making the case for trustworthy autonomic computing. Definition of relevant autonomic terminologies has also been provided. This is important to ensure adequate understanding of the concepts and ideas presented in this book. The self-CHOP autonomic functionalities are at the core of autonomic computing. These have been introduced, with examples.

A general introductory discussion on trustworthy autonomic computing and a review of the research in trustworthy autonomic computing are discussed. Trustworthy autonomic computing is built on three pillars, covering validation, dependability and architecture considerations. These pillars would ensure, amongst other things, fit-for-purpose results, continuous evaluation of control actions and will support the definition of systems in universal language at both system design and post system design. Trustworthiness support will need to be conceived during system design and so should be integrated into the autonomic architecture.

Chapter 2

Evolution of autonomic computing

The major theme in this book deals with identifying and developing techniques to make autonomic computing systems trustworthy. To achieve this, it is important to first understand the level of work that has already gone into the autonomic computing research and how that can be harnessed. This chapter starts with an overview of the autonomic computing architecture and its life cycle. A broad analysis of autonomics research to show the trends in and direction of the autonomic computing research and where the work needs to be concentrated to address open challenges and achieve trustworthiness is presented. It is also important to take a holistic view of the entire field of research in order to gain a clearer picture of the need for and lack of effort towards trustworthy autonomic computing.

In this chapter, you will learn the following:

- the design of autonomic systems
- the life cycle of autonomic architecture
- key factors of trustworthy autonomic computing design
- major trends and direction in the autonomic computing research
- about key studies and researchers that have shaped the study of autonomic computing

2.1 Importance of understanding the evolution of autonomic computing

The evolution of autonomic computing can be tracked based on what it promises to achieve (the original intended goal of the concept), the design and the actual implementations – from conceptual ideas to actual developments and implementations. The idea of trustworthiness was not part of the initial thinking in the development of the autonomic computing concept. Our earlier study [2] has shown how important this has become.

2.2 Autonomic architecture

Trustworthiness cannot be reliably retrofitted into systems; it must be designed into system architectures. The design of an autonomic system is fundamental to its operations. The autonomic architecture is key to autonomic trustworthiness, and that is why it is important to start by discussing the development in the autonomic architecture. This section tracks the autonomic architecture (leading to trustworthiness), pictorially and in detail, in a number of progressive stages addressing it in an increasing level of detail and sophistication. Figure 2.1 provides a key to the symbols used.

- Sensor and actuator

These are the touchpoints where the autonomic manager connects with the managed system or monitored environment. The autonomic manager takes in relevant context data (from the managed system or monitored environment), processes it for a decision and then executes that decision. The sensor represents a source of ambient/context data for the autonomic manager, while the actuator provides capacity for executing the adaptation decision of the autonomic manager.

- Console

  Autonomic systems come in maturity stages – from basic autonomic (requiring a level of human interference and/or control) to complete autonomic (requiring no human interference or control) systems. The console represents a

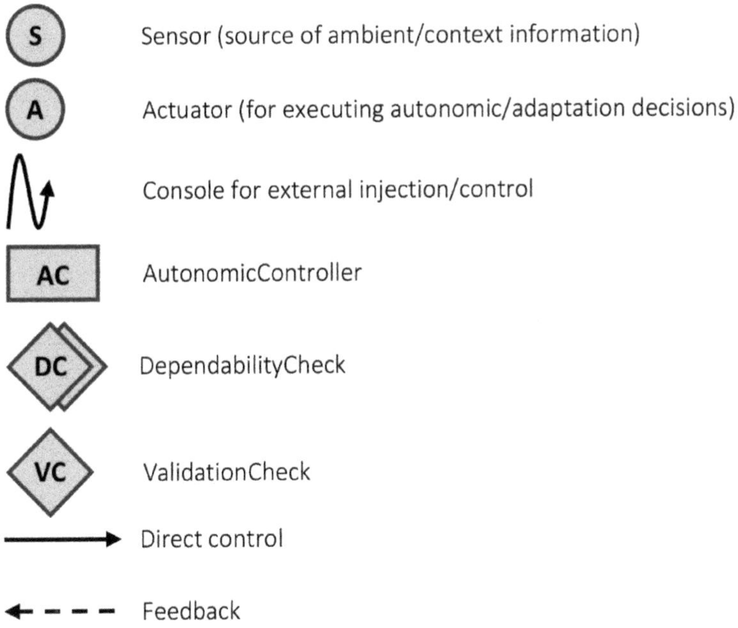

Figure 2.1 Pictographic key used for the autonomic architecture life cycle

touchpoint for human interference and interaction with the autonomic manager. This could be one-way or bi-directional, e.g.,

1. One-way: This could be a dashboard for the autonomic manager to display information intimating the user of its actions. It could also be a control panel for the user to interfere with (e.g., configure, reconfigure or override) the autonomic manager after observing its actions.
2. Bi-directional: This could be a provision for the autonomic manager to provide feedback to the user with a possibility for the user to override or compliment the decisions and actions of the autonomic manager. There are several possible variations of this.

- Autonomic controller

The autonomic controller (AC) represents basic autonomic manager control logic. It analyses input from the sensor and decides an adaptation action based on the chosen autonomic control logic.

- Dependability check

The dependability check (DC) provides the capability of staying on course to achieve the goal of the autonomic manager. It takes a holistic view of adaptation decisions and considers the short- and long-term effects of those decisions in order to efficiently guide the autonomic manager towards its intended goal.

- Validation check

The validation check (VC) represents the ability to verify adaptation decisions before they are executed. This helps in ensuring that decisions conform to the policies behind the control logic and that there are no errors in the process. It is important to note that the type of validation defined by the VC is runtime-based (i.e., runtime validation).

- Direct control

This arrow indicates the flow of control – the preceding object or component passes control to the succeeding object.

- Feedback

This indicates feedback from one object to another. This can be in any form, e.g., control or [re]calibration feedback.

Figure 2.2 illustrates the progression, in sophistication, of autonomic architectures and how close they have come to achieving trustworthiness. Although this may not be exhaustive as several variations and hybrids of the combinations may exist, it represents a series of discrete progressions in current approaches.

Two distinct stages of sophistication are identified. The first stage represents the traditional autonomic architecture (Figure 2.2 levels (i) and (ii)), basically concerned with direct self-management of a controlled/monitored system following some basic sense-manage-actuate logic defined in the AC component. For the prevailing context, AC is just a container of autonomic control logic, which could be based on **M**onitor-**A**nalyse-**P**lan-**E**xecute (Figure 1.3) or any other autonomic control logic. The original autonomic architecture, proposed with the introduction of autonomic computing [7] falls within this level. This achieves basic self-management capability and has since been adapted in several studies to offer more smartness and sophistication. To add a degree of trust and safeguard, an external interface for user control input is introduced in Figure 2.2 level (ii). This chronicles such approaches that provide a console or touchpoint for external administrative interactions (e.g., real-time monitoring, tweaking, feedback, knowledgebase source, trust input) with the autonomic process. An example of level (ii) is work in Reference [14] where, in addressing the problem of human–computer interactions raised by the autonomic computing vision, the authors proposed a solution where system's actions

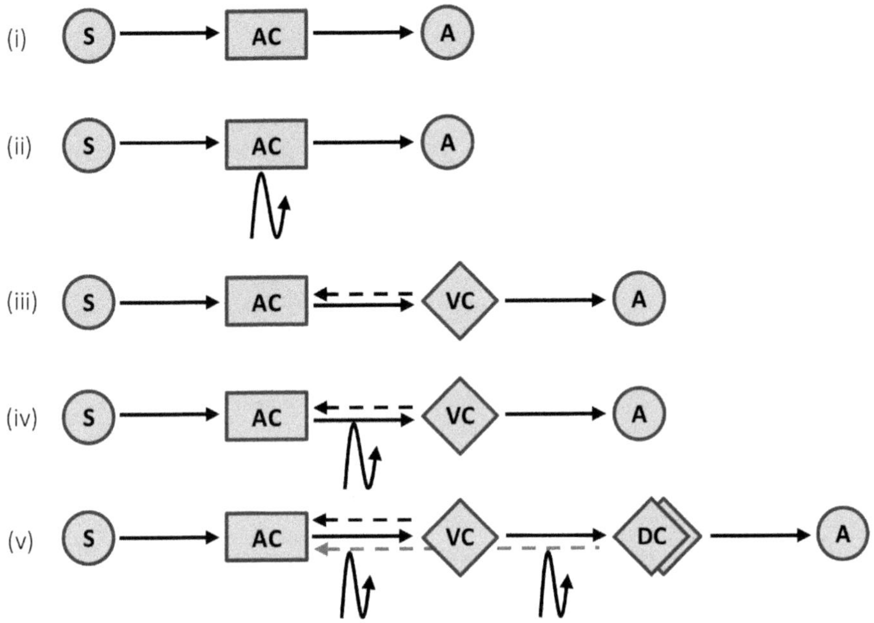

Figure 2.2 *Pictorial representation of trustworthy autonomic architecture life cycles. This is not exhaustive but represents major themes identified in research. Finer-grained sub-stages and design may exist.*

are transparent to the user and the user can moderate the behaviour of the system by allowing or disallowing system decided actions. The system has a console that offers the user the privilege of authorising or not authorising a particular process. Another example in this category is unmanned vehicles (UVs). In UVs, there are provisions for activating auto piloting and manual piloting. The user can decide when to activate either of the two or run a hybrid.

The second stage (Figure 2.3) represents efforts towards addressing runtime validation. Instrumentations to enable systems to check the conformity of management decisions are added. This includes such approaches that are capable of runtime self-validation of autonomic management decisions. The self-validation check is done by the VC component and this results in either a pass (in which case the validated decision is actuated) or a fail. Where the check fails, VC sends feedback to AC with notification of failure (e.g., policy violation) and a new decision is generated. An additional layer of sophistication is introduced in level (iv) with external touchpoint for higher level of manageability control. This can be in the form of an outer control loop monitoring, over a long-time frame, an inner short-time frame control loop. The work in Reference [18] (see section 1.2.1, Figure 2.4), which is an extension of the **M**onitor-**A**nalyse-**P**lan-**E**xecute control to include a 'Test' activity

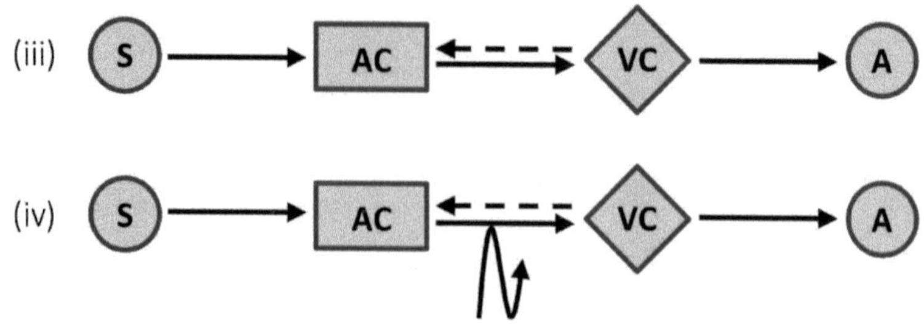

Figure 2.3 *Second stage representation of trustworthy autonomic architecture life cycles. The major improvement of this stage is the consideration for runtime validation.*

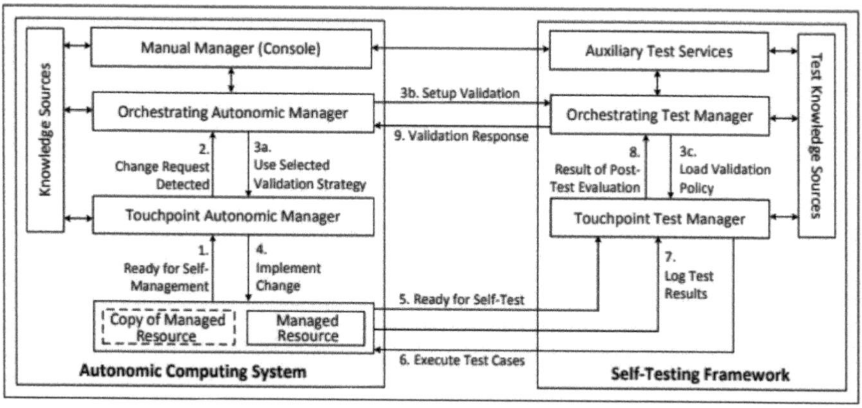

Figure 2.4 *High-level architectural model for an integrated self-testing framework for autonomic computing systems [22] (with permission)*

corresponds to level (iii). The test activity tests every suggested action (adaptation decision made) by the plan activity for conformity before the action is executed – leading to a new **M**onitor-**A**nalyse-**D**ecision-**T**est-**E**xecute control. If the test fails, the action is dropped and a new one is decided again.

The work in Reference [22], which corresponds to level (iv) of Figure 2.3, is an extension of the work in Reference [18] to include auxiliary test service components that facilitate manual test management and a detailed description of interactions between test managers and other components (see Figure 2.4). Here, test managers implement closed control loops on autonomic managers (such as autonomic managers implement on managed systems/resources) to validate change requests generated by the autonomic managers. Notice also that touchpoints are provided as manageability interfaces.

At the level of current sophistication (state-of-the-art), there are techniques to provide runtime VC (for behavioural and structural conformity), additional

(v) 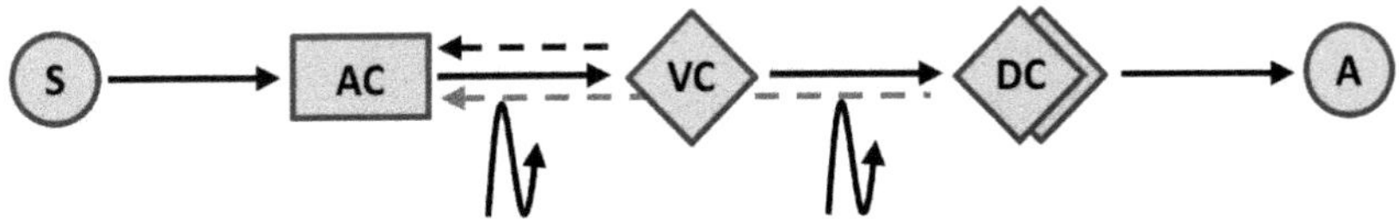

Figure 2.5 *Design for a trustworthy autonomic architecture addressing the identified issues and ensuring dependability. The sensor (S) receives inputs (context information) into the system; the AC analyses these inputs and based on the outcome of the analysis decides an adaptation action. The VC validates the decided action and returns feedback if validation fails, and the DC monitors the behaviour of the system over time and compares that with the general goal of the system and may inhibit the actuator (A), which executes the adaptation decision. The touchpoints allow for user intervention.*

console for higher level (external) control, etc. Emerging and needed capabilities include techniques for managing oscillatory behaviour in autonomic systems. These are mainly implemented in isolation. What is required is a holistic framework that collates all these capabilities into a single autonomic unit. Policy autonomics is one of the most used autonomic solutions. Autonomic managers follow rules to decide on actions. As long as policies are validated against set rules, the autonomic manager adapts its behaviour accordingly. This may mean changing between states. And when the change becomes rapid, despite meeting validation requirements, it is capable of introducing oscillation, vibration and erratic behaviour – all in the form of noise into the system. This is more noticeable in highly sensitive systems. So, a trustworthy autonomic architecture needs to provide a way of addressing these issues. Level (v) of Figure 2.2, shown in Figure 2.5, falls within the next stage of sophistication required to address the identified issues and ensure dependability.

2.3 Autonomic computing: trends and direction

This section covers the analysis of research efforts towards achieving the goal of autonomic computing in the first two decades of the introduction of the concept. The nature of the analysis is geared towards identifying recurring themes, trends, vital areas to be covered to achieve the goal of autonomic computing, where the research should be heading and the open/emerging challenges.

An analysis-by-problem approach is used to show the pattern, in terms of maturity stages, of how researchers have attempted addressing the autonomic computing challenge. This is addressed in two broad periods: the first decade, covering years 2001–2011 and the second decade, covering studies and developments from years 2012 to 2019. Note that the autonomic computing concept was introduced by IBM in 2001. The analysis in this section is drawn from proceedings of the International

Conference on Autonomic Computing (ICAC) and the International Conference on Autonomic and Autonomous Systems (ICAS). These were the early leading international conferences on the general concept of autonomic computing, and I believe that they both give a true representation of the distribution of interest, work done and trends in autonomic computing research.

2.3.1 Background

Computing systems, including hardware, software and communications, started growing exponentially in terms of increasing heterogeneity, scale and ubiquity, becoming exceedingly complex for human management. Computing devices got more pervasive, embedded in everyday objects and exposed to environments where system working conditions are dynamic, uncertain and unpredictable. Managing such systems, which are heterogeneously knitted together and pervasively ubiquitous, became daunting and utterly complex. With highly limited expertise to address this concern, the cost of system ownership and management rose exponentially. To deal with such complexity necessitated the introduction of a new concept, namely Autonomic Computing, by IBM in 2001 [1],[7],[23].

The autonomic computing concept was introduced to address the complexity of managing ever-growing and evolving systems by shifting the responsibility for low-level tasks from the human to the system. This is achieved by building self-managing systems that are capable of self-configuring, self-healing, self-optimising and self-protecting, for a start. These are widely referred to as the autonomic self-CHOP or self-* functionalities. With such capabilities, autonomic systems are able to manage themselves and thereby reduce the computing system management complexities for humans. This created a new research area with many challenges. Earlier autonomic computing researchers like Salehie and Tahvildari [24] proposed a categorisation of complexity in computing systems and presented an overview of autonomic computing research area. The work in Reference [24] captures the fundamental IT complexities and the autonomic capabilities that would address them and then outlines the underlying research issues/challenges from a practical and theoretical point of view.

Researchers took on the challenge of developing this new concept. The autonomic computing concept is now well-understood, and a lot has been achieved since it was introduced. The efforts of academic and industry researchers have gone a long way in addressing the goal of the concept. However, there are still open and emerging challenges. It is therefore important to continuously assess the extent to which the original vision of the concept has been accomplished, understand the trends and explore ideas for addressing the open and emerging research challenges. This is one of the focus points in this chapter.

The number of dedicated conferences and journals in this research area has continued to increase. These provide a good source of data for analysing and understanding the extent of work done in the autonomic computing research area. ICAC and ICAS are two leading autonomic computing conferences and have together published about 1,050 high quality research papers in the first two decades of autonomic computing research.

The work in this chapter is based on the review of the 1,050 ICAC and ICAS publications. Because of their unique composition, it is believed that these two conferences will give a true representation of the distribution of interest, work done and trends in autonomic computing research. ICAS is academia dominated while ICAC is industry dominated and both have a good blend of academia–industry collaborations.

The analysis of the first decade of autonomic computing study [2] reveals a progressive result in terms of what was achieved. However, there are gaps that need to be addressed. It has been established that towards the end of the first decade, emphasis shifted to addressing the bigger picture, dealing with the issues of large-scale systems and creating re-usable solutions using already established techniques. This led to new challenges, including issues of heterogeneity of services and platforms, interoperability of ever-growing coexisting multi-agent systems and trustworthy autonomics. The case is made, of particular interest, to address users' need for assurance that autonomic managers can reliably manage today's systems of increased scale and complexity.

There is a lack of effort in offering a holistic analysis and evaluation of how the actual work has progressed in achieving the original vision of the autonomic computing concept. Jeffrey Kephart, one of the leading autonomic computing researchers and a researcher with IBM, in a keynote during ICAC 2011 presented an excellent analysis of the extent to which the original autonomic computing vision had been realised with some discussions and speculations about the remaining research challenges [25]. While Kephart concentrated more on the various technological threads, their origins and how they have progressed, the focus in this book is mainly on the level of maturity in terms of the types of, and scale of, problems targeted at the various stages. This enables us to reflect on the overall progress in the field, and to be able to identify current and emerging challenges. This work is not just a review but also a substantiation of an earlier proposed roadmap (pathway) to achieving the goal of autonomic computing [26]. We had posited (and explained how) that the journey to the goal of autonomic computing would proceed from defining systems and autonomicity to ultimately achieving certifiable autonomic computing systems. This is corroborated in this report.

Although limited, studies evaluating the trends in autonomic computing have largely focused on specific applications and autonomic functionalities. Out of the 1,050 publications reviewed in this study, only 12 (9 in the first decade and 3 in the second) are somewhat related to evaluating the trends in autonomic computing. A significant chunk of these References [27–31] focuses on the comparison of approaches and techniques for autonomic computing. Krupitzer *et al.* [27] define self-improvement as an adaptation of an autonomic system's adaptation logic and present a comparison of approaches for self-improvement in autonomic computing and self-adaptive systems. Maggio and Hoffmann [28] present a comparison of decision-making approaches to self-optimising autonomic systems, while Alhaisoni, Liotta and Ghanbari [29] compare two popular Live and Video-on-Demand P2P streaming applications. Mohamed, Romdhani and Ghedira [30] evaluate the concepts in Meta-Object Facility and Eclipse Modelling Framework meta-models for model transformation. Gjørven, Eliassen and Aagedal [31] examine different approaches for self-adaptation. None of these is a comprehensive analysis covering the generality of trends and efforts in autonomic computing research as in this book.

Other slightly related studies, within the study window, include surveys that categorise existing autonomic computing research efforts as well as highlight open challenges [24,32,33,34] and those that focus on specific topics [35,36]. An overview of academic- and industry-led autonomic projects and autonomic characteristic-based comparison of those projects is presented in Reference [24]. Nami and Bertels [32] provide a general survey of autonomic computing systems, the underlying features, architectures and challenges. It also highlights the challenges of achieving autonomicity in systems. An analysis of the requirements of context adaptation in autonomic computing, evaluation of approaches for autonomic context adaptation and a survey of existing work on context adaption in autonomic computing are presented in Reference [33]. The survey in Reference [34] presents a review, focusing on existing autonomic computing frameworks, architectures and self-management techniques. On more whittled focus, Higgins *et al.* [35] present a survey on security challenges for swarm robotics (multiple autonomous agents), while Ding *et al.* [36] evaluate and characterise service level objectives performance goals for autonomic cloud applications. While these studies have addressed reviews of various isolated and specific areas of autonomic research, this book considers the general key areas and presents the review in a way that shows the research stages against a maturity timeline.

The analyses in the following sections 2.2.2 and 2.2.3 are based on the review of about 1,050 research publications using webometrics and direct analysis techniques. These are analysed in terms of main application domain, emphasis and technical approach as well as author distribution (Table 2.1). This classification is chosen based on the observed interest of researchers and sponsors. The result is an empirical evaluation of the overall impact, trends and state-of-the-art of autonomic computing research activity. An analysis-by-problem approach reveals a particular pattern (problem definition to issues of scale) in addressing the autonomic computing vision.

2.3.1.1 Data and methodology for the trend analysis

In order to be able to recreate this study, it is important to understand the source of data and the method employed. This study involves the review of all the proceedings

Table 2.1 Classification, in terms of focus area, for the reviewed publications

Authoring	Main application domain	Others
Academic	*Data centre*	*Design and architecture*
Industry	*Distributed systems*	*Learning and knowledge*
Joint (academic and industry)	*Networks*	*Performance management*
	Robotics	*Policy autonomics*
	Storage and database management	*Self-CHOP*
		Survey
		VT(Validation and Trustworthiness)
		Actual VT proposal

of ICAC and ICAS in the first two decades, covering autonomic computing research from 2001 to 2019. These are two leading autonomic computing conferences with widespread distribution of academic and industry participation. Publications used in this work are sourced from ThinkMind[*], IEEE Xplore[†] and IEEE Computer Society[‡] digital libraries. A total of 1,050 research publications, including keynotes (626 of which are from ICAC and 424 from ICAS), were reviewed using webometrics and direct analysis techniques. Figure 2.6 is the distribution of the reviewed papers.

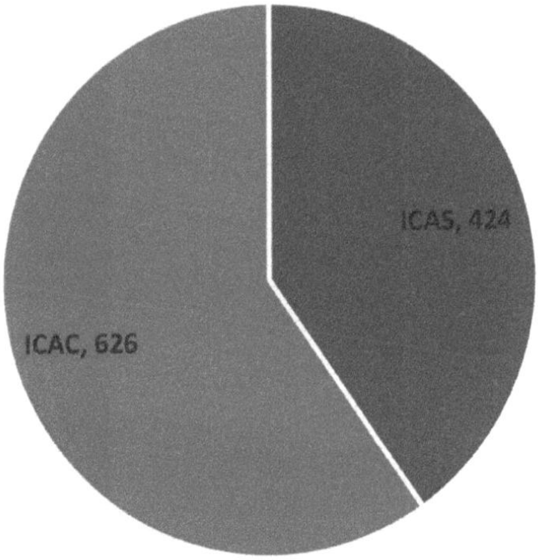

Figure 2.6 Conference distribution of publications. This represents autonomic computing research published in both ICAC and ICAS from 2001 to 2019.

[*]ThinkMind Digital Library via http://www.thinkmind.org/
[†]IEEE Xplore Digital Library via https://ieeexplore.ieee.org/Xplore/home.jsp
[‡]IEEE Computer Society Digital Library via http://www.computer.org/portal/web/csdl/proceedings

Table 2.2 Grouping of the reviewed papers

Distribution	Description
Authoring	This considers the affiliation of the authors and is classified according to academic (authors from an academic institution), industry (authors from the industry) and joint (collaboration between academic and industry authors) – regardless of location. If all authors are from same category, say Industry, but one is also affiliated to an academic institution, the paper is classed as Joint
Emphasis	This group consists of studies that prominently focus on specific themes – autonomic computing focus areas
Main application domain	Studies in this category focus on the application of autonomic computing in different domains. In most cases, this is about applying the autonomic functionalities in specific systems
Technical approach	These are technological approaches to autonomic computing. This is about mainly using known and established techniques to achieve or enable autonomic functionalities

These are analysed in terms of main application domain, research emphasis, technical approach as well as author distribution as shown in Table 2.1 and explained in Table 2.2 and Table 2.3. The grouping of these papers is not exhaustive but reflects recurring major themes from both conferences (ICAC and ICAS). The following result is an empirical analysis of the overall state-of-the-art of autonomic computing research activity, covering key themes, in the first two decades.

Every paper is reviewed and allocated to the relevant group and category (e.g., Tables 2.4 and 2.5). Some papers, depending on content, are allocated to more than one category. The analysis considers the first and second decades of autonomic computing research both separately and jointly. An analysis-by-problem approach reveals a noticeable pattern (from problem definition to issues of scale) in tackling the autonomic computing vision. A number of open and emerging challenges are identified – these include runtime validation, trustworthiness, interoperability (coexistence of autonomic managers) and certification, requiring solutions specifically tailored for runtime self-adaptive systems.

Overall, by the end of the second decade, very impressive progress has been made and this has been driven by widespread effort and collaborations from academic and industry players.

2.3.2 Autonomic computing in the first decade

The first ten years after the introduction of the autonomic computing concept saw an increasing show of interest by researchers to grasp and make the most of the concept. It was not as though there was no self-management computing at that time,

Table 2.3 Categorisation of the grouping of reviewed papers

Category	Description
Authoring	
Academic	All authors are from the academia
Industry	All authors are from the industry, government and non-academic organisations
Joint	At least one author from academic and one from industry or same author from both academic and industry
Emphasis	
Storage and database management	Using autonomic computing to improve data storage and database management
Design and architecture	Proposing and demonstrating autonomic architectures and design
Performance management	Demonstrating performance management goals, e.g., using autonomics to improve quality of service
Self-CHOP	Studies in this category also touch on one or more of the self-Configuring, Healing, Optimisation and Protection autonomic functionalities in particular
Survey	Surveys and reviews
VT	VT-related studies
Actual VT	Studies proposing actual validation and/or trustworthiness methods
Main application domain	
Data centre	Studies using data centres as case studies
Distributed systems	Studies using distributed systems as case studies
Networks (+ wireless sensor networks)	Studies focusing on networks, including wireless sensor networks
Robotics	Studies involving robots
Technical approach	
Policy	Studies utilising policies and rules to enable autonomicity – rule-based or policy autonomics
Learning and knowledge	Studies utilising learning and knowledge techniques, e.g., artificial intelligence, machine learning, cognitive computing, etc.

but the concept opened a new dedicated door for addressing self-management computing. Overall, very impressive progress was made in the first decade, and this was driven by the interest of the main sponsors – industry leaders such as IBM, Sun, Motorola, Google, Microsoft and Hewlet Packard, amongst others. A detailed work in this regard is published in Reference [2].

Figure 2.7 shows the stages (A, B and C) adopted by researchers in addressing autonomic computing and the emerging challenges (D and E) towards achieving the overall goal of autonomic computing. This is a high-level view as finer-grained sub-stages may exist. The stages are classified against a maturity timeline as shown in Figure 2.8. This study is based on the review of 647 proceedings (publications – Tables 2.4 and 2.5) from ICAC and ICAS. These were the early major collation of generic autonomic computing-based publications.

Table 2.4 ICAC proceedings distribution (first decade) [2]

Distribution	icac 04	icac 05	icac 06	icac 07	icac 08	icac 09	icac 10	icac 11	Total	%
Authoring										
Academic	39	30	20	15	15	18	18	32	**187**	**55.6547619**
Industry	17	18	09	06	05	10	04	01	**70**	**20.8333333**
Joint	08	16	14	11	06	06	05	13	**79**	**23.5119048**
Total	**64**	**64**	**43**	**32**	**26**	**34**	**27**	**46**	336	
Emphasis										
Storage and database management	05	05	04	02	00	00	01	04	**21**	**6.25000000**
Design and architecture	07	12	01	02	04	03	03	03	**35**	**10.4166667**
Performance management	09	05	05	03	01	06	03	08	**40**	**11.9047619**
Self-CHOP	11	09	04	05	07	06	04	02	**48**	**14.2857143**
Survey	00	00	00	00	00	00	00	01	**01**	**0.29761905**
VT	04	03	03	04	02	03	00	00	**19**	**5.6547619**
Actual VT	01	01	01	03	01	01	00	00	**08**	**2.38095238**
Main application domain										
Data centre	03	11	11	11	09	10	09	12	**76**	**22.6190476**
Distributed systems	17	06	05	04	00	01	02	04	**39**	**11.6071429**
Networks (+ wireless sensor networks)	08	02	00	01	00	00	01	03	**15**	**4.46428571**
Robotics	01	00	00	00	00	00	00	02	**03**	**0.89285714**
Technical approach										
Policy	02	06	03	02	02	00	01	00	**16**	**4.76190476**
Learning and knowledge	08	04	03	01	06	03	01	03	**29**	**8.63095238**

Table 2.5 ICAS proceedings distribution (first decade) [2]

Distribution	icas 05	icas 06	icas 07	icas 08	icas 09	icas 10	icas 11	Total	%
Authoring									
Academic	20	39	53	34	48	27	23	**244**	**78.4565916**
Industry	01	10	13	00	04	01	01	**30**	**9.64630225**
Joint	02	09	03	09	05	02	07	**37**	**11.8971061**
Total	**23**	**58**	**69**	**43**	**57**	**30**	**31**	**311**	
Emphasis									
Storage and database management	00	04	03	01	03	00	01	**12**	**3.8585209**
Design and architecture	03	15	07	02	09	03	07	**46**	**14.7909968**
Performance management	01	05	07	03	06	02	00	**24**	**7.7170418**
Self-CHOP	00	01	01	01	03	03	01	**10**	**3.21543408**
Survey	00	01	02	01	03	00	01	**08**	**2.57234727**
VT	01	03	01	00	00	01	03	**09**	**2.89389068**
Actual VT	00	00	01	00	00	00	00	**01**	**0.32154341**
Main application domain									
Data centre	01	06	04	03	03	04	02	**23**	**7.39549839**
Distributed system	05	12	07	01	05	01	02	**33**	**10.6109325**
Networks (+wireless sensor networks)	04	07	06	02	05	03	01	**28**	**9.00321543**
Robotics	01	03	01	04	04	01	03	**17**	**5.46623794**
Technical approach									
Policy	00	02	02	03	03	02	00	**12**	**3.8585209**
Learning and knowledge	00	01	04	06	04	00	01	**16**	**5.14469453**

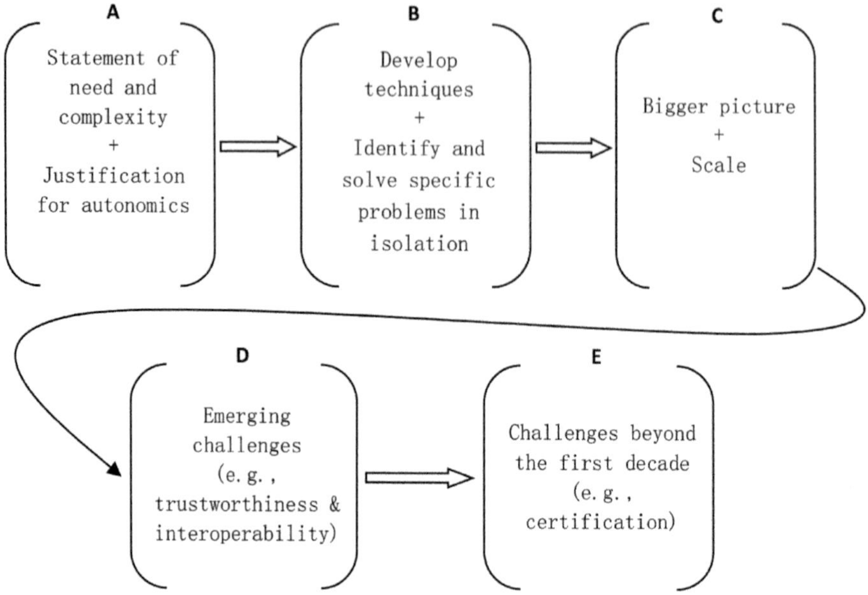

Figure 2.7 *Observed trend and direction of autonomic computing research in the first decade of its inception (2001–2011)*

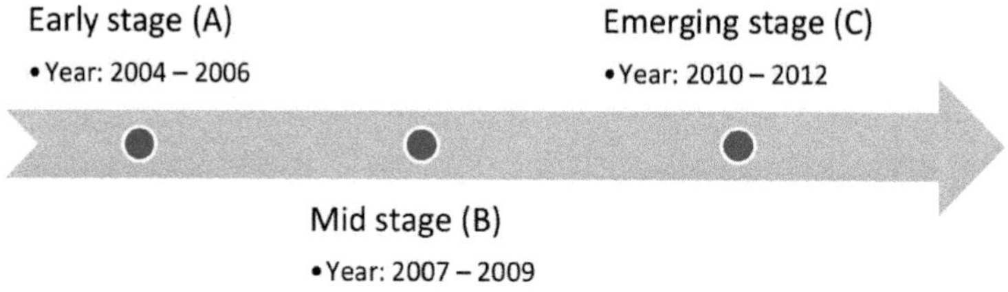

Figure 2.8 *Stage classification for all reviewed publications*

Tables 2.4 and 2.5, adapted from Reference [2], are high level analysis of ICAC and ICAS conference proceedings, covering autonomic computing research in the first decade. These were analysed in a way of showing research stages against a maturity timeline.

At this stage of autonomic computing research, the foremost focus of the research community, in terms of application scenario and emphasis, was mostly data centre, distributed systems, storage and database management, design and architecture, learning and knowledge, and self-CHOP. Validation and trustworthiness (VT) with its methodologies is one critical area that received less attention.

In terms of main application domain, the data centre clearly tops the ranking in terms of interest to the community. This is partly because the autonomic computing vision is industry-borne and has continued to be driven by the industry. This is evidenced by the number of papers (including on data centres) that are authored, co-authored or sponsored by the industry partners. Data centres are very complex; in fact, they have many dimensions of complexity, which arise from their scale, necessary speed of operation and large number of tuning parameters. In addition, they have high power costs, including a significant cost component for the cooling systems. Autonomic computing arose because of the need for automatic management of such complexity and successful autonomic techniques in this domain translate into significant financial reward for the owners and users of such systems. There is now a social responsibility dimension to it – to reduce the carbon footprint of data centres as a response to climate change. This high complexity is also attractive to academic researchers as it provides a rich domain to evaluate a wide range of techniques, tools and frameworks for autonomic computing.

Investigation [2] reveals that, shortly after the introduction of the autonomic computing concept, initial research focus was mainly on stating the problem and challenge of the ever-growing system complexity [37,38] and justifying autonomic computing as a reliable [39,40] solution. Most of the work in this area was industry sponsored and widely based on dynamic resource allocation, e.g., References 41 and 42. Some major industry players then were IBM, HP, Sun, etc. Following the early stage, after establishing the case for autonomic computing as a promising solution, research efforts shifted to developing and applying techniques which were then established and increasingly used, e.g., policy autonomics [43,44], utility functions [45,46], fuzzy logic [47,48], dead-zone logic [20,49], etc. These autonomic enabling techniques are discussed in Chapter 3. Progress was also made in identifying and solving specific problems in isolation. A significant number of studies offered specific solutions to specific problems. Some examples of the variety of these include References [50–54]. In Reference [53], authors propose a control scheme for dynamic resource provisioning in a virtualised data centre environment to address issues of power management without trading performance. Experiments report that the controller, while still maintaining quality of service goals, is able to conserve power by 26 per cent. References [52,54] investigate the use of thermal load management to address heating in data centres. While Moore *et al.* [52] concentrated on predicting the effects of workload distribution and cooling configurations on temperature (deducing heat profile), Ghanbari *et al.* [54] based their work on workload scaling. Calinescu in Reference 51 implements an earlier proposed generic autonomic framework (based on service-oriented architecture) and demonstrates the effectiveness of his framework in resource allocation, while Benoit [50] presents an automatic diagnosis framework to dynamically identify bottlenecks in large systems. At this stage, studies largely comprise implementations, demonstrations and presentation of experimental results of proposed ideas.

Towards the end of the first decade, emphasis shifted to addressing the bigger picture, dealing with the issues of scale [55–57] and creating re-usable solutions using already established techniques. This led to fresh challenges, including issues of heterogeneity of services and platforms [58, 59]. Solutions were then proposed for addressing large-scale systems with varying heterogeneous platforms. The increase in scale and size of systems, coupled with heterogeneity of services and platforms, leads to further complexity and means that more autonomic managers could be integrated to achieve a particular goal. With more autonomic managers integrated, working together towards a particular goal comes the need for interoperability between autonomic managers. As in the nature of technology, the addressing of one problem always leads to new challenges. As expected, this growth of systems in scale and complexity led to reliability (and by extension trustworthiness) concerns for large-scale systems [60]. There is no way we can succeed in self-managing large-scale complex systems without addressing trustworthiness (reliability) concerns. So, interoperability and trustworthiness became some of the emerging major challenges at the end of the first decade. These needed, and still need, to be addressed if we are to attain the full goal of autonomic computing.

> ***[There is no way we can succeed in self-managing large-scale complex systems without addressing trustworthiness (reliability) and interoperability concerns.]***

Interoperability was somewhat neglected as a challenge in this era. Earlier studies were fundamentally concerned with getting autonomic computing to work and establishing relevant concepts and demonstrating viability. Many mechanisms and techniques were explored but focus started shifting, towards the end of the decade, to the next level, e.g., how to reliably manage multi-manager scenarios, to govern interactions between managers and to arbitrate when conflicts arise. These are the kind of solutions needed to address the challenges arising from the increased availability of large systems with multiple autonomic agents. When more than one autonomic manager is needed to coordinate a system, there may be situations where one manager counters the decision of another. Although there were some mentions and general discussion around this area, significant progress was not made. For example, Anthony *et al.* [61] evaluate the nature and scope of the interoperability challenges for autonomic computing systems, identify a set of requirements for a universal solution and propose a service-based approach to interoperability to handle both direct and indirect conflicts in a multi-manager scenario.

In another example, Beran *et al.* [62] examine the web services solution developed as a part of the Consortium of Universities for the Advancement of Hydrologic Science, Inc. (CUAHSI) Hydrologic Information System (HIS) project. CUAHSI HIS is a web services solution that standardises access to cross-domain hydrologic data repositories (of disparate semantic and syntactic definitions and hosted on heterogeneous platforms) to facilitate data discovery and enable cross-domain interoperability. The project emphasises the idea of a seamless interface through which access can be gained to hydrologic data from multiple heterogeneous data sources. An architecture-led interoperability solution, based on the extension of the trustworthy autonomic architecture discussed in Chapter 4, is presented in Chapter 6. The idea is that interoperability support should be designed in and integral at the architectural level as doing otherwise (retro-fitted solution) may lead to further complexities and unreliability.

> ***[Evidence has shown that while the industry community (and by the way, the originator of the autonomic computing research) set the pace for the research, the academic community expatiated the research and is playing huge collaborative role in achieving the research goal.]***

The second decade and beyond would need to start from addressing the issues of self-validation, trustworthiness, certification and many more. Questions that need addressing include the following:

- *What are the processes to ensure that component upgrades that are tested and confirmed in isolation will not cause harm in a multi-system environment?*
- *How can certified autonomic systems be achieved?*
- *How can users be confident that a system does what it says?*
- *How can consistency and reliability be achieved, over longer time frames, beyond attaining self-management?*

Such challenges and questions are acknowledged and discussed in [Reference 9]. Figure 2.9 shows an analysis of the reviewed publications in the first decade, in terms of their topic areas. Only about 4.3 per cent of these papers are VT related and out of these, only a few, about 1.2 per cent of the papers, are actual VT methodologies. This number includes mainly those studies that incorporate validation, testing and reliability into their architectures, frameworks or implementations and not necessarily as a core or critical feature. This shows an understanding of the challenges of VT but yet to be fully grasped. Some of the very few publications that actually propose actual VT methodologies are non-generic and tackle application specific problems. Figure 2.9 shows the low-level research into trustworthy autonomics in the first decade.

Moving forward, it is important to note that making autonomic systems trustworthy is not optional – it is an essential prerequisite for the ultimate success of autonomic computing.

2.3.3 Autonomic computing in the second decade

The first decade of autonomic computing summarily shows a progressive result in terms of what was achieved. Emerging challenges, e.g., large-scale systems, increasing heterogeneity of services and platforms, interoperability of systems etc., from the first decade started receiving attention in the second decade. Tables 2.6 and 2.7 are high level analysis of ICAC and ICAS conference proceedings, covering

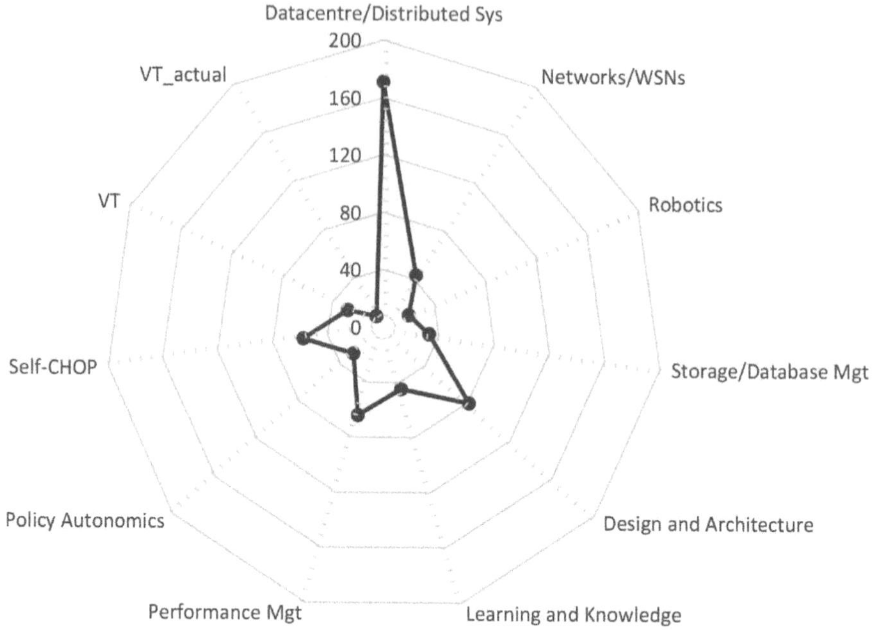

Figure 2.9 Reviewed the first decade publications in terms of major focus areas. The focus areas, which are not exhaustive, represent recurring major themes from both ICAC and ICAS conferences.

autonomic computing research in the second decade. As in the first decade, these are analysed to show research stages against a maturity timeline.

In terms of author distribution, the academic community continues to dominate the research effort, with the most publications. There is a 5 per cent reduction in contribution from the industry category. However, there is a significant increase in collaboration between academic and industry researchers. On the average, 26 per cent of all publications in the second decade are classed as joint. This represents an increase of over 8 per cent from 17.9 per cent in the first decade. This shows a growing synergy between the academia and the industry in achieving the autonomic computing goal as the challenges are well-understood.

In terms of emphasis, there is significant increase in storage and database management (by 10 per cent), performance management (by 22 per cent) and self-CHOP (by 18 per cent) related publications. This is expected as it corroborates the trend identified towards the end of the first decade. The significant jump in applying autonomic computing to address these areas is a direct response to the challenge of large-scale systems identified towards the end of the first decade. This shows how the second decade responds to the emerging challenges of the first decade. The increase in scale and size of systems (e.g.,

Table 2.6 ICAC proceedings distribution (second decade)

Distribution	icac 12	icac 13	icac 14	icac 15	icac 16	icac 17	icac 18	icac 19	Total	%
Authoring										
Academic	18	17	20	19	40	30	18	13	**175**	**60.3448276**
Industry	10	3	3	5	3	3	0	1	**28**	**9.65517241**
Joint	19	14	6	14	11	10	5	8	**87**	**30**
Total	**47**	**34**	**29**	**38**	**54**	**43**	**23**	**22**	**290**	
Emphasis										
Storage/Database management	14	11	8	11	5	5	2	4	**60**	**20.6896552**
Design and architecture	10	2	0	8	10	6	3	1	**40**	**13.7931034**
Performance management	20	21	19	11	17	6	14	8	**116**	**40**
Self-CHOP	7	8	5	11	25	17	8	5	**86**	**29.6551724**
Survey	0	0	0	0	1	0	0	1	**2**	**0.68965517**
VT	2	1	1	1	3	2	0	1	**11**	**3.79310345**
Actual VT	2	0	0	1	2	1	0	0	**6**	**2.06896552**
Main application domain										
Data centre	8	7	10	5	6	3	7	1	**47**	**16.2068966**
Distributed system	26	12	11	22	17	8	9	9	**114**	**39.3103448**
Networks (+ wireless sensor networks)	4	7	2	2	7	8	4	3	**37**	**12.7586207**
Robotics	0	0	0	0	0	0	0	0	**0**	**0**
Technical approach										
Policy	0	1	0	4	2	3	2	3	**15**	**5.17241379**
Learning and knowledge	1	4	7	5	15	10	8	9	**59**	**20.3448276**

Table 2.7 ICAS proceedings distribution (second decade)

Distribution	icas 12	icas 13	icas 14	icas 15	icas 16	icas 17	icas 18	icas 19	Total	%
Authoring										
Academic	14	13	6	17	3	9	9	11	**82**	**72.5663717**
Industry	2	1	1	1	1	3	2	2	**13**	**11.5044248**
Joint	3	3	1	5	1	5	0	0	**18**	**15.9292035**
Total	**19**	**17**	**8**	**23**	**5**	**17**	**11**	**13**	**113**	
Emphasis										
Storage/Database management	1	0	0	0	0	0	0	0	**1**	**0.88495575**
Design and architecture	3	2	1	5	0	1	0	3	**15**	**13.2743363**
Performance management	1	2	2	4	1	2	1	0	**13**	**11.5044248**
Self-CHOP	11	8	2	1	0	0	0	0	**22**	**19.4690265**
Survey	1	0	0	0	0	0	0	0	**1**	**0.88495575**
VT	3	2	0	2	0	1	0	1	**9**	**7.96460177**
Actual VT	0	0	0	0	0	0	0	1	**1**	**0.88495575**
Main application domain										
Data centre	4	2	2	1	0	0	0	0	**9**	**7.96460177**
Distributed system	2	7	3	8	1	4	1	1	**27**	**23.8938053**
Networks (+wireless sensor networks)	0	1	1	0	0	1	6	1	**10**	**8.84955752**
Robotics	1	2	1	4	3	2	1	7	**21**	**18.5840708**
Technical approach										
Policy	3	0	1	1	0	0	0	1	**6**	**5.30973451**
Learning and knowledge	2	2	3	1	0	4	6	4	**22**	**19.4690265**

cloud computing, online services and big data applications) has led to increased demand and management of storage systems [63–66] – these studies also propose solutions. Several other studies have proposed autonomic solutions to workload scaling [52–54]. Performance management saw the second highest jump (22 per cent) of all the categories. Studies in this category are widespread, ranging from variety of performance metrics [67–71] to specific considerations, e.g., quality of service and service level agreement [72–77] to energy efficient [78–83] related performance management. There is no significant change in any of the design and architecture, survey, VT and actual VT categories from the first decade. These unchanged categories are discussed in detail in the general trend discussion section below.

Findings in the analysis of the second decade largely corroborate those of the first decade, (Figure 2.10). In terms of main application domain, the data centre continues to dominate in the ranking of interest to the community. However, this time we have noticed an increase in the consideration of energy efficiency for data centres [78-83], encouraging green computing as a way to manage climate change. Network and robotic categories saw a minor increase in consideration from the first decade. There is no massive interest in these areas from the analysis. Data centre/distributed systems remains the main application domain for autonomic computing. This is an area that is witnessing exponential growth, due to increasing reliance on cloud computing, leading to more complexities. As a result, there is a significant upsurge in learning and knowledge, reflecting the application of modern technologies, like machine learning and artificial intelligence, to address those complexities. This also reflects current line of thinking and direction in technology solutions – 'artificial intelligence to the rescue of everything difficult'. This explains the significant rise, by 13 per cent, in the number of learning and knowledge–related publications in this decade. Although other autonomic enabling techniques like fuzzy logic [47, 48, 84, 85], utility functions [86–89], etc., still exist and continue to help in pushing the autonomic boundary, policy autonomic remains the dominant technique.

There is reduction in the focus on design and architecture as there is now a good hang on the design of autonomic systems. Trustworthy autonomics (VT and VT_Actual) remains an area of real concern and importance but still largely unexplored. Recurring themes include autonomic power management in ever growing data centres and distributed systems. Effort towards reducing data centre's contribution to climate change is taking centre stage.

/Trustworthy autonomics (VT and VT_Actual) remains an area of real concern and importance but still largely unexplored. Only about 3 per cent of the over 1,000 reviewed publications are VT related. Far fewer than this are actual proposals for trustworthy autonomics solution./

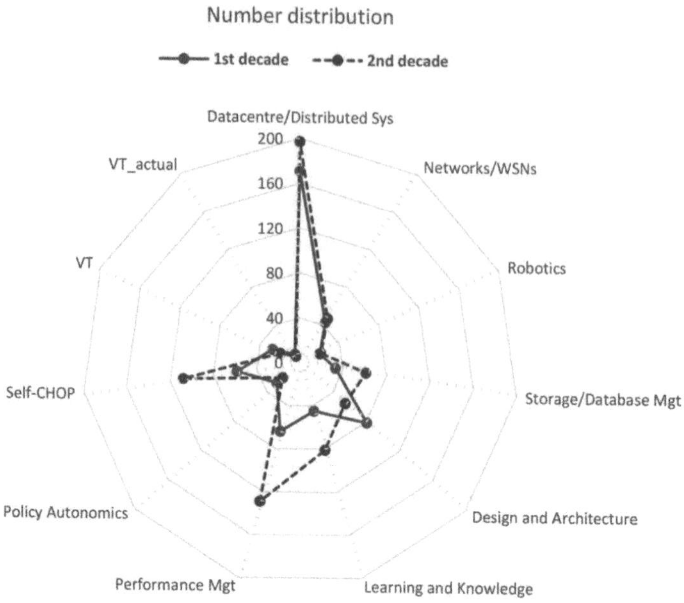

(a)

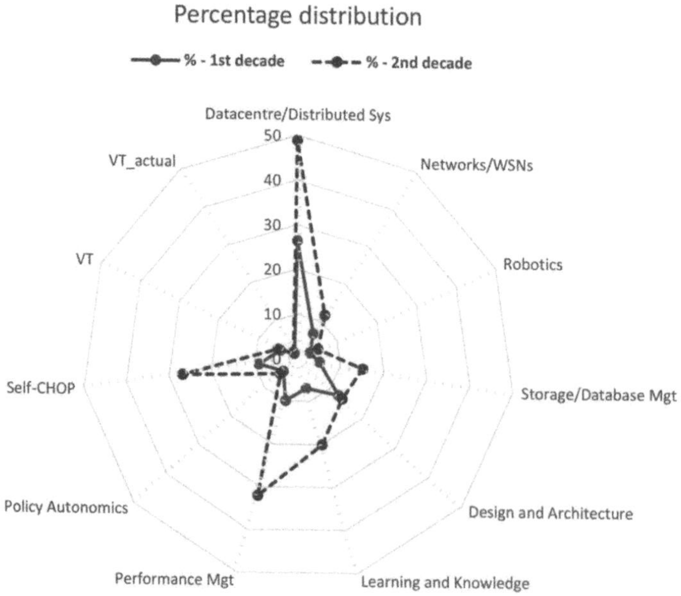

(b)

Figure 2.10 *Reviewed first and second decade publications in terms of major focus areas. The focus areas, which are not exhaustive, represent recurring major themes from both ICAC and ICAS conferences. Analysis considers actual number of publications (a) and percentage of all publications (b).*

It is important to note the insignificant shift in the study of trustworthy autonomics. We are well into the second decade of the study of autonomic computing, and the general effort focusing on trustworthy autonomics has barely changed. Only about 3 per cent of the over 1,000 reviewed publications are VT related. Far fewer than this are actual proposals for trustworthy autonomics solution. There is still a wide gap in our appreciation of the need for trustworthy autonomics and the availability of the appropriate solutions. This further strengthens the case for this book.

2.3.4 *First and second decades of autonomic computing research at a glance*

A general overview in the first two decades of the study of autonomic computing in terms of major focus areas shows that survey and distributed systems are the least and most considered areas, respectively (Table 2.8 and Figure 2.11). This shows the level of understanding there is, in these considerations, of the extent of work done in achieving the goal of autonomic computing. The second least considered category, *Actual VT*, raises a concern. The dynamic nature of autonomic systems means that it is close to impossible to comprehensively predict possible outcomes at design time, making it difficult to predetermine whether the autonomic manager's decisions are or will be in line with the overall system's goal. As a result, there is a vital need for runtime validation of autonomic decisions which also contributes to trustworthy autonomics. This area is still largely unexplored.

Analysis so far shows a progressive result in terms of what has been achieved in the autonomic computing research. The academia is clearly leading the effort. There is significant and increasing reduction in the number of publications in both conferences (Figure 2.12). This can be due to a number of factors, including acceptance rate (this usually modulates according to uptake), visibility of conferences (publicity outlets), proliferation of conferences, etc. It is suggested that this continuous decrease is largely due to the number of other publication avenues – conferences and journals that accept similar topics. These avenues, including those dedicated to autonomic computing, have continued to emerge following the introduction of the autonomic computing concept. It would be interesting to know if this trend will continue or whether these two conferences will bounce back in the coming years. However, it is preferable to have dedicated topic-specific conferences. This would help in tracking efforts being made in those research areas.

As can be seen in Figure 2.11, trustworthy autonomics is still largely unexplored. Note that some of these publications only touched on some specific aspects of the categories. The analysis results of the second decade largely corroborate those of the first decade. These correctly reflect the identified trend and direction towards the end of the first decade.

Table 2.8 ICAC and ICAS proceedings distribution in the first two decades of autonomic computing research

Distribution	icac icas 04	icac icas 05	icac icas 06	icac icas 07	icac icas 08	icac icas 09	icac icas 10	icac icas 11	icac icas 12	icac icas 13	icac icas 14	icac icas 15	icac icas 16	icac icas 17	icac icas 18	icac icas 19	Total	%
Authoring																		
Academic	39	50	59	68	49	66	45	55	32	30	26	36	43	39	27	24	**688**	**65.52**
Industry	17	19	19	19	5	14	5	2	12	4	4	6	4	6	2	3	**141**	**13.43**
Joint	8	18	23	14	15	11	7	20	22	17	7	19	12	15	5	8	**221**	**21.05**
Total	**64**	**87**	**101**	**101**	**69**	**91**	**57**	**77**	**66**	**51**	**37**	**61**	**59**	**60**	**34**	**35**	**1050**	**100**
Main application domain																		
Data centre	3	12	17	15	12	13	13	14	12	9	12	6	6	3	7	1	**155**	**14.76**
Distributed systems	17	11	17	11	1	6	3	6	28	19	14	30	18	12	10	10	**213**	**20.29**
Networks	8	6	7	7	2	5	4	4	4	8	3	2	7	9	10	4	**90**	**8.57**
Robotics	1	1	3	1	4	4	1	5	1	2	1	4	3	2	1	7	**41**	**3.90**
Storage and database management	5	5	8	5	1	3	1	5	15	11	8	11	5	5	2	4	**94**	**8.95**
Others																		
Design/ Architecture	7	15	16	9	6	12	6	10	13	4	1	13	10	7	3	4	**136**	**12.95**
Learning/ Knowledge	8	4	4	5	12	7	1	4	3	6	10	6	15	14	14	13	**126**	**12**
Performance management	9	6	10	10	4	12	5	8	21	23	21	15	18	8	15	8	**193**	**18.38**
Policy	2	6	5	4	5	3	3	0	3	1	1	5	2	3	2	4	**49**	**4.67**
Self-CHOP	11	9	5	6	8	9	7	3	18	16	7	12	25	17	8	5	**166**	**15.81**
Survey	0	0	1	2	1	3	0	2	1	0	0	0	1	0	0	1	**12**	**1.14**
VT	4	4	6	5	2	3	1	3	5	3	1	3	3	3	0	2	**48**	**4.57**
Actual VT	1	1	1	4	1	1	0	0	2	0	0	1	2	1	0	1	**16**	**1.52**

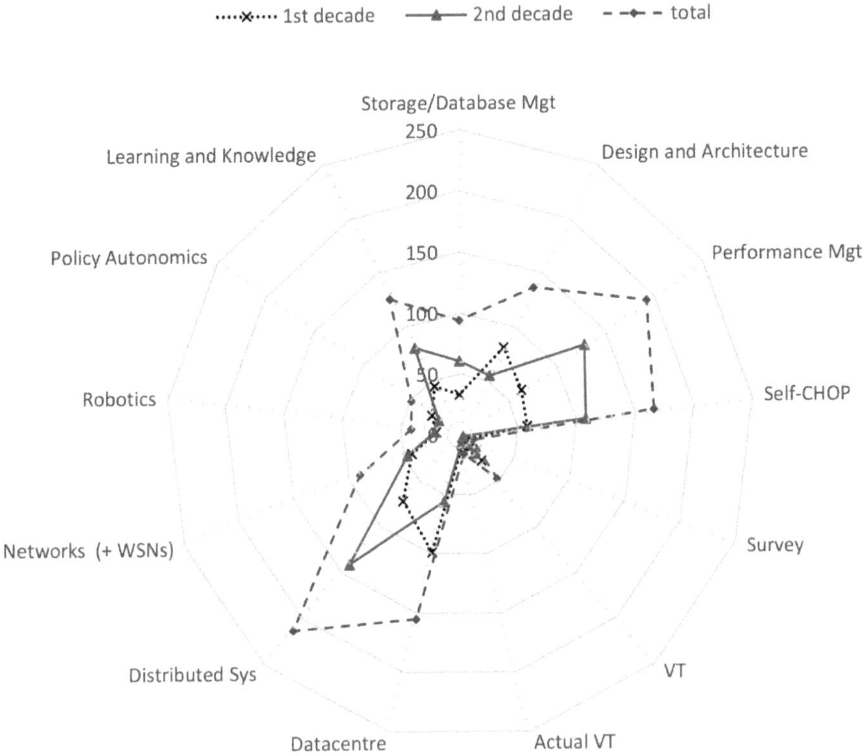

Figure 2.11 *General overview in the first two decades (2004–2019) of the study of autonomic computing. This analysis is based on the review of about 1,050 conference (ICAC and ICAS) paper publications.*

2.4 Trends, direction and open challenges

In this section, the analysis-by-problem approach (Figure 2.13) is used to show the pattern (in terms of maturity stages) that the autonomic computing research community follows in tackling the research challenge. This is useful in identifying the direction of travel and open/remaining research challenges and helps to focus the minds of researchers. Figure 2.13 shows the observed stages (A–C) the research community has adopted in addressing autonomic computing and a view of the current and open challenges (D) towards achieving the goal of autonomic computing. Stage D represents themes that are considered open challenges based on the direction of research.

The analysis here is kept to a high level; however, finer-grained sub-stages may exist. The stages are classified against a maturity timeline, as shown in Table 2.9 Figure 2.8. Although there are possible overlaps, only major and recurring themes are considered for these stages.

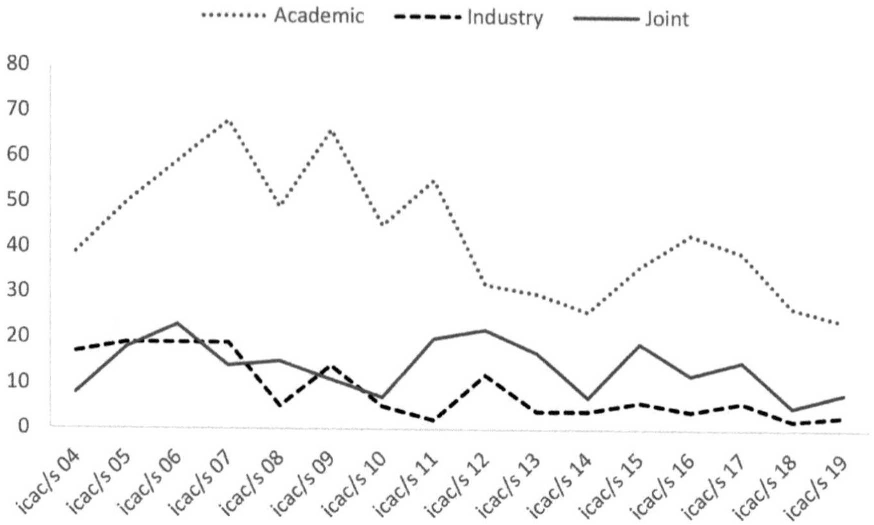

Figure 2.12 Number of ICAC and ICAS conference publications

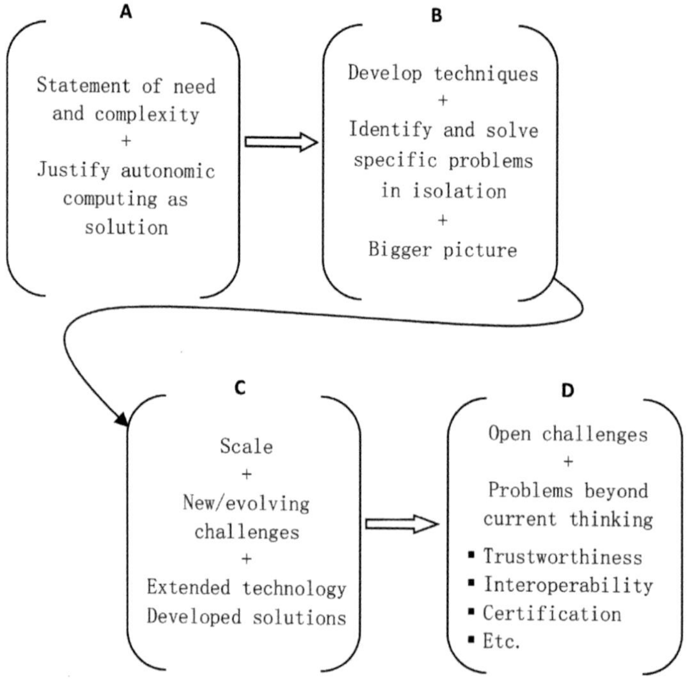

Figure 2.13 Stages showing observed trend and direction of research after the first two decades

Figure 2.14 shows the classification of proceedings used for determining the information in Figure 2.13. Stage A represents research efforts (in this case proceedings of both conferences) from 2004 to 2009. This is the early stage of the research. The middle stage, Stage B, represents efforts from 2010 to 2014 – a time covering towards the end of the first decade and the early years of the second decade. Stage C covers efforts well into the second decade.

2.4.1 Trends and direction

In the early stage (Figure 2.14), investigation reveals that research focused mainly on stating the problem/challenge of evergrowing system complexity [37, 38], the need for solution and justifying autonomicity as that solution [40, 90]. Majority of work in this area, data centre and distributed systems, e.g., were hinged on dynamic resource allocation [41, 42, 91] and were industry (e.g., IBM, HP, Sun) dominant. Towards the middle stage, the research community intensified effort in developing and applying techniques that have now been established and are increasingly used in today's research, e.g., policy-driven autonomics [43, 44], utility functions [46, 92], fuzzy logic [47, 48]. There was also a huge effort in understanding the self-CHOP autonomic functionalities. Although there has been debate on the actual composition of autonomic functionalities and the list substantially growing [3, 5], it is a choice to limit it to the original and generally accepted four self-CHOP functionalities in this chapter.

By the middle stage, many of the autonomic enabling techniques, e.g., policy autonomics, utility functions, fuzzy logic, etc., were fully developed and widely accepted/used. Progress was now made in identifying and solving specific problems in isolation and a significant number of papers offered specific solutions to specific problems. This stage saw an increase in studies specifically devoted to demonstrating the autonomic functionalities in different application domains – examples include self-configuration in distributed systems [93] and for autonomic managers [94], self-healing in control theory [95], self-optimisation-based architecture [96]

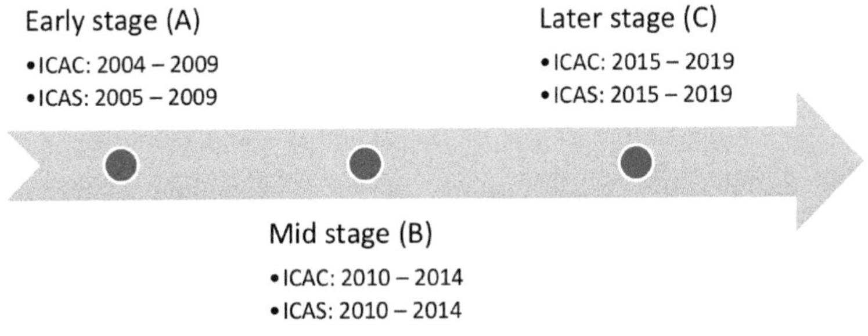

Figure 2.14 Stage classification for all conference proceedings. This is the classification of proceedings used for determining the observed trend and direction of research after the first two decades.

and self-protection in pervasive systems [97]. Other specific areas of focus include virtualisation for distributed systems and data centres [98–100], performance management – especially quality of service [73, 101, 102] and autonomic energy management [103]. The establishment of the composition of autonomic functionalities led to interests, e.g., in how autonomic systems can be described in a universal language that allows for a way to measure the extent of autonomicity exhibited by a particular system [104]. Studies in this stage largely consist of implementations, demonstrations and presentation of experimented results of proposed ideas.

Towards the beginning of the second decade saw the community starting to address the bigger picture with concern now more to do with scale [56, 105] and generalisation of techniques so as to make re-usable solutions. At this stage issues of heterogeneity of services and platforms also began to arise. For example, the community was now faced with addressing large-scale data centres with diverse heterogeneous platforms. This increase in scale and size of systems (e.g., data centres/distributed systems) coupled with heterogeneity of services and platforms means that more autonomic managers could be integrated to achieve a particular goal. This bringing together of many autonomic managers for a common goal led to the need for interoperability between autonomic managers – this became one of the new challenges for the second decade. It is still an open challenge.

Interoperability was somewhat neglected as a challenge in the first decade. Earlier work, within the research community, was fundamentally concerned with getting autonomic computing to work and establishing fundamental concepts and demonstrating viability. Many mechanisms and techniques were explored. Now, in the second decade, that the concept of autonomic computing is well understood and widely accepted, the focus can shift to the next level; e.g., interoperability – how to manage multi-manager scenarios, to govern interactions between managers and to arbitrate when conflicts arise. These are the kind of problems that arose with the increasing scale of systems [65, 66]. For example, when more than one autonomic manager is needed to coordinate a large-scale system, there may be situations where one manager counters the decision of another. There were a few mentions and general discussion around this challenge [12, 106, 107] towards the end of the first decade.

The community had not yet made good progress on interoperability though there were efforts on the way. For example, Anthony *et al.* [61] evaluate the nature and scope of the interoperability challenges for autonomic computing systems, identify a set of requirements for a universal solution and propose a service-based approach to interoperability to handle both direct and indirect conflicts in a multi-manager scenario. In this approach, an interoperability service interacts with autonomic managers through a dedicated interface and is able to detect possible conflicts of management interest. In this way, the interoperability service manages all interoperability activities by granting or withholding management rights to different autonomic managers as appropriate. Another example is the work in Reference [62] which examines a web services solution that standardises access to cross-domain hydrologic data repositories (of disparate semantic and syntactic definitions and hosted on heterogeneous platforms) to facilitate data discovery and enable cross-domain interoperability. The project emphasises the idea of a seamless interface through which access can be gained to hydrologic data from multiple heterogeneous data sources.

There has now been an increased focus in the autonomic research community on interoperability. Several studies [36, 108, 109, 110, 36, 111] in the later stage (Figure 2.14) have addressed the challenge of interoperability in many ways. The study in Reference [108] looks at interoperability within autonomous swarms of unmanned systems, another study in Reference [109] focuses on autonomic conflict management between coexisting applications, while the study in Reference [110] addresses interference-aware load balancing. The research in Reference [36] looks at interoperability in achieving service level objectives, and Reference [111] is interested in multi-agent interaction within supply scheduling.

One recurring theme in the later stage is power management. Climate change awareness/campaign has become popular in the last decade. This is also reflected in the direction of research within the autonomic computing community as increasingly several studies are focused on autonomic power management of data centre. Efforts towards reducing the data centre's contribution to climate change are taking centre stage [79–83]. It is important to remember that the current stage is characterised by increased scale, new challenges and extended technologies (Figure 2.13). As a result, there is a significant jump in learning and knowledge (Figure 2.11), reflecting the application of modern technologies, like machine learning, to address those complexities [63][112][113]. This explains the increase in learning and knowledge in Figure 2.11. Also noticeable in Figure 2.11 is the decrease in the focus on design and architecture as there is now a good hang on the design of autonomic systems compared to the first decade.

2.4.2 *Open challenges*

On the other hand, beyond current mainstream focus are evolving and open challenges, including issues of validation, trustworthiness and certification. The following set of questions identified earlier [9] are yet to be fully answered:

- *What are the processes to ensure that component upgrades that are tested and confirmed in isolation will not cause harm in a multi-system environment?*
- *How can certified autonomic systems be achieved?*
- *How can users be confident that a system does what it says?*
- *How can consistency and reliability be achieved, over longer time frames, beyond attaining self-management?*

Out of the 1,050 reviewed publications, only 48 are VT related while only 16 are actual VT methodologies. The number for VT includes mainly those papers that incorporated validation, testing and reliability into their architectures, frameworks or implementations and not necessarily as a core or critical feature. For example, in the two decades under review, only two ICAS papers [12, 114] propose a method. The work in Reference [12] presents a framework (based on model checking) for verifying and detecting constraint violation when two or more workflows are executed on the same system as a way of ensuring system trustworthiness. Page *et al.* [114] propose a methodology to analyse and test autonomous systems in hazardous environments, with the aim of verifying safe decision-making.

The few VT-related papers in ICAC include [9][115][116][117]. Hoi *et al.* [9] ask the critical question of *'How can we trust an autonomic system to make the best decision*?' and proposes a 'trust' architecture to win the trust of autonomic computing system users. The proposal is to introduce trust into the system by assigning an 'instantaneous trust index' (ITI) to each execution of a system's autonomic manager – where ITI could be computed, e.g., by examining what fraction of autonomic manager suggested actions the user accepts unchanged, or by examining how extensive the changes that the user makes to the suggested actions are. The overall trust index, which reflects the system administration's level of trust in the autonomic manager, is computed as the function $f(ITI_i)$ where $i = 1, 2, 3, \ldots$ and ITI_i are the individual ITIs for each autonomic manager execution. Kikuchi *et al.* [115] propose a policy verification and validation framework that is based on model checking to verify the validity of administrator's specified policies in a policy-based system. Because a known performing policy may lead to erroneous behaviour if the system (in any aspect) is changed slightly, the framework is based on checking the consistency of the policy and the system's defined model or characteristics. In all the reviewed first decade papers, this is the only VT method implemented with data centre case study. Landauer and Bellman [116] present a methodology that facilitates the evaluation of design choices at system definition time while Reference [117] concentrates on computational trust.

It should be noted that autonomic system trustworthiness goes beyond secure computing. It is result oriented, not focusing on how a goal is achieved but the dependability of the output. All systems, no matter how simple, are designed to meet a need, but not all systems have security concerns. So, trustworthiness is not all about security and validation; on the other hand, it is not about showing that a system or process works but ensuring that it does exactly what it is meant to do. It is also important to note that validation here needs to be runtime.

We have identified the problems of robust design, validation and related issues on trustworthiness leading to certification [26]. In Reference [26], we outline the challenges in current autonomic system validation methods and propose a strategy leading to the achievement of autonomic systems certification. This strategy is a roadmap defining the stages or processes in the journey towards full autonomic computing. We posit that there are significant limitations to the way in which autonomic systems are validated, with heavy reliance on traditional design-time techniques, despite the highly dynamic behaviour of these systems in dealing with runtime configuration changes and environmental and context changes. These limitations ultimately undermine the trustability of these systems and are barriers to eventual certification. Shuaib *et al.* [11] propose a framework that will allow for proper certification of autonomic computing systems. Central to this framework is an alternative autonomic architecture based on intelligent machine design which draws from the human autonomic nervous system. It is strongly believed that certification is critical to achieving the full goal of autonomic computing.

> ***[There are significant limitations to the way in which autonomic systems are validated, with heavy reliance on traditional design-time techniques, despite the highly dynamic behaviour of these systems in dealing with runtime configuration changes and environmental and context changes]***

Another open challenge is interoperability, discussed in Chapter 6. Effort here will include evaluating the nature and scope of the interoperability challenges for autonomic computing systems, identifying a set of requirements for a universal solution and proposing a service-based approach to interoperability to handle both direct and indirect conflicts in a multi-manager scenario. An efficient solution, e.g., stigmergic-based interoperability [118], will need to be seamless and consider interoperability as an integral part of the system.

These are only a few main open challenges. As technology evolves, leading to new complexities and issues, the autonomic computing solutions will need to evolve too.

2.5 Conclusion

This chapter has discussed the evolution of autonomic computing, focusing on the autonomic architecture life cycle and the trend and direction of research towards addressing the autonomic computing challenge.

For autonomic architecture, at the level of current state of practice, there are techniques to provide runtime validation (for behavioural and structural conformity) and additional console for higher level (and external) control. What is missing are techniques for managing, e.g., in a longer time frame, instability and oscillatory behaviour in autonomic systems. A holistic framework that collates all these capabilities into a single autonomic unit is required. These are proposed in this book.

A broad and general analysis of autonomic computing research, in terms of identifying trends in the research from 2004 to 2019, has also been presented. This gives a thorough review of the state-of-the-art in trustworthy autonomics. Results show that trustworthy autonomics, which is essential to the success of autonomic computing, has received very little attention compared to other focus areas. Only 9 per cent of over 1,000 reviewed research publications identify trustworthiness as a challenge while only about 3 per cent propose actual methodologies targeting validation and trustworthiness although majority of these methodologies are application dependent.

A roadmap towards achieving trustworthy autonomic systems, identifying stages of layered autonomic solution within which appropriate processes and instrumentations are defined, needs to be followed. The stages can also be seen as concrete autonomic developmental phases (in terms of maturity timeline) that lead to achieving certifiable autonomic systems. These stages should include the following:

- Defining an autonomic system – what makes a system autonomic? This will include a description of autonomicity and a means to measure the level of autonomicity required for or attained by the system.
- Setting out validation requirements, appropriate to the system's definition, that will meet runtime conditions.
- Defining robust techniques and measures that ensure the system remains consistent and reliable under almost all perceivable operating and contextual circumstances.

The trend seen in the analysis in this chapter seems to be revealing a kind of plan that is consistent with the roadmap towards achieving trustworthy autonomic systems.

Chapter 3
Autonomic enabling techniques

Autonomic computing has been powered by a combination of many established and new techniques. These include different algorithms, logics, functions, mechanisms, routines, tools, etc., which are used to deliver desired autonomic functionalities. This chapter presents some of these techniques and shows examples of how they can be used to achieve relevant autonomic computing features.

In this chapter, you will be able to:

- Study different autonomic enabling techniques
- Understand how autonomic enabling techniques can be used to achieve autonomic functionalities
- Practice with autonomic enabling techniques
- Understand how autonomic enabling techniques can be combined to achieve trustworthy autonomics

3.1 About autonomic enabling techniques

Autonomic computing leads to the creation of systems that are capable of self-management – autonomic systems. This has been widely accepted to mean that such systems are able to demonstrate some level of autonomic functionalities. So, autonomic systems are defined by the autonomic functionalities they provide. These autonomic functionalities, arguably not exhaustive, depending on domain application, were originally limited to self-configuration, self-healing, self-optimisation and self-protection (self-CHOP).

Each of the autonomic functionalities can be enabled by a single technique or a combination of different techniques. For example, self-healing can be achieved by implementing any fault-tolerant technique. Self-healing can also be achieved by specifying relevant behaviours as policies (or rules). Building autonomic systems requires imbedding these autonomic enabling techniques into the design of the systems.

3.2 Simple exponential smoothing

Autonomic systems are designed to make decisions and adapt based on contextual information. Relevant inputs from the operating environment are fed into the autonomic system, which are processed for the system's adaptation. Sometimes, these inputs are erratic, irregular and could lead to instability in the system's behaviour. Making decisions based on erratic inputs can lead to unreliable outcomes. To enable an autonomic system make reliable decisions with highly irregular inputs, the system needs to be able to sanitise the inputs first. This sanitisation may involve analysing the inputs for trends and removing noise before acting on them. Sometimes, it may be necessary to be able to forecast or have an idea of the subsequent data inputs (next expected values) and take those into consideration for more efficient adaptation decisions. One way of doing this is to find a way of forecasting future values (data points) with reference to the most recent data points. This is especially relevant in situations, like autonomic computing, where data values have no form of trend or seasonality.

Simple exponential smoothing (SES) is a technique for extrapolating patterns and trends in time-series data. This is used in analysing time-series data to smooth the data stream, remove noise and forecast the next data in the sequence. In signal processing, for example, the signal may fluctuate with high-frequency (noise), and SES can be used to remove the noise and smooth the data. The SES (S_t) of a data sequence (x) at time (t) is defined by the following:

$$S_t = (\alpha \cdot x_t) + ((1 - \alpha) \cdot S_{t-1})$$
$$\text{where, } S_0 = x_0, t > 0 \text{ and } 0 < \alpha < 1$$

The smoothed value S_t is a forecast for the next data sequence x_{t+1} . The smoothing constant (α) controls the closeness of the forecast value to the actual value. The sequence begins at $t = 0$, allowing for at least one observation before forecast can start. The result is that S_t smoothens the data sequence, generating new values that are stable and close to x_t as possible. The idea here is to use a weighted average of previous values in a particular series to forecast future values. This idea is very useful in autonomic computing for making reliable decisions with unstable data inputs.

3.2.1 *Implementing an SES using python*

SES is one out of three types of exponential smoothing techniques. It is suitable for series that are unpredictable, i.e., series with no trend or seasonality. Holt's exponential smoothing is suitable for series with trend and no seasonality while Winter's exponential smoothing is suitable for series with trend and seasonality. These can be implemented in Python using the Statsmodels package:

```
from statsmodels.tsa.holtwinters import SimpleExpSmoothing
from statsmodels.tsa.api import ExponentialSmoothing
from statsmodels.tsa.api import SimpleExpSmoothing
from statsmodels.tsa.api import Holt
import statsmodels.tsa.holtwinters as ets
// Any or a combination of the above will suffice
import matplotlib.pyplot as plt
// you can use the matplot library for plotting the chart of the forecast

data = [dat1, dat2, dat3, …, datn]
// prepare data. This can be hardcoded or received as a csv file
model = SimpleExpSmoothing(data).fit()
model = SimpleExpSmoothing(data).fit(smoothing_level=0.2,optimized=False)
// specifying the smoothing constant (in this case α=0.2) if needed
fcast = model.forecast()
// make the forecast
```

The smoothing constant (α) can be specified using smoothing_level, but if this is not specified or set to None, the model will automatically optimise the value – Statsmodels will automatically find an optimised α value for the forecast. However, since a satisfactory forecast value is application domain dependent, an 'optimised' value may not always be the best value for α. So, it may be necessary to specify different α values and then choose a smoothed forecast option that best meets the goal of the system in the case scenario – see the next section 3.2.2. For more details about SES, see References 119, 120 and 121.

3.2.2 Basic implementation of an SES using microsoft excel sheet

Implementing SES in Microsoft Excel is very straightforward. We need to note the SES function, which is computed in order to generate the required forecast.

$$S_t = (\alpha \cdot x_t) + ((1 - \alpha) \cdot S_{t-1})$$

Figure 3.1 is a Microsoft Excel computation of SES for a fictitious sample data series (column C). Different α values (column A: 0.2, 0.3, 0.5, 0.8 and 0.25) are used to generate different forecasts. As highlighted, the SES function (=(A2*$C3)+((1-$A$2)*D2)) that is computed for Cell D3 is replicated for all the other cells in that column. The '$' notation is used to keep those values constant when replicating the

D3   fx   =(A2*$C3)+((1-$A$2)*D2)

	A	B	C	D	E	F	G	H
1	α		Actual value	α=0.2	α=0.3	α=0.5	α=0.8	α=0.25
2	0.2							
3	0.3		20	4	6	10	16	5
4	0.5		2	3.6	4.8	6	4.8	4.25
5	0.8		5	3.88	4.86	5.5	4.96	4.4375
6	0.25		15	6.104	7.902	10.25	12.992	7.078125
7			8	6.4832	7.9314	9.125	8.9984	7.308594
8			4	5.98656	6.75198	6.5625	4.99968	6.481445
9			9	6.589248	7.426386	7.78125	8.199936	7.111084
10			3	5.871398	6.09847	5.390625	4.039987	6.083313
11			12	7.097119	7.868929	8.695313	10.408	7.562485
12			5	6.677695	7.00825	6.847656	6.081599	6.921864
13			25	10.34216	12.40578	15.92383	21.21632	11.4414
14			12	10.67372	12.28404	13.96191	13.84326	11.58105
15			1	8.73898	8.89883	7.480957	3.568653	8.935786
16			8	8.591184	8.629181	7.740479	7.113731	8.70184
17			2	7.272947	6.640427	4.870239	3.022746	7.02638
18			6	7.018358	6.448299	5.43512	5.404549	6.769785
19			9	7.414686	7.213809	7.21756	8.28091	7.327339
20			15	8.931749	9.549666	11.10878	13.65618	9.245504
21			2	7.545399	7.284766	6.55439	4.331236	7.434128
22			18	9.636319	10.49934	12.27719	15.26625	10.0756

Figure 3.1 Microsoft Excel computation of simple exponential smoothingSES with different values

function. For example, the SES function becomes =(A2*$C12)+((1-$A$2)*D11) for Cell D12. However, the column A values are changed for the other columns to capture the different values of α. For example, the SES function for Cells E3 and F3 becomes =(A3*$C3)+((1-$A$3)*E2) and =($A$4*$C3)+((1-A4)*F2), respectively. The chart for the forecast is shown in Figure 3.2.

Figure 3.2 shows the SES of a sample series using different smoothing constants. Ideally, the closer the smoothing constant is to 1, the closer the forecast will be to the actual (expected) value. However, a value of $\alpha = 1$, which would return the exact expected actual value, does not necessarily mean that the forecast is optimised. For studies showing how to determine optimal values of exponential smoothing constants, see References 122, 123, 124, 125 and 126.

It is important to note that an optimised value of α is relative. In a situation where it is useful to generate a more accurate forecast, an *optimised* value of α, for example, generated by default as explained in the Python implementation, would be one that produces forecasts that are satisfactorily close to the actual value. In another instance, say where the series is highly erratic and unpredictable, it may be preferred to choose a smoothing constant that generates forecasts that are more stable as well as close to the actual value. In the example of Figure 3.2, a smoothing constant value of $\alpha = 0.5$ may be preferred as it represents a more fine-tuned outcome. This choice may be justified because it smoothens out unwanted cyclical and irregular values. It may also be the case that even a more stable outcome is desired, in which case a smoothing constant value of $\alpha = 0.3$ is preferred. As can be seen in Figure 3.2, a value of $\alpha = 0.3$ leads to an outcome that is well within the standard deviation of the series, i.e., between data values of 3 and 15.

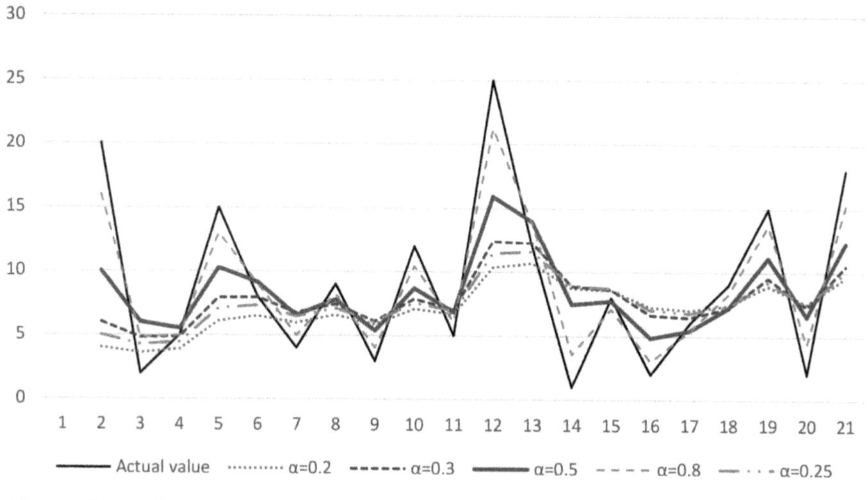

Figure 3.2 Sample series showing SES. Different smoothing constants (0.2, 0.25, 0.3, 0.5 and 0.8) are used

The smoothing constant value may also depend on the standard deviation of the data series, considering the amount of variation of the forecast from the expected. The important thing is to choose a smoothing constant value that enables the system in which it is applied to achieve its intended goal. For example, in trustworthy autonomic computing, having different values of the smoothing constant is useful for dynamic tuning of behaviours. This is the focus of the implementation in this book as explained in section 3.2.3. It is important to then note that the choice of a smoothing constant value should be application dependent.

3.2.3 Implementing SES in autonomic computing

SES is used in this book in Chapter 6 for analysing interoperability in a multi-autonomic manager datacentre scenario. The model of the datacentre used in the experimentation is as follows.

The datacentre model comprises the following:

- A pool of resources S_i (live servers) – a collection of servers available to the autonomic manager.
- A pool of shutdown servers $\check{S}_i$. These are ready to be powered and restored to S_i as needed.
- A list of applications A_j – a collection of applications supported (as services) by the datacentre.
- A pool of services Ṳ. This is a combination of applications and their provisioning servers.
- Two autonomic managers that optimise the entire system.

As service requests arrive, the autonomic manager dynamically populates Ṳ to service the requests. Service (application) requests arrive and are queued. If there are enough resources to service a particular request, then it is serviced; otherwise, it remains in the queue (or may eventually be dropped). The autonomic manager checks for resource availability and deploys server(s) according to the size of the request.

[In order to efficiently provision for service requests, the autonomic manager needs a way of having an idea of the level of expected requests so as to prepare for them. A trustworthy autonomic manager would require the ability to forecast these expected requests.]

The size of application requests and the capacity of servers are defined in million instructions per second. When a server is deployed, it is placed in a queue for a time defined by a particular time variable. This queue simulates the time (delay) it takes to load or configure a server with necessary application before provisioning. Any server can be (re)configured for different applications and so servers are not pre-configured. Servers are then 'provisioned' after spending time in the queue. The provisioning pool is constantly populated as requests arrive. As requests are fully serviced (completed), servers are released into the server pool and redeployed as may be needed.

A basic system without any form of smartness can barely go far before the whole system is clogged due to inefficient and unstructured resource management. The level to which any autonomic manager can successfully and efficiently manage the process defined above depends on its level of sophistication. This largely depends on how each autonomic manager is wired (in terms of architecture and not necessarily the scheduling algorithm or actual component logic used) and may include, in this case, the ability to *optimally* forecast requests for efficient adaptation. For example, two autonomic managers, differently wired, may employ the same scheduling algorithm but achieve different results. Results here may be looked at in terms of, say, '*with such level of available resources how many requests were successfully serviced over a period of time?*'. These are the kinds of considerations for trustworthy autonomic managers.

In this scenario, resource requests are sometimes erratic and the autonomic managers need to be able to *forecast* requests and be able to plan for what is coming. The smoothing constant variable (α) for calculating SES is used to forecast the size (capacity) of arriving or expected requests. The autonomic managers with interoperability solution use SES in calculating when it is safe to start restoring servers or stop shutting servers down as the case may be. The smoothing average is implemented on the capacity (million instructions per second) of arriving requests, which sometimes can be highly erratic. Taking decisions based on erratic behaviour can destabilise the entire system and so appropriate smoothing constant (α) is needed to stabilise the system. An experiment with different smoothing constant values is shown in Figure 3.3.

It is important to choose a smoothing constant value that will not result in exponential smoothed average that is very close to the actual data as that will not smoothen the system's behaviour. For the experiments in Chapter 6, exponential results using three smoothing constants (0.05, 0.15 and 0.25) are analysed (Figure 3.3). Using any of 0.15 or 0.25, as shown, will result in exponential smoothed average very close to the actual data with no significant difference and so does not smoothen the system's behaviour. However, the smoothing constant of 0.05 proves best in smoothing the system behaviour and using this will enable the autonomic managers to take more reliable decisions. The experimental analyses presented in Chapter 6 are based on smoothing constant value of 0.05.

3.3 Dead-zone logic

In system design considerations, there are broadly two types of systems. These are systems with predetermined behaviour, leading to predictable outcomes, and systems whose behaviour may not be predetermined and whose outcomes are

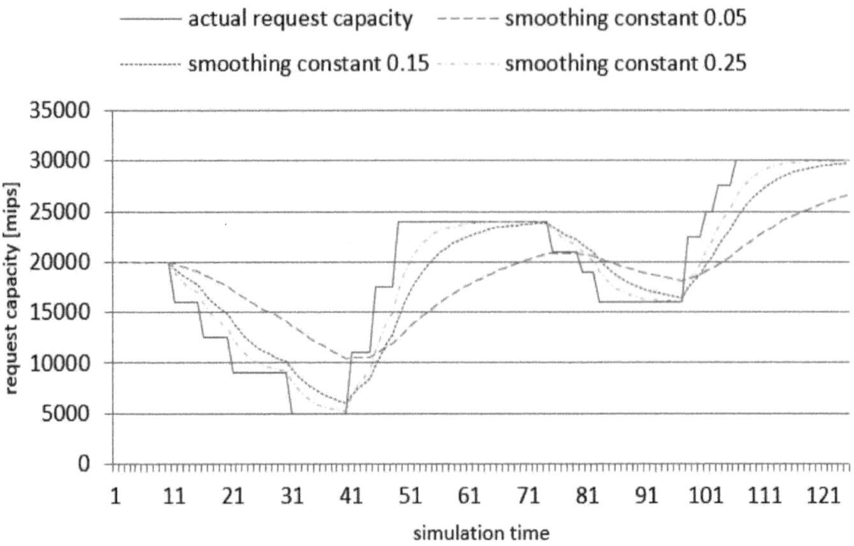

Figure 3.3 *Simple exponential smoothed results with three values of* α *(the smoothing constant). It is important to have a justification for the choice of* α

unpredictable. The operating and environmental conditions of predictable or fixed systems are well-known. These conditions are adequately captured when configuring the systems so that their behaviour and outcomes are always predictable under almost all conceivable conditions.

On the other hand, flexible systems are exposed to environments where system working conditions are dynamic, uncertain and most times, unpredictable. For these systems, it is impracticable to fully predetermine their operating and environmental conditions. These systems are designed to adapt their behaviour dynamically. Such systems, for example, autonomic systems, are getting more pervasive and being embedded in everyday objects. To adapt their behaviour, these systems are influenced by contextual input – environmental condition, direct data input, etc. However, these contextual inputs are not always predetermined and cannot be planned for during system design time. Also, they are sometimes erratic or sporadic, and this can lead to unstable behaviour and unreliable outcomes. Trustworthy autonomic systems should be able to handle sporadic inputs and yet remain stable and produce reliable outcomes.

Consider two systems – a basic radiator controller with fixed input and conditions and a driverless car with unpredictable inputs and conditions, for example. Heating controllers are connected to a central heating system and are used to control the overall ambient temperature of the environment, e.g., the home. They come in all forms of shapes and with different features. There are 'smart controllers' these days, like the Hive Active Heating (Figure 3.4). Regardless of all the smartness of new heating controllers, they are based on a simple device called thermostat.

Figure 3.4 *Hive Active Heating 2 control – an example of a fixed system with predetermined behaviour*

A thermostat senses the temperature of an environment and controls the switching ON or OFF of a heating system to maintain a desired temperature setpoint. Heating controllers like Figure 3.4 are simply called thermostats.

The basic function of a thermostat is to sense ambient temperature and maintains it at a setpoint. Once a target temperature is set, the system maintains that temperature. For example, in Figure 3.4, the TARGET temperature is set to 20 degrees and the ACTUAL ambient is 18 degrees. As shown, heating is turned ON and will remain so until ACTUAL temperature gets up to 20 degrees. As long as this system is in use, it will not let the ambient temperature to fall below the TARGET temperature without switching heating ON. This is a typical example of a fixed system with known environmental conditions and predictable outcomes. The design of such system can predetermine all conceivable environmental conditions (ACTUAL temperature is either below or above TARGET temperature), making the system predictable (heating is turned ON or OFF). Thermostats are reliable candidates for home heating controllers because home temperature does not fluctuate frequently, meaning that it is okay to have a system with a binary decision line.

In a different system, e.g., a driverless car (Figure 3.5), it is almost impossible to predetermine all the driving conditions the car will face. This makes the design of such cars very complex because designers cannot completely determine how the car should react. Even with experience and research, human knowledge of driving conditions is still limited. Machine learning and artificial intelligence may help the driverless car make some important decisions; however, as driving conditions also include considerations for human behaviour (e.g., the decision process of other road users – drivers, cyclists, pedestrians, bystanders, etc.) which is highly unpredictable, it is difficult to predict outcomes. It is also important to note that some of the ambient inputs the driverless car uses for its decision-making are erratic and volatile, and decisions based on such inputs can lead to undesirable outcomes not anticipated at design. This is a typical

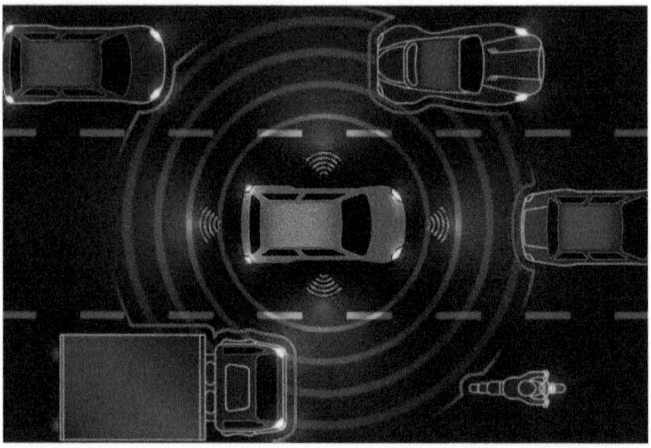

Figure 3.5 *RAC's illustration of a driverless car – an example of a flexible system whose behaviour may not be predetermined (Image from RAC.co.uk)*

example of a flexible system, which is exposed to environments where system working conditions are dynamic, uncertain and most times, unpredictable.

Dead-zone (DZ) logic is a simple mechanism to stabilise an erratic behaviour. It was originally introduced by Dr. Richard Anthony [20, 43] and extensively demonstrated in Reference 49. It prevents unnecessary, inefficient and ineffective control brevity when an adaptive system is sufficiently close to its target state. This can be used in designing fixed and flexible systems, where input-based decisions change quite regularly, in order to calm system behaviour. This is widely relevant for trustworthy autonomic systems.

DZ logic is implemented using a tolerance range check object which controls the choice of action to be taken, depending on specified or learned rules. These adaptation-related actions could be as simple as increase value, decrease value or do not change value. This logic is used in configuring the dependability check component of trustworthy autonomic architecture (TrAArch – see Chapters 4, 5 and 6) to enable the autonomic manager achieve stability by mitigating oscillation and unwanted erratic behaviours. The DZ width, demarcated by the DZ boundaries, defines an area (or state) within which the autonomic manager does not allow a system to change its action.

Figure 3.6 is a representation of a system behaviour on a behaviour space divided into two zones (A and B). A particular policy or adaptation action is activated within each zone, demarcated by a decision boundary. So, for example, the policy action for zone A is activated when the system's state falls within the boundaries of zone A. Within each zone, at decision or state points (represented by x and y), actions are changed or maintained and these are persisted until the decision boundary is crossed. For the behaviour in Figure 3.6, there seems to be stability in the system as the points of behaviour change (state points – x and y) are reasonably far from the decision boundary. This shows that the system does not change its behaviour frequently.

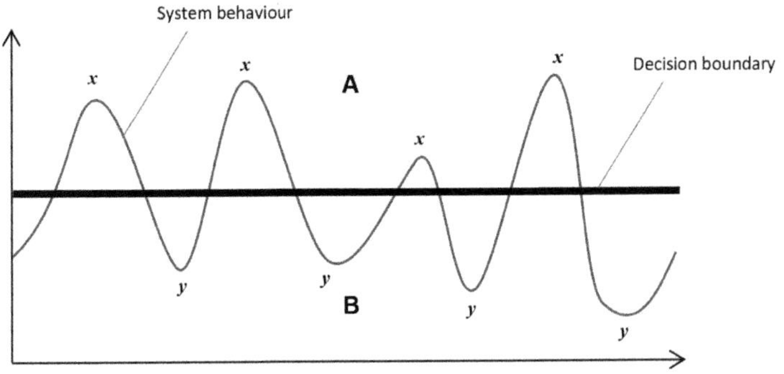

Figure 3.6 *System behaviour space showing stable outcome. The behaviour of the systems, represented by the graph, is not erratic*

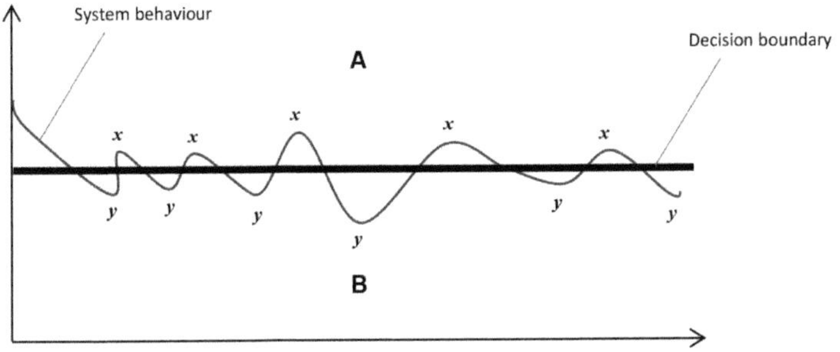

Figure 3.7 *System behaviour space showing unstable outcome. The system behaviour may be erratic*

However, this cannot always be guaranteed as some systems are dynamic with fluctuating and erratic behaviour caused by sporadic contextual inputs, for example. This is the case with the example in Figure 3.7.

In Figure 3.7, the points of behaviour change are sometimes very close to the zone boundary. This shows that the system changes its behaviour quite frequently. This kind of performance might not be desirable in situations where each change has significant overall implications. Take for instance, a system that helps in making stock trading decisions might not be profitable if it frequently changes its decisions in a volatile market condition. Such sensitive systems need to be able to tune out erratic contextual inputs that could cause oscillation and instability in the process. This is where the DZ logic is helpful.

In Figure 3.8, the system's behaviour space is further divided into different zones (A, B, C and D). This introduces DZ boundaries, defining DZ widths within which a change of action is not allowed, which reduce the rate of action change and thereby increasing stability. In this case, the points of behaviour change (state points) indicate which zone action is activated or running – a, b, c and d indicate

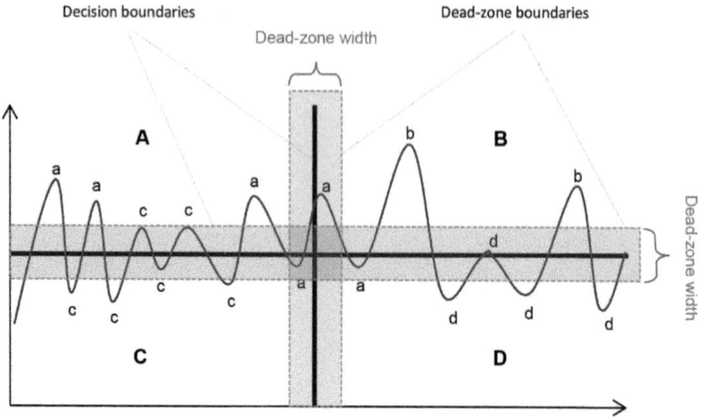

Figure 3.8 Illustration of DZ logic over a system behaviour space divided into different zones and expressed in two dimensions of freedom. The system behaviour is erratic in some places and a bit stable in other places

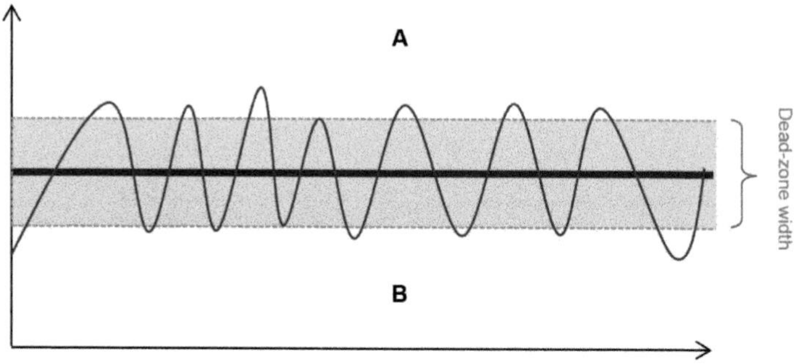

Figure 3.9 Dynamic tuning of DZ width to reduce adaptation

actions for zones A, B, C and D, respectively. Ideally, without the DZ boundaries, a new action is activated each time the system behaviour crosses the decision boundary. Without the DZ boundaries in Figure 3.8, there would have been 18 action changes, which are now reduced to 9 by implementing DZ logic.

However, there are situations where it might be necessary to dynamically adjust (tune) the DZ width to allow the system some flexibilities in decision-making based on current (unplanned and learned) realities. Consider Figures 3.7–3.8 as good examples of when it may be necessary to dynamically tune the DZ widths. In Figure 3.9, the system's state points are very close to the edges of the DZ boundaries. At this behaviour, it may be necessary to dynamically increase the DZ width – this is known as dynamic tuning (e.g., $DZWidth + \alpha$). On the other hand, in Figure 3.10, where most of the state points are far from the DZ boundaries which means that the system rarely adapts, it may be necessary to reduce the DZ width ($DZWidth - \alpha$) if the

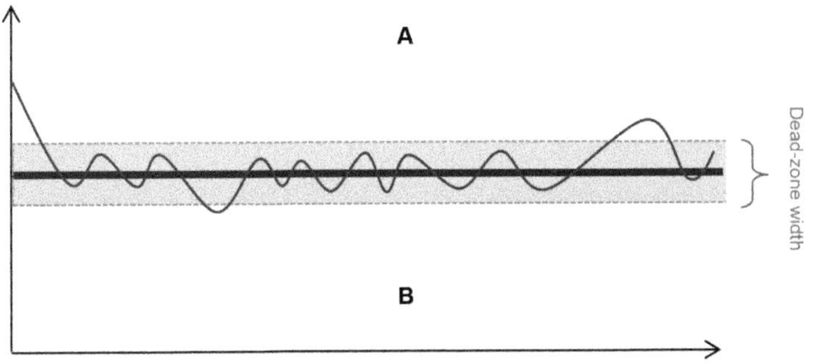

Figure 3.10 Dynamic tuning of DZ width to increase adaptation

system is desired to adapt more frequently. It is important to note that the dynamic tuning of DZ widths is application dependent. See Reference 49 for a detailed presentation of DZ logic.

3.3.1 Implementing dead-zone logic in autonomic computing

Consider an experiment in which an autonomic manager is monitoring a system behaviour to track a particular goal over time. A random number generator is used to generate numbers between and including 15 and 25. An autonomic manager monitors the number generation, tracking the value of 20, and performs one of three actions at every number generation cycle – *if generated number < 20, perform action A, if > 20, perform action B and if = 20, perform no action.* This can be an example representation of so many smart systems, e.g., a heating controller monitoring the fluctuating temperature of an environment, a sensor-powered system monitoring the humidity around a preserved item, a sensor monitoring the movement of a fragile cargo during transportation, etc. The role of the autonomic manager is to perform some actions based on the outcome of the number generator (representing some environmental conditions), and this can be implemented using the following code:

```
Random randomGen = new Random();
int num = randomGen.Next(15, 26); // random number generator
                                   //generating values from 15 to 25

if (num < 20)
{
    AutonomicManagerAction.ActionA;
}
else if (num > 20)
{
    AutonomicManagerAction.ActionB;
}
else
{
    AutonomicManagerAction.NoAction;
}
```

This is a very basic implementation of the system and, depending on the rate of the number generation, if the outcome frequently fluctuates around 20, the autonomic manager will change its action frequently as well. That level of decision change might be considered instability in some applications. Implementing a DZ logic will help the autonomic manager calm the situation as follows:

```
Random randomGen = new Random(); // global intialisation
public int Counter = 0; // global intialisation
public int DecisionChangeCount = 0; // global initialisation
public int DZWidth = 1 // global initialisation

private void timerGeneral_Tick(object sender, EventArgs e) // implement as a timer
{
        int num = randomGen.Next(15, 26); // random number generator
                                          //generating values from 15 to 25
        Counter += 1

        if (num < (20 + DZWidth)) // dead zone is added to the decision boundary
        {
            AutonomicManagerAction.ActionA;
            DecisionChangeCount += 1; // incrementing decision change count
                                   // by 1 each time a decision is changed
            if (Counter == 10)
            {
               if (DecisionChangeCount > 3)
                  {
                      DZWidth += 1; // increase dead-zone width by 1
                  }
               if (DecisionChangeCount < 1)
                  {
                      DZWidth -= 1; // decrease dead-zone width by 1
                  }
               Counter = 0; // re-initialises counter
               DecisionChangeCount = 0; // re-initialises counter
            }
        }
        else if (num > (20 + DZWidth)) // dead zone is added to the decision boundary
        {
            AutonomicManagerAction.ActionB;
            DecisionChangeCount += 1; // incrementing decision change count
                                          // by 1 each time a decision is changed
            if (Counter == 10)
            {
               if (DecisionChangeCount > 3)
                  {
                      DZWidth += 1; // increase dead-zone width by 1
                  }
               if (DecisionChangeCount < 1)
                  {
                      DZWidth -= 1; // decrease dead-zone width by 1
                  }
               Counter = 0; // re-initialises counter
               DecisionChangeCount = 0; // re-initialises counter
            }
        }
        else
        {
            AutonomicManagerAction.NoAction;
        }
}
```

> ***Note:*** *this is an adaptation of a C# script for implementing the experiment explained above. To be able to plot the graph shown in Figure 3.11 in real time, you would need to use graphics class (e.g., the System.Drawing Namespace) that provides for drawing to the display device. You can always Google how to plot graphs in C# using System.Drawing or any other Namespace.*

In this second implementation, the autonomic manager implements DZ logic. By implementing DZ logic, it becomes sensitive to the effects of its actions on the system. This means that the manager looks at the impact of its actions on the system over a long-term time frame and decides whether to retune itself. In this case, for example, if the actions of the autonomic manager cause the system to oscillate, e.g., frequently changing its action, it creates a tolerance behaviour range within which actions are not changed, i.e., actions are persisted. In order to manage erratic behaviour, the autonomic manager decides whether to reduce its rate of action change by increasing the DZ width and thereby making the decision boundary (20 + DZWidth) instead of 20 following some defined policy. The policy ensures that for every 10 decision cycles, decision change count of 4 or above is considered unstable while no decision change is considered inactive. So, the autonomic manager is configured to dynamically throttle the size of the DZWidth to only allow minimum of 1 and maximum of 3 decision changes in every 10 decision cycles. Figure 3.11 shows the result of this experiment.

Figure 3.11 represents the behaviour trend (in terms of action change) of the autonomic manager with and without dead zone. The autonomic manager implemented with DZ logic is represented by *AutonomicManager_WithDZ* while

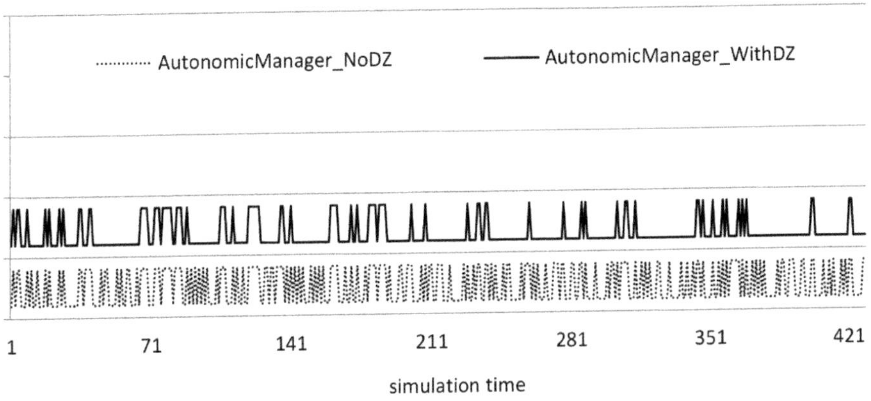

Figure 3.11 *System behaviour analysis of an autonomic manager with and without DZ logic. The autonomic manager implemented with DZ logic is represented by AutonomicManager_WithDZ while the same autonomic manager implemented without DZ logic is represented by AutonomicManager_NoDZ*

the same autonomic manager implemented without DZ logic is represented by *AutonomicManager_NoDZ*. The trend, indicated by the graph, shows the state of each autonomic manager over a period of time – it alternates between crest and trough each time the autonomic manager changes its decision. Results of the experiment show that while *AutonomicManager_NoDZ* changed its decision a total of 236 times, *AutonomicManager_WithDZ* changed its decision 93 times. This represents a significant improvement with DZ logic. Imagine, for example, how inefficient it will be for a real-life smart system to make 236 decisions whereas it can make only 93 efficient decisions within the same time frame and conditions by simply implementing DZ logic. It is obvious then that DZ logic can reduce instability and this is useful in building trustworthy autonomic systems.

3.4 Stigmergy

Stigmergy was first introduced in 1959, in reference to termite behaviour, by a French biologist Pierre-Paul Grassé who defined it as 'Stimulation of workers by the performance they have achieved' [127]. This has since inspired a wide range of research and application in computer science leading to more accessible definitions, understanding and implementations. Two interesting definitions of stigmergy by Wiktionary are as follows:

> ***"A mechanism of spontaneous, indirect coordination between agents or actions, where the trace left in the environment by an action stimulates the performance of a subsequent action."***
>
> ***"A mechanism of indirect coordination between agents or actions, in which the aftereffects of one action guide a subsequent action."***

Stigmergy is a self-organisation technique that enables coexisting agents (sometimes unaware of the existence of others) to achieve seamless coordination without external control, planning or direct communication between agents. This is similar to what is observed in ant colony. When an ant finds food, it leaves traces (pheromones) on its way back to the ant hill. These traces will guide other ants and itself back to the food source. This type of collaboration also helps the ants to find and establish shortest paths to food. The idea of stigmergy is simple – in a multi-agent environment, the actions of one agent leave signs (*traces*) in the environment, which are sensed by other agents and which influence their subsequent actions.

3.4.1 Natural stigmergy: wildlife

Ever wondered how school/swarm of fish, birds, ants, termites, etc. (Figure 3.12) coordinate their activities? Observing a bird flock, flying very closely and synchronously in their hundreds and even thousands, perform some amazing choreographic display can be satisfyingly intriguing. There are three important features to observe

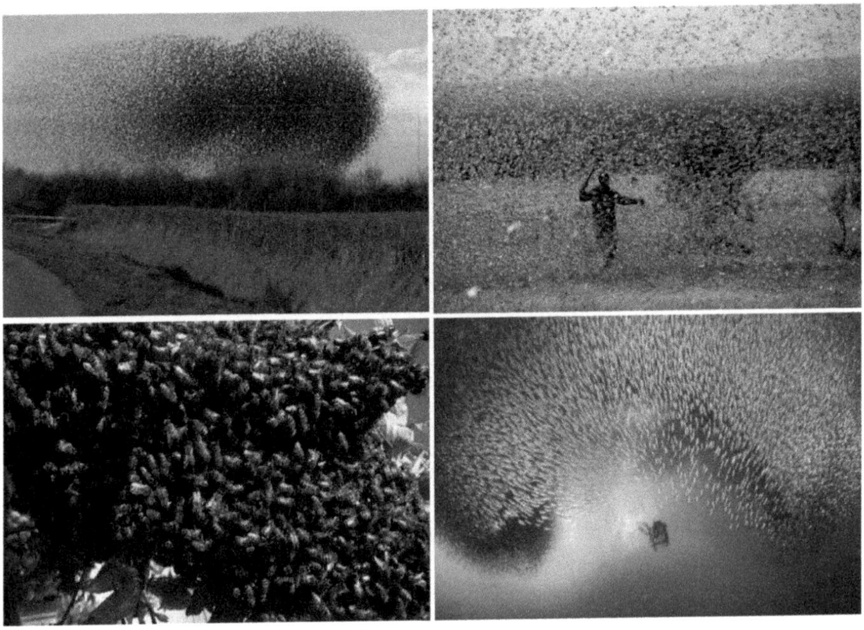

Figure 3.12 *Images showing swarm of birds, locusts, bees and fish. Image credit: for birds, John Holmes (rs-online.com); for locusts, Reuters; for bees, Deb Conway (GirlzWurk); for fish, Jamie Smith (storytrender.com)*

here: the size of the individual bird is significantly so small compare to the size of the swarm, a bird at the tail of the swarm does not see the one at the front and no individual bird is in charge. Similar features are also observed in a school of fish. Millions of tiny fish can move with such a 'coordinated' precision that when a predator attacks, without warning and in split-second, the school move in the same direction and speed. There appears to be a set of 'natural' simple rules that individuals follow which leads to a collective intelligence.

This kind of behaviour where a synchronised coordination is achieved without a dedicated or centralised leadership is possible because of stigmergy. Work done by individuals leave guides for others in the environment. This is an example of collective intelligence, which is achieved by a group of individuals working together, sometimes unaware of the existence of others in the group, to achieve a common goal. This is also known as swarm intelligence. This can result in a group of simple devices following simple rules (e.g., policies) to efficiently achieve complex tasks.

3.4.2 Natural stigmergy: humans

Stigmergy can also be observed in the way humans behave. Countless social experiments have shown how easy it is for humans to be influenced in the way they behave by the environment in which they find themselves. Take a roadside trash pileup for example. If a driver pulls up at a roadside and finds a trash nearby, instinctively something suggests to them that 'it is okay to drop your trash here'. There is a big chance that the driver will drop their trash in that same location. Although not all drivers will behave in this way, it is likely that most drivers will, and with time there will be enough contribution of trash to form a concentration of litter in that location. Whereas this is an unwanted outcome, it shows how information or trace left in the environment can influence the behaviour of other users and collectively, without any conscious coordination, a noticeable outcome that also affects the environment (for all the users) will be achieved. This sounds like a perfect example of Pierre-Paul Grassé's definition of stigmergy as the 'Stimulation of workers [users] by the performance they have achieved'.

Pierre-Paul Grassé's idea of stigmergy, a process in which termites achieve order (building a home) from disorder (mud) through a cooperative process, has been studied and used to explain how some disordered systems can self-organise into ordered systems without a plan or a central control [128, 129]. A special edition of Cognitive Systems Research on Human Stigmergy [129] has documented some important studies and discussions on the theoretical developments and new applications in this area.

Just like stigmergy enables ants to use trails to find the shortest path between points, human stigmergy also has the property of finding the shortest paths. While 'shortest path', for ants, might be the shortest path from their home to a food source, for humans, it might be finding the most relevant or useful information. Take Google Search* for example. Each time we conduct a search we expect the search to return the most useful and relevant output following our search term. To achieve this, Google Search engine deploys a number of complex algorithms to seek out the 'most desired' output. One of the algorithms that power this is Google PageRank (Figure 3.13). This algorithm is based on popularity measure of webpages. Webpages contain links (hyperlinks) to one another and thereby providing information about which pages are most desired. The number of webpages that reference (contain links to) a particular webpage is an indication of how important that particular webpage is. As shown in Figure 3.13, the size of each webpage is proportional to the number of links pointing to it. Google Search uses this popularity measure information to place the most sought-after pages in the search result. The important property to note here is that without any form of control, millions of webpages developed and used by humans collectively 'work together' to improve the user experience of everyone on the internet. This is an example of human stigmergy, achieved through uncoordinated collective effort of different web developers.

It is natural to assume that more people using a particular thing is an indication of how good that thing is. Human behaviour and decision-making are usually influenced by the experience of others and their feedback. We love to go where others have gone before. In the research community, for example, the quality of a

*https://www.google.com/search/howsearchworks/

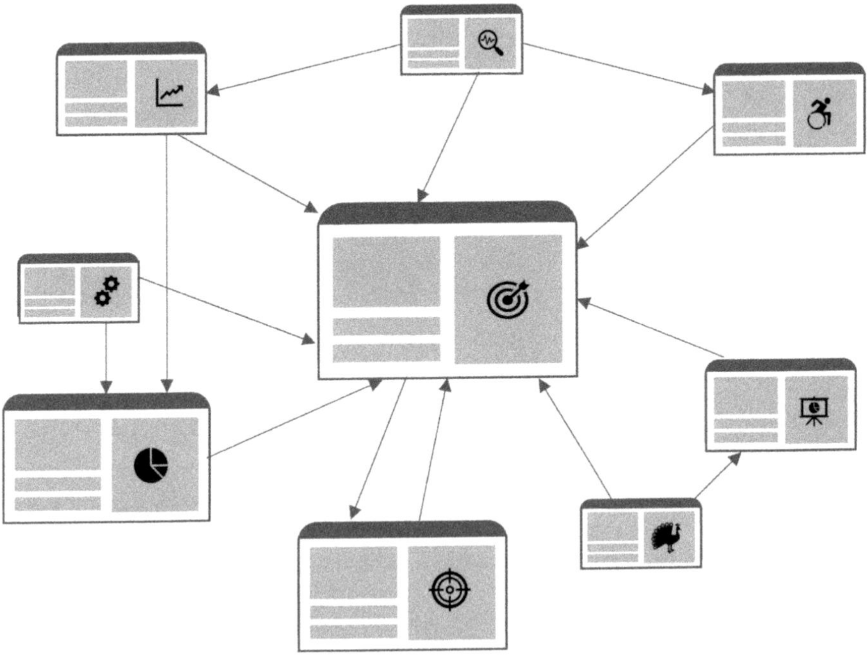

Figure 3.13 *Example illustration of Google PageRank used in Google Search engine. This represents different webpages with links to (referencing) other webpages. The more webpages pointing to a particular webpage, the more important that webpage is and the more likely that it will be returned, in a search, as the most sought-after source. In this case, the webpage in the middle (with a dartboard) would certainly be returned as the most relevant and useful webpage for the search*

research publication is measured using some indices and metrics. These indices and metrics mostly rely on number of citations. Research papers with more researchers and other papers referencing them (i.e., with more citations) are regarded as high quality. Figure 3.14 shows the Google Scholar popularity/quality measure of a researcher and IEEE Xplore popularity/quality measure of the IEEE Transactions on Computers journal.

Stackoverflow†, a website that provides quick answers to computer science-related questions, is another example of human stigmergy. Users ask questions and other users provide answers. Users who find a particular answer useful upvote that answer. According to Stackoverflow, 'Upvoting helps exceptional content to rise to the top and bring awareness to useful responses'. The system uses the upvotes and date of posts to keep the most relevant contents on top. This way, through the

†https://stackoverflow.com/

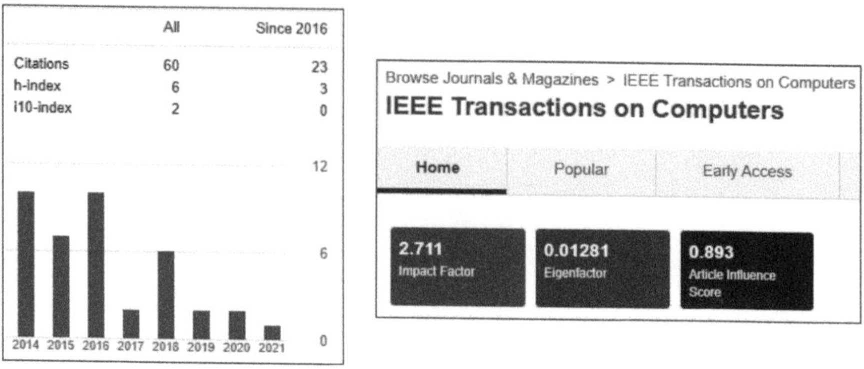

Figure 3.14 Google Scholar and IEEE Xplore popularity/quality measure of a researcher and a journal respectively. h-Index is the largest number h such that h publications have at least h citations. i10-index is the number of publications with at least 10 citations. Impact factor is the average number of times articles from a journal published in the past two years have been cited in the Journal Citation Reports (JCR) year. Eigenfactor™ Score considers the number of times articles from a journal published in the last five years have been cited in the Journal Citation Reports year while also considering which journals have contributed these citations. Article Influence™ Score is also a prestige measure and has all the features of the Eigenfactor Score, with an additional normalisation to the number of published papers. Explanations taken directly from Google Scholar and IEEE Xplore

uncoordinated actions of users on the environment (in this case Stackoverflow), the users help themselves to find best question and answer match.

3.4.3 Stigmergy in autonomic systems

Stigmergy in computer science involves modelling the behaviour of social animals, especially ants, in which individual entities cooperate to solve complex problems. In this organic cooperative arrangement, individuals work as if they were alone while their collective activities appear to be coordinated [127]. A study in Harvard has demonstrated how collective behaviour in biological systems can be applied to computing and robotics [130, 131]. In this study, a thousand identical tiny robots were programmed to mimic the collective behaviour of biological systems in forming different patterns (Figure 3.15). Although these robots were given the same rules, they were programmed with stigmergic properties to behave differently. With this, they were able to achieve collective intelligence in completing tasks like formation of different patterns without any central control. Although these formations are not as natural and swift as observed in that of swarm of birds, the same idea is demonstrated. It took the robots about 12 hours to complete each of the formations shown in Figure 3.15.

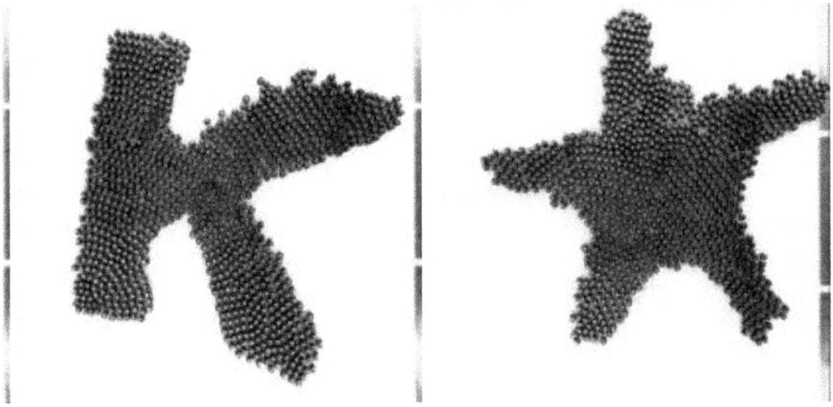

Figure 3.15 *A thousand self-organising robots forming different patterns through the cooperation of all. This is a demonstration of swarm intelligence as shown in Reference 130. The robots were able to collectively complete different formations without a central control*

This technique can be useful for multi-agent coordination and control. Stigmergy-based coordination is a rich and wide area of research that can be explored in many forms. The potential of utilising stigmergy by software agents to interact with each other and to collectively solve a common task is presented in Reference 132. A multi-agent stigmergic coordination in manufacturing control system has been discussed in Reference 133. Coordination amongst the agents in the manufacturing control system is a direct reflection of the pheromone-based stigmergy in ant colony.

One of the important observations here is that the robots in Figure 3.15 were able to complete these tasks without any chaos. Notwithstanding the small space, a thousand tiny robots, without the express knowledge of the presence of each other, were able to collectively complete such tasks without counteracting one another. This is a good idea and provides a promising solution for managing complex interactions between coexisting autonomic systems in a multi-autonomic system environment. This is a required feature for trustworthy autonomic systems. In trustworthy autonomic computing, there is need for a level of confidence in successful coexistence of autonomic systems whether they are aware of the presence of others or not.

In this book, Chapter 6, stigmergy-based interoperability solution for managing complex interactions between autonomic managers in a multi-manager scenario is presented. Two autonomic managers are used in this arrangement (Figure 3.16). The scenario is a datacentre managed by two autonomic managers: a power manager responsible for optimising power usage and a performance manager responsible for handling resource allocation. A basic conflict could arise, for example, when the power manager tries to take off a server that the performance manager is about to deploy. With stigmergy, both autonomic managers could be designed to collectively

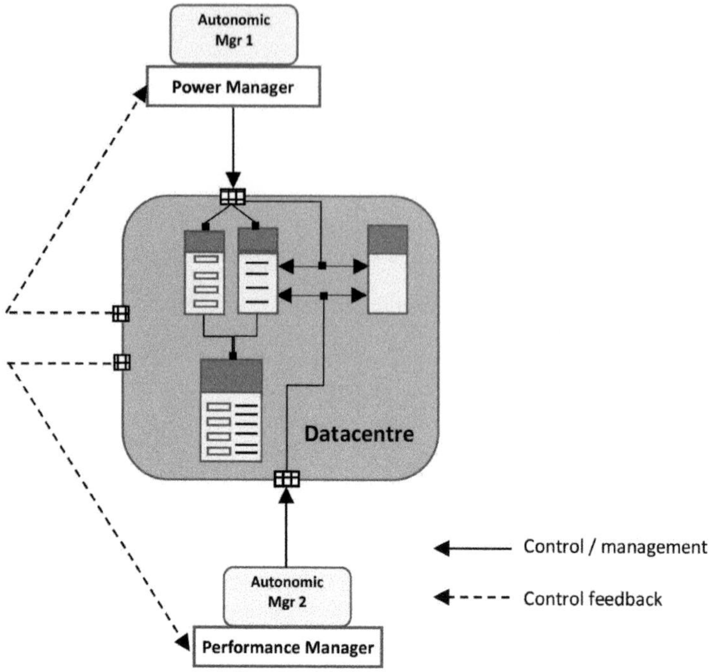

Figure 3.16 An illustration of a datacentre that is managed by two autonomic managers. The power manager is responsible for optimising power usage while the performance manager is responsible for handling resource allocation

compliment rather than conflict each other even without the express knowledge of the presence of each other. With the existence of large and complex datacentres, managed by multiple autonomic systems, stigmergy can help in achieving reliable interoperability. See Chapter 6 for more discussions on multi-agent interoperability and experiments.

Autonomic managers are designed by different vendors and may not have been wired at design to coexist with other autonomic managers. Although they may perform brilliantly in isolation, but when they coexist with others may counter each other's actions. A stigmergic inspired solution, built into the system's design, will enable different autonomic managers to coexist and to achieve seamless coordination without even direct communication between them.

3.5 Policy autonomics

Generally, a policy is a system of propositions, sometimes expressed as procedures, for achieving desired outcomes. In computing, a policy can be used to express rules that define a system's goal. In autonomic computing, these are context-sensitive rules that determine runtime behaviour of the autonomic system. An autonomic system takes in context data, analyses them and takes decisions for action. This process can be captured in a policy as shown, for example, in the policy pseudocode for a sensor below:

```
Initiate sensor capture

Receive input from sensor

Analyse data for possible decisions

Make an adaptation decision

Issue a conditional instruction for actuating
      adaptation decision

if Condition
{
      Relevant instructions within Condition
}
else
{
      Relevant instructions outside Condition
}
```

3.5.1 Policy-based networking

In networking, a policy is a formal set of statements, sometimes written in natural language, that define how traffic should be routed or how resources should be managed or allocated. For resource allocation, network management systems retrieve policy statements stored in a policy repository during operation. A policy statement can be as simple as:

```
Give the fast internet connection to everyone on VLAN1

Give network priority to traffic from 10.20.2.1/24

Use shortest path to a destination

Route through the most efficient path
```

Policy-based routing is a technique used in making routing decisions based on pre-decided policies written by network administrators. All network devices, for example, routers and network hosts, usually use routing tables to decide how to move packets across a network. A routing table contains a set of rules and necessary information for determining where and how network packets will be directed. These include routes/paths to destinations, metrics associated with those routes, best and/or default path towards packet destinations, etc. Figure 3.17 is an illustration of a network consisting of five Cisco routers (R1, R2, R3, R4 and R5).

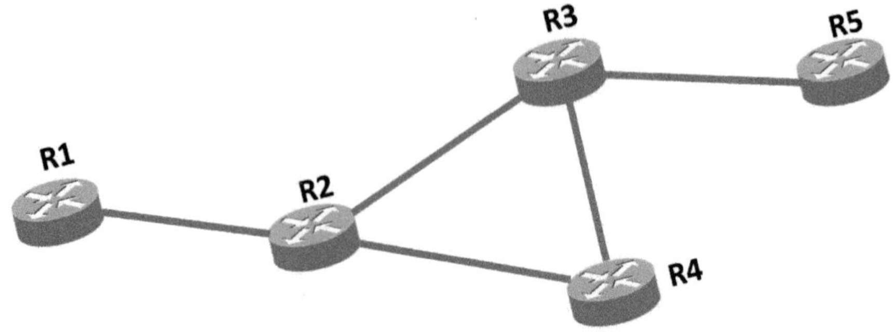

Figure 3.17 *An illustration of policy-based routing. The routers will forward data packets to target destinations based on default routing information or based on defined routing policy*

A router receives and forwards data packets to other network destinations. When a router receives a packet, it checks the destination address of that packet and then looks up on the routing table to decide the best or favoured route to the identified network destination. So, the default routing decision here is based on the destination address. However, there might be need to base this routing decision on other criteria. For example, the network administrator may want to define special routing for certain types of traffic based on certain conditions. This is achieved using policy-based routing. It enables network administrators to override the default settings of a routing table.

Let us assume that the default arrangement in Figure 3.17 is that a packet from router one (R1) to router five (R5) travels from router one (R1) to router two (R2) to router three (R3) and then to router five (R5) – R1 → R2 → R3 → R5. Policy-based routing allows the administrator to override this arrangement. For example, the network administrator can tell R2 to check for the source address, as well as the destination address, of any packet and use R4 as the next hop if the source address is R1. In this case, the packet from R1 to R5 will follow R1 → R2 → R4 → R3 → R5 instead of R1 → R2 → R3 → R5. This will ensure that all packets from R1 will avoid the R2 ↔ R3 interface. Whereas an interface is avoided in this basic example, this may be used to avoid passing certain traffic through certain networks.

Achieving policy-based re-routing as explained above will involve creating an access control list that will be used to identify the traffic/packet of interest, creating a route map using conditional (e.g., IF … THEN … ELSE) statements based on the created access control list and then applying the route map using IP policy commands. Below is a basic policy-based routing sample for achieving R1 → R2 → R4 → R3 → R5:

```
access-list 50 permit ip host <R1 IP or relevant interface> any
      //identifying traffic from R1

route-map exampleMap

      //creating a route map called exampleMap

match ip address 50

      //identifying traffic that match access list 50

set ip next-hop <R4 IP address or relevant interface>

      //if the above condition is met, R4 is set as the next hop
```

3.5.2 Policy-based autonomics

Policy-based autonomics is about using policies to achieve required autonomic functionalities. This entails automating the process of achieving a task based on the known or defined rules governing that task. A policy can be used to express the structure and sequence of logical steps to be followed in achieving a specific task. Methods for building policies for autonomic functionalities (e.g., self-CHOP) have been explored in References 20 and 134. Richard Anthony [20] describes a policy expression language which helps in building policies for autonomic systems. A framework for building self-CHOP policies and performing policy-based autonomic actions is presented in Reference 134.

The design of autonomic systems has fundamentally been based on the use of policies and rules. This is one of the earliest autonomic enabling techniques. It has been adapted, over time, with new technologies in the design of autonomic systems and it is still very relevant today. One of the easiest ways of delivering autonomic behaviours and functionalities is to express the desired goal using policies or rules and getting the system to adapt its behaviour accordingly. A desired feature of a trustworthy autonomic system is proactive adaptation. It enables the autonomic system to recognise or forecast adaptation concerns in advance and prepares for it. This helps the autonomic system to deal with the peculiar context dynamism in autonomic computing which places unique and complex challenges on trustworthy autonomic computing systems. Marwin Zufle *et al.* [135] proposed a rule-based forecasting method for autonomic systems. The proposed method supports dynamic rule learning which enables the autonomic system to adapt its forecasting according to runtime conditions. The authors argue that 'the uncertainty that results from the gap between design time and runtime for adaptive systems, as well as the environmental uncertainty at runtime, decreases the possibility that a forecasting method chosen at design time can cope with runtime demands' [135].

> ***[A desired feature of a trustworthy autonomic system is proactive adaptation. It enables the autonomic system to recognise or forecast adaptation concerns in advance and prepares for it. This helps the autonomic system to deal with the peculiar context dynamism in autonomic computing which places unique and complex challenges on trustworthy autonomic computing systems.]***

Policy autonomics has been well-studied and demonstrated. It has been used in the actual design of autonomic systems as well as in different domain-based applications. For example, policy autonomics is used in the design of autonomous agents in environments with uncertainties and different levels of complexity [136]. One major challenge, with growing complexity, in business computing of today is efficient management of cloud computing resources. Many studies and implementations have relied on the use of historical data to forecast future cloud system states and resource requirements. Whereas this has helped, to some extent, in managing resource scheduling, there are still challenges – one example is to do with scaling. This is because resource demand, in cloud computing, remains heterogeneous and varies over time. Autonomic policy-based autoscaling has been proposed as an efficient autoscaling scheduling solution [137, 138]. Policies are set and modified by system designers or admins and the autonomic systems execute these policies by adapting their behaviour accordingly in order to achieve the set goal.

Policy autonomics has been well-studied and demonstrated. It has been used in the actual design of autonomic systems as well as in different domain-based applications. For example, policy autonomics is used in the design of autonomous agents in environments with uncertainties and different levels of complexity [136]. One major challenge, with growing complexity, in business computing of today is efficient management of cloud computing resources. Many studies and implementations have relied on the use of historical data to forecast future cloud system states and resource requirements. Whereas this has helped, to some extent, in managing resource scheduling, there are still challenges – one example is to do with scaling. This is because resource demand, in cloud computing, remains heterogeneous and varies over time. Autonomic policy-based autoscaling has been proposed as an efficient autoscaling scheduling solution [137, 138]. Policies are set and modified by system designers or admins and the autonomic systems execute these policies by adapting their behaviour accordingly in order to achieve the set goal.

One advantage of policy autonomics is that the system behaviour can easily be modified. Since the policies determine the way the autonomic system behaves, the system's behaviour can be modified at any time by updating the policies. Note that policies can be implemented as modules, which are fed into the system. These simply comprise rules and actions. Consider the following basic room temperature monitoring example.

3.5.2.1 Room temperature monitoring example

Consider how you might implement a very simple room temperature monitoring and control system. The rule is that the room temperature should not go below 15 degrees. The following set of C# pseudocode will perfectly implement this system.

```
Random Rnd = new Random(); // instantiates random number generator
int RoomTemperature = Rnd.Next(); // generates a random number

if (RoomTemperature < 15)
{
  Heating.ON = True
}
else
{
  Heating.ON = False
}
```

The rule for achieving the system's goal, which is 'room temperature should not go below 15 degrees', is expressed using a set of policy commands that ensures that heating is turned ON whenever room temperature goes below 15 degrees. The random number generation here represents inputs (room temperature measurements) from sensors. Every time this code is called upon (the interval can be implemented using a Timer class), the system checks the room temperature and decides whether to switch heating ON or OFF.

3.6 Utility function

In economics, utility is a simple concept for representing worth. The usage of this concept has evolved and become very handy in may application domains – for defining individual preferences. A utility function (UF) is a relative measure of how much, to an individual, an option is preferred over another option. This measure is relative because worth is defined by the individual. It provides a means of choosing from several options, which are expressed as a series of weighted terms [20]. Terms are values representing the options while weights represent worth. Actual utility is then defined as the combination of the terms and weights. The higher utility is always preferred.

Example

Let Utility $= U$, Term $= T$ and Weight $= W$, we can present the utilities of two options, x and y, severally as follows:

- If $U_x = 5$ and $U_y = 10$, then y is preferred over x (doesn't mean y is twice better)
- $U_x = (T_{x1}, W_{x1}, T_{x2}, W_{x2}, \ldots, T_{xn}, W_{xn})$
- $U_y = (T_{y1}, W_{y1}, T_{y2}, W_{y2}, \ldots, T_{yn}, W_{yn})$

- $U_x = \{(T_{x1} * W_{x1}), (T_{x2} * W_{x2}), \ldots, (T_{xn} * W_{xn})\}$
- $U_y = \{(T_{y1} * W_{y1}), (T_{y2} * W_{y2}), \ldots, (T_{yn} * W_{yn})\}$
- $U_x = \{(T_{x1} + W_{x1}), (T_{x2} + W_{x2}), \ldots, (T_{xn} + W_{xn})\}$
- $U_y = \{(T_{y1} + W_{y1}), (T_{y2} + W_{y2}), \ldots, (T_{yn} + W_{yn})\}$

The higher utility is always preferred. However, it does not necessarily mean that the higher utility is better by the magnitude of the difference. It is possible for an option to have more than one term and associated weight. Utility can be expressed in many ways, and the products of each term and its associated weight are combined, in a certain way, to determine the worth of each option. There are several ways of representing preferences and these are the basic ones:

- $U_x > U_y$ — x is strictly preferred to y
- $U_x = U_y$ — either x or y can be chosen as both are equally preferred
- $U_x \geq U_y$ — x is preferred at least as much as y
- $U_x \geq U_y \geq U_z$ — x is preferred at least as much as y and z
- $U_x \geq U_y = U_z$ — x is preferred at least as much as y or z

So, utility is a measure of preferences amongst options while UF is a rule that assigns importance to the available options. This explanation, illustrated using Figure 3.18, is a very basic and simplistic representation of the concept. However, this economic concept can be borrowed and adapted for decision-making process in autonomic computing.

Figure 3.18 is an illustration of how we can calculate the utilities of two systems to decide our preference. Both systems have Terms defined as $SysA_{Ti}$,$SysB_{Ti}$

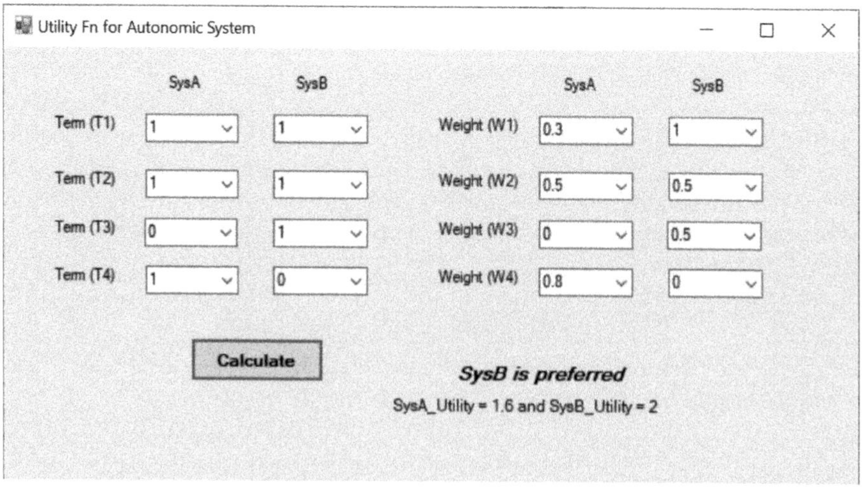

Figure 3.18 Basic utility calculator, programmed in C#

and Weights defined as $SysA_{Wi}$ and $SysB_{Wi}$. The terms can be seen as important or required features of a system – if a system exhibits a particular feature (i), then a value of 1 is selected otherwise 0 is selected. The weights represent the degree of importance of the terms to the system. So, the utility for both systems is calculated as follows:

$$\begin{aligned} SysA_{Utility} &= (SysA_{T1} * SysA_{W1}) + (SysA_{T2} * SysA_{W2}) + (SysA_{T3} * SysA_{W3}) \\ &+ (SysA_{T4} * SysA_{W4}) \end{aligned}$$

$$\begin{aligned} SysB_{Utility} &= (SysB_{T1} * SysB_{W1}) + (SysB_{T2} * SysB_{W2}) + (SysB_{T3} * SysB_{W3}) \\ &+ (SysB_{T4} * SysB_{W4}) \end{aligned}$$

The utility calculator (Figure 3.18) is developed using C#, and the commented code is presented below. This is for the benefit of those who are new to programming, showing how a simple concept can be coded.

```
private void button1_Click(object sender, EventArgs e)
{
   double SysA_Utility; double SysB_Utility; //declaring these variables as double

   //SysA_T1-4 and SysA_W1-4 are all comboBoxes and their values are hereby
   //represented as strings (.toString()) before being converted to numbers
   //(int/double.Parse()). Same is repeated for SysB. UtilityA1-4 are
   //declared as double and used to hold the calculated values
   double UtilityA1 = (int.Parse(SysA_T1.SelectedItem.ToString()) *
      double.Parse(SysA_W1.SelectedItem.ToString()));
   double UtilityA2 = (int.Parse(SysA_T2.SelectedItem.ToString()) *
      double.Parse(SysA_W2.SelectedItem.ToString()));
   double UtilityA3 = (int.Parse(SysA_T3.SelectedItem.ToString()) *
      double.Parse(SysA_W3.SelectedItem.ToString()));
   double UtilityA4 = (int.Parse(SysA_T4.SelectedItem.ToString()) *
      double.Parse(SysA_W4.SelectedItem.ToString()));

   double UtilityB1 = (int.Parse(SysB_T1.SelectedItem.ToString()) *
      double.Parse(SysB_W1.SelectedItem.ToString()));
   double UtilityB2 = (int.Parse(SysB_T2.SelectedItem.ToString()) *
      double.Parse(SysB_W2.SelectedItem.ToString()));
   double UtilityB3 = (int.Parse(SysB_T3.SelectedItem.ToString()) *
     double.Parse(SysB_W3.SelectedItem.ToString()));
   double UtilityB4 = (int.Parse(SysB_T4.SelectedItem.ToString()) *
      double.Parse(SysB_W4.SelectedItem.ToString()));

      //Computing the utilities
    SysA_Utility = UtilityA1 + UtilityA2 + UtilityA3 + UtilityA4;
    SysB_Utility = UtilityB1 + UtilityB2 + UtilityB3 + UtilityB4;
           //Using if statement to determine preference
          if (SysA_Utility > SysB_Utility)
             labelResult1.Text = "SysA is preferred";

           else
             labelResult1.Text = "SysB is preferred";
     //Formatting what is printed on the screen
     labelResult2.Text = "SysA_Utility = " + SysA_Utility + " and SysB_Utility =
     " + SysB_Utility;
}
```

3.6.1 UF in autonomic systems

Below are some UF implementation considerations for autonomic systems.

3.6.1.1 Autonomic system with multiple input sources – one or more sources can be used

A simple illustration of the adaptation of UF in autonomic computing is shown in Figure 3.19. The basic operation of an autonomic system is based on a sensor generating inputs (context information) into the system and an autonomic controller analysing these inputs to decide on adaptation actions, which are then executed by an actuator (Figure 3.19(a)). Assuming we have a scenario where inputs are generated by multiple sensors (Figure 3.19(b)), we are left with deciding which input the autonomic controller should use per time. This may be a situation of having redundancy to ensure high-availability, in which case input from any of the sensors can be used. However, we can go further to achieve a better result as well as high-availability.

As shown in Figure 3.19(c), we can use UF to combine all input sources, instead of using one per time, for a better outcome. It doesn't matter if a particular source

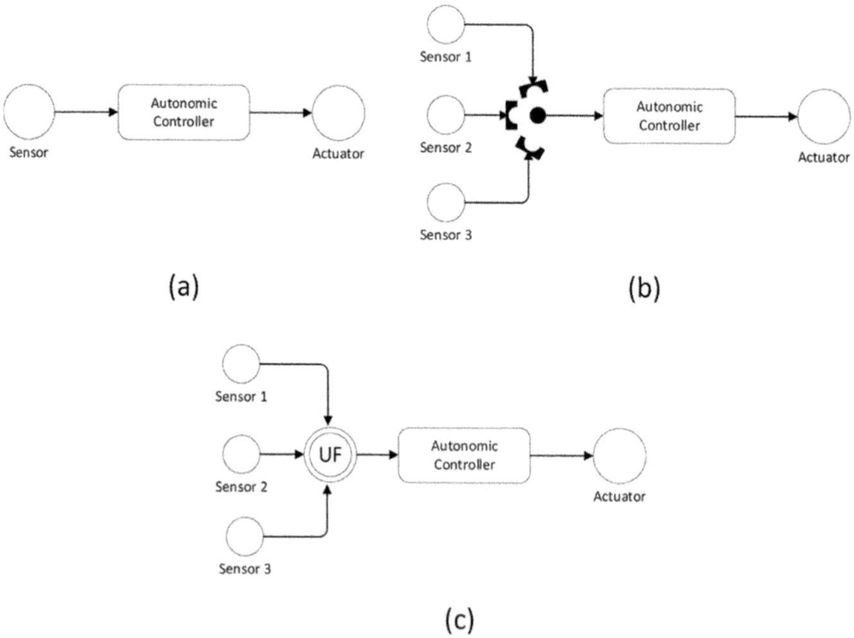

Figure 3.19 Adaptation of UF in autonomic computing: Panel (a) is a basic illustration of an autonomic system. Panel (b) is an autonomic system with multiple alternate input sources. Panel (c) combines all input sources using UF for a better outcome

is down – if only one source is available, its input is used, otherwise all available inputs are combined so that the best, say two out of three, sources are used. In this kind of setting, it is desirable and feasible to use one or more out of all available sources. A case example where it is important to use the most reliable source is presented below.

3.6.1.2 Autonomic system with multiple input sources – only most reliable source can be used

In autonomic computing, the UF concept can be useful in a scenario where, for example, the autonomic manager has several sources of input and needs to decide on preferred input before acting on it. In this case, the term values are supplied by environment sensors and the weights are set to reflect the application's interpretation of utility, as used in Reference 20. In the example presented in Reference 20, the autonomic manager receives two signals from two sensors and needs to determine which signal to use. Each signal has two terms (*SpikeLevel* and *NoiseLevel*) with associated weights (*W_spike* and *W_noise*), respectively. A UF is used to determine which signal to use.

According to Figure 3.20, the two signals are received and processed to generate their individual *SpikeLevel* and *NoiseLevel* values. These two values are combined with their associated weights in a UF to determine which signal is preferred at that time. The utility of the signals (U_i) is determined by the tuple $\{ T_{i1} , W_{noise} , T_{i2} , W_{spike} \} \rightarrow \{(T_{i1} * W_{noise}), \{(T_{i2} * W_{spike})\}$ or $\{(T_{i1} + W_{noise}), \{(T_{i2} + W_{spike})\}$. This process is repeated each time the autonomic manager requires input from the sensors. The preferred signal is used as input for the actual self-management process.

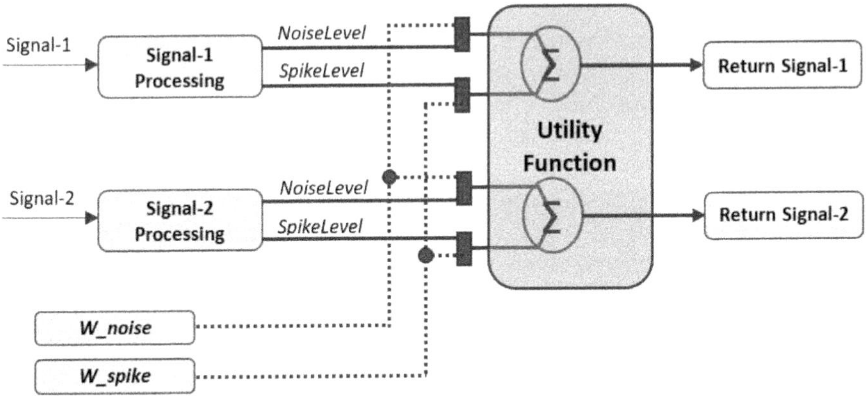

Figure 3.20 Example of an autonomic manager using UF to choose between signals (adapted from Reference 20). Autonomic decision can be based on ether Signal-1 or Signal-2 and UF is used to decide on the best signal to use

This kind of setting is useful when it is important to ensure the reliability of the input. Having more than one sensor helps in reducing input error – if one sensor is unstable, obstructed or generates *unreliable* input, an alternative is used.

3.6.1.3 Measuring autonomic systems

Another important application of UF in autonomic computing is in the area of measuring the autonomicity of autonomic systems. Take Figure 3.18, for example, we can use this system to measure the level of autonomicity (LoA) of both SysA and SysB – that is, the degree to which both systems are autonomic. If we assume that any autonomic system is defined by the self-CHOP functionalities (the important features of an autonomic system), we can represent these functionalities as terms. We then assign weights to the terms to define their level of importance for the different systems in a particular context. Note that in order to effectively compare two systems, you need to define their capabilities in the same context or application domain. The utilities of both systems can now be calculated to establish their levels of autonomicity.

Measuring the LoA of autonomic systems is an important idea in the study of autonomic systems and achievement of trustworthy autonomic computing. LoA provides a quantitative approach to classifying autonomic systems according to extent of autonomicity. See Chapter 7 for more details on this topic.

3.7 Fuzzy logic

Traditionally, decision-making is based on binary logic – '0 or 1', 'yes or no', 'true or false', etc., without consideration of any degree of truth – the extent to which a state is represented. For example, a cup of tea might be considered to be 'cold' or 'hot'. But because the definitions of 'cold' and 'hot' are relative, we need some 'degree of truth' to put it in context – the tea could be very cold, cold, warm, hot, very hot, etc. This is mostly how things are represented in real life and how the human brain rates things. We do not live in a 'yes or no' world. There are usually some level of vagueness and imprecise information when it comes to decision-making and addressing these properly will lead to more reliable decisions and outcomes.

Fuzzy logic is a technique for representing vagueness and imprecise information. It allows for modelling of uncertainties in decision-making where conditions are not precise and a lot of different factors need to be considered. It takes relevant factors in decision-making and presents them as fuzzy sets and fuzzy rules, which are combined for a more efficient decision. Fuzzy sets and rules reveal the vagueness in those factors and express them in degrees of truth.

3.7.1 Moving vehicle case example

Consider the example of a moving vehicle that needs to apply the brakes when it is close to an object. The decision here is to stop the vehicle to avoid a collision while the factors are 'close' and 'brake'. Table 3.1 shows two decision-making logic

Table 3.1 *Ordinary versus fuzzy logic-based decision-making*

Ordinary logic	Fuzzy logic
IF the vehicle is close **to the object THEN apply the** brakes	Sets • Distance to object (range): $D = (1–5)$ • Weight of the vehicle (range): $W = (1–5)$ • Force on brake pedal (range): $F = (1–5)$ • … Rules • IF $D > 3$ THEN $F = 2$ • IF $D < 3$ THEN $F = 4$ • IF $D < 3$ AND $W >= 4$ THEN $F = 5$ • IF $D \geq 2$ AND $W < 4$ THEN $F = 3$ • …

options for the vehicle stopping example. In the ordinary logic situation, the goal is stated and the human driver decides, while considering a lot of imprecise factors, when and how hard to apply the brakes. This sort of decision-making is quite relatively straightforward for humans because they possess the natural ability to easily deal with vague and imprecise data. In a world of growing automation, we would like to replicate such ability in machines. However, this is not as easy or straightforward. We need to be able to let the machine in on how to deal with imprecise data in decision-making. This is where the fuzzy logic option comes in (Table 3.1). It is easier for the machine to deal with vague and imprecise data if they are defined as sets and rules as shown. Note that sets are ideally expressed as a range of 0 (element not belonging at all) to 1 (element fully belonging). However, we have used the range of 1–5 in this example for easy explanation. Generally, fuzzy sets require minimum value, maximum value and resolution (number of steps between minimum and maximum values).

In this example, decision-making in the 'ordinary logic' case is Boolean based – it is either the vehicle is close to the object or not and the response is to apply the brakes or not. However, this does not entirely represent real-life situations. Ideally, we would want to know how close the vehicle is to the object in order to decide how fast or hard to apply the brakes. This is where fuzzy logic comes in. Fuzzy logic considers how close (the degree of closeness is expressed as a range, in this case) the vehicle is to the object as well as the weight of the vehicle (which affects how the brakes perform) before deciding how fast or hard to apply the brakes. More rules can be defined to take care of more possibilities. Also, more factors like vehicle height, vehicle speed, other vehicles approaching behind, etc., may be considered to define additional sets. This is closer to how humans make decisions – considering 'all possible' factors. By applying fuzzy rules on fuzzy sets, computers or automated systems are able to represent knowledge in a way that allows them mimic human decision-making process.

3.7.2 *Fuzzy logic controller*

Figure 3.21 is an example of a fuzzy system, showing a typical fuzzy logic controller for the moving vehicle case example. The system, which comprises four different modules, processes some input sets to generate actionable output sets. The inputs and outputs are crisp sets, i.e., precise values. For example, the weight of the vehicle and its distance to an object are precise values. Also, the decision at the other end (the output) is a definite action. The system takes in crisp inputs, fuzzifies them by representing them in degrees of possibilities, applies some rules to generate fuzzy decisions and then defuzzifies the decisions into crisp actions.

The fuzzification module converts the crisp inputs into fuzzy sets. These, in this case, are several possible representations of the weight of the vehicle and its distance to an object. From the example in Figure 3.21, it shows that the vehicle is significantly heavy ($W = 0.7$) and not too close to the object ($D = 0.4$). The fuzzification module also has defined fuzzy set for force on the break. The rules module defines several possible fuzzy rules, which are used in making the final decision. The Inference module is the brainbox – it takes inputs from the fuzzification module and decides which rule that best suits the condition defined by those inputs. The output(s) of the inference module, which are still fuzzy values, are defuzzified by the defuzzification module.

3.7.3 *Fuzzy logic in autonomic system*

Fuzzy logic, in reflecting human reasoning, attempts to model the human decision-making and thought process. This is widely used in computing, especially expert systems. The idea is to recreate, as close as possible, the human natural instinct in terms of reasoning, and use that to build more reliable intelligent systems.

Fuzzy logic is a very important technique for autonomic computing, especially trustworthy autonomic computing. It is desirable that autonomic managers are

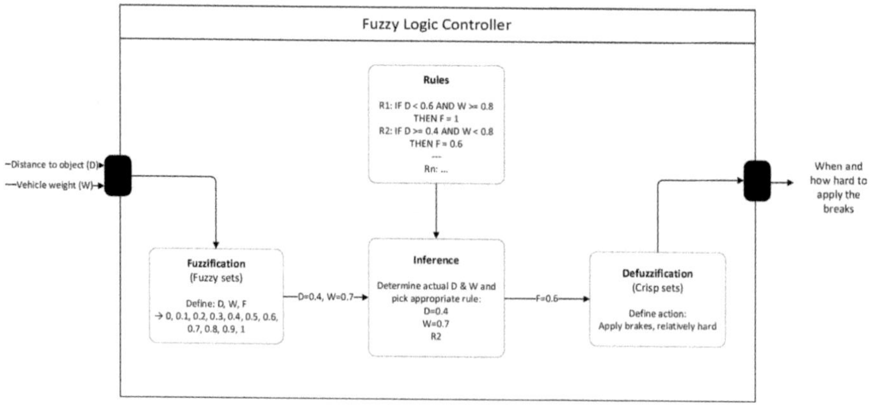

Figure 3.21 Fuzzy logic controller for a moving vehicle (Table 3.1)

able to make reliable decisions. With fuzzy logic, autonomic managers make more informed decisions as they are exposed to 'all the facts' about the situation. The idea is to factor fuzzy logic into the design of autonomic systems. For example, let us consider an autonomic stock trading system. The system should be able to consider relevant factors and then decide when best to sell/buy, by what margin, and by what magnitude. The system needs to track changes (e.g., in trade volumes, price, rates, market mood, etc.) in real time in order to make profitable trading decisions.

Figure 3.22 is an example of implementing a fuzzy logic-powered autonomic stock trading system. The fuzzy sets and rules can be as many as possible to reflect as diverse and many conditions (or realities) and responses as possible. The more fine-grained these are, the better the trading decision. This sits well with trustworthy autonomic computing.

The fuzzy logic concept is about mapping a set of inputs onto a set of possible outputs and combining them in a fuzzy function, which is capable of capturing the imprecise, vague and overlapping concepts in an efficient manner [139].

3.8 Autonomic nervous system

The autonomic nervous system is part of the human nervous system which controls key functions without conscious awareness or involvement of the human. It coordinates and organises how the activities of the body's major organs and glands are stimulated or inhibited. Take for example, an athlete running for the Olympic 10,000 m Gold does not have a say on their heartbeat rate, rather they concentrate on executing their planned technique for achieving the goal at hand. The job of regulating the heart rate is done in the background without the athlete's consciousness.

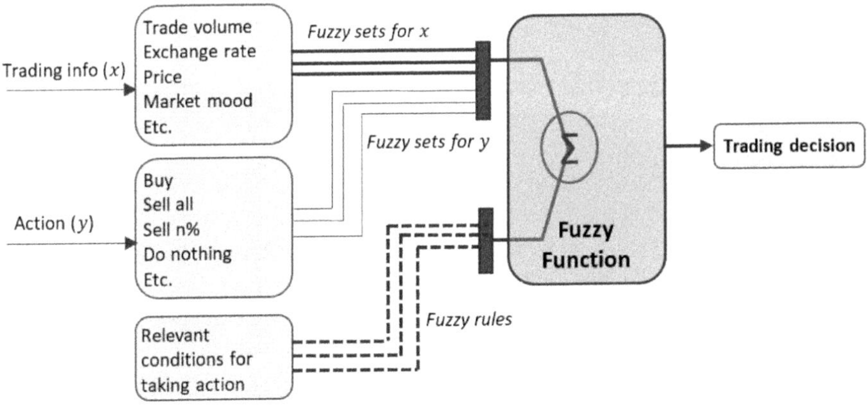

Figure 3.22 Fuzzy logic implementation for autonomic stock trading. Efficient decisions are reached by processing imprecise information

The autonomic nervous system is an independent control mechanism within the human body that monitors body changes and affects appropriate regulatory response to ensure survival amongst other things. To achieve this, the autonomic nervous system autonomically regulates a number of parameters within 'predetermined' safe or operational limits. These parameters have a bearing on survivability and examples include blood–glucose concentration, sweat, food digestion, blood pressure, heart rate and so on. However, all parameters are not uniformly related to lethality. To survive, all essential parameters must be kept within their defined safe limits. Ashby [140] has described those parameters that are closely linked to survival and are also closely linked to each other such that changes in one lead to changes in others as essential parameters. Observing that the human internal mechanisms, by working together, continuously maintain the body's essential parameters within their safe limits, Ashby concludes that a system is adaptive only if it maintains its essential parameters within the bounds required for 'survival'.

> ***[This is typically the idea mimicked by the autonomic computing concept – setting a boundary (safe limits) within which parameters, sometimes predetermined, can be dynamically maintained to achieve a specific goal. This is then powered by the self-* autonomic functionalities.]***

The autonomic nervous system is a very complex system. The scope of this section does not cover its intricate details and so, readers are encouraged to conduct personal studies on that if required. However, the main idea here is that mundane tasks are completed in the background without the human consciously getting involved. This allows the human to concentrate on other actions that require consciousness. This is the idea that inspired autonomic computing. Autonomic computing is all about mimicking the human autonomic nervous system, giving autonomic systems the capability to manage some routine tasks by themselves while the user focuses on achieving the system's goal. With such capabilities, self-managing (autonomic) systems are able to 'automatically' (autonomically) manage mundane tasks in the background so the administrator can focus on the system's goal – that is why they are called self-managing systems. Any system that is capable of mimicking the human autonomic nervous system, even in parts, can be considered an autonomic system.

While the runner focuses on the goal, Figure 3.23, a number of other things are going on in the body (e.g., elevated heart rate, adrenaline release, sweat release, increased breathing, etc.), without the runner's control. In real life, the goal might be a fixed target, as in in this case, the finish line. However, there are situations where the goal is a moving target, dynamically changed or influenced by wide-ranging (e.g., contextual) factors. This concept is very critical for trustworthy autonomic computing. Trustworthy autonomic systems are goal-centric, i.e., the system focuses on its goal and does any and everything within its capabilities to ensure that the defined goal is achieved. This is why the definition of a goal, for trustworthy autonomic systems, needs rethinking in order to cater for dynamic goals.

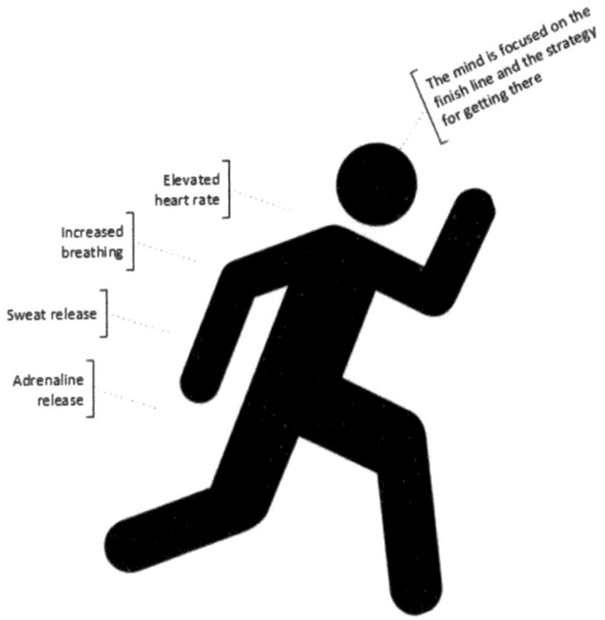

Figure 3.23 *A runner naturally focuses on their goal and strategy while their body works on taking them there*

3.9 Combining autonomic techniques

The autonomic enabling techniques can individually be adapted to achieve some level of autonomic functionalities. For example, DZ logic can be used to build a self-optimising autonomic system. Also, the whole idea of autonomic computing is based on adapting the autonomic nervous system. It is also possible to achieve greater autonomic functionality by combining techniques. For example, stigmergy has been used, in combination with trend analysis and DZ logic, to implement multi-agent interoperability in autonomic computing – see Chapter 6. The proposed stigmergy-based dynamic interoperability solution allows for indirect coordination, through the operating environment, between coexisting autonomic managers.

Trustworthy autonomic computing is about strengthening the capability of the autonomic system to make consistent and reliable decisions. There are many ways of combining autonomic enabling techniques.

One example of combining techniques is where utilities are rendered using policies. A working example of combining UF and policy autonomics, where UFs are specified within policy logic, is presented in Reference 20. Figure 3.24 shows how UF, fuzzy logic and policy autonomics can be combined. Using the autonomic stock

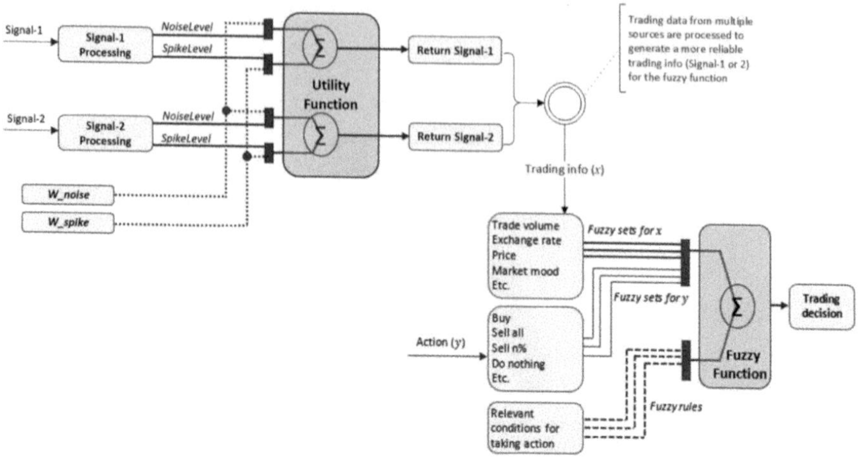

Figure 3.24 *A combination of UF, fuzzy logic and policy autonomics. UF is used to select the best input from different sources and the selected input is processed using fuzzy logic whose rules are expressed using policies*

trading example (see section 3.7.3 and Figure 3.22), a UF-based system can be used to generate more accurate trading information.

So, Figure 3.24 is a combination of Figures 3.21.–3.22 to demonstrate the combined effect of UF and fuzzy logic in building a more reliable autonomic stock trading system. The system can take input (trading information – represented as Signal-1 and Signal-2) from different sources. These inputs are processed to generate relevant terms (T_i – represented as NoiseLevel and SpikeLevel), which are combined with associated weights (W_i – represented as *W_noise* and *W_spike*) in a UF to return a reliable trading information (x – which represents the preferred of the two sources or aggregated information from both sources). This is then fed into the fuzzy logic module. The fuzzy rules can be presented using policies. An autonomic stock trading system that is based on this kind of combination will more likely lead to reliable outcomes.

Another possible combination that is capable of resulting in more reliability is shown in Figure 3.25. The combination of SES and DZ logic can lead to greater stability in autonomic systems. Recall that DZ logic uses the DZ width to determine when and when not to take adaptation action. Dynamically tuning the DZ width, as discussed in section 3.3.1, can enable the autonomic system achieve self-stability (see Figure 3.11). The value of the DZ width can be dynamically determined using SES calculation, and as demonstrated in Chapter 6, the smoothing constant α can influence the dynamical tuning of system behaviour, when combined with a DZ logic, in order to achieve greater self-stability.

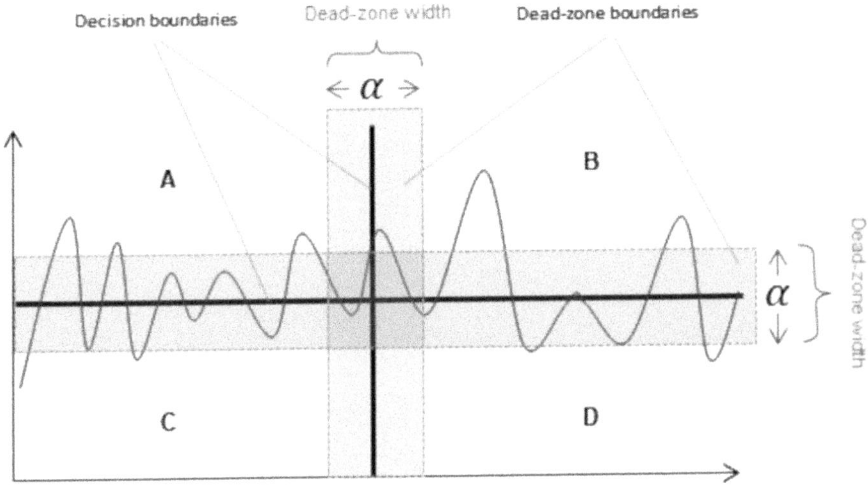

Figure 3.25 *A combination of SES and DZ logic. The smoothing constant influences the size of the DZ width. With this, the DZ width can be tracked dynamically*

The combination of SES and DZ logic, as explained above, can be crucial in dealing with dynamic goals. Sometimes, the goal of an autonomic system is a moving target and tracking such a goal requires dynamic decision-making and adaptation.

3.10 Conclusion

There are many autonomic enabling techniques and this chapter has only considered a few. These techniques are the building blocks that make autonomic systems what they are. If you consider these as standalone components with connection and interoperability interfaces, they can be used to define autonomic systems of varying functionalities. Deploying one component is capable of achieving at least one of the self-* autonomic functionalities and combining more components results in even more functionalities. There is probably no limit to how autonomic enabling techniques can be combined – examples have been discussed in this chapter. The more efficiently these can be combined, the more trustworthy the resulting autonomic systems will be. So, trustworthy autonomic computing will require some level of leveraging the capabilities of different autonomic enabling techniques.

There are other relevant techniques that can be used to achieve some level of autonomic capabilities. For example, fault tolerance, which gives a system the ability to continue operating despite failure in some parts of the system, can be used to achieve self-healing autonomic functionality. Trend analysis helps in deducing useful trends and information from a continuous stream of data, and this can help in adaptation decision-making process of autonomic systems. The use of trend analysis is shown in Chapter 6. Load balancing is another important technique. It enables the efficient distribution of tasks across resources and can be used to achieve self-optimisation autonomic functionality.

Chapter 4
Trustworthy autonomic computing

Trustworthy autonomic computing (TAC) looks beyond the basics of successfully achieving an autonomic system to establishing basis for trusting that the autonomic system does 'what it says it will do'. This chapter introduces the trustworthy autonomic architecture (TrAArch) and covers the following:

- The importance of TAC
- The differences between TAC and Trusted Computing
- How a TrAArch can be designed
- Overview of the TrAArch framework

4.1 About trustworthy autonomic computing

As we have seen, in Chapter 2, TAC has not been at the top of the list of priorities for autonomic researchers. Efforts have mainly concentrated on design and methodology. Trustworthy autonomics entails **a rethink – from** just thinking **'*how do we build autonomic systems*' to '*how do we build dependable autonomic systems*'**. The perception of users on the reliability of autonomic systems may be reflected in the level of the public's acceptance of autonomic systems. For complete reliance on autonomic computing systems, the human user will need a level of *trust* and confidence that these systems will satisfy specified requirements and will not fail. It is also not sufficient that systems are safe, secure and perform within requirement boundaries; outputs must also be seen to be reliable and dependable. Trustworthy autonomics is a non-negotiable priority for researchers, developers and users.

This chapter looks at the differences between TAC and Trusted (or Trustworthy) Computing and then presents a framework for a trustworthy autonomic architecture. This trustworthy architecture will form the basis for several implementations in this book.

4.2 Trustworthy autonomic computing vs trusted computing

In 2002, 1 year after the introduction of autonomic computing, Microsoft launched the Trusted Computing (TC) paradigm with four pillars (security, privacy, reliability and business integrity) for achieving trustworthy systems [141]. The same drive for trustworthy systems also led to the formation of the Trusted Computing Group (TCG), successor to the Trusted Computing Platform Alliance (TCPA), whose aim is to improve the trustworthiness and security of future computer systems.

However, autonomic systems are unique in context when compared to ordinary computing systems. For example, when a security-tight system pushes out unstable outputs as a result of adaptive-borne oscillations, the system may be secure but has not yet achieved trustworthiness. The peculiarity of context dynamism in autonomic computing places unique and different challenges on TAC systems from those on TC systems. Validation, e.g., which is an essential requirement for trustworthiness, can be design-time based for ordinary computing systems but must be runtime based for autonomic systems. This shows that achieving TC systems and TAC systems take different courses.

> ***[The peculiarity of context dynamism in autonomic computing places unique and different challenges on Trustworthy Autonomic Computing systems from those on Trusted Computing systems. Validation, for example, which is an essential requirement for trustworthiness, can be design-time based for ordinary computing systems but must be runtime based for autonomic systems.]***

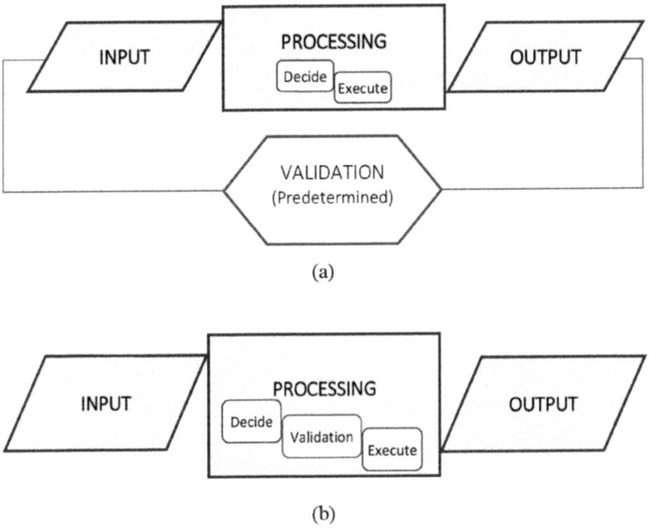

Figure 4.1 *Validation processes in normal and autonomic computing systems. Validation is predetermined in normal systems but not in autonomic systems*

Computing has always been defined as the whole idea of a system taking an input, processing that input and then outputting a result. This is illustrated using some basic flowchart symbols in Figure 4.1. For ordinary computers, Figure 4.1a, validation would rely on coded rules based on predetermined and expected conditions. This means that validation processes, represented by the *Preparation* symbol, can be determined at design time for validating the system's behaviour based on known and expected conditions. For autonomic systems, Figure 4.1b, validation would rely on adaptive procedures based on context dynamism. This means that validation processes, now represented by the *Alternate Process* symbol, have to be able to deal with unexpected conditions.

The Committee on Information Systems Trustworthiness in a publication defines a trustworthy system as one ***which does what people expect it to do – and nothing more – despite any form of disruption*** [142]. This definition has been the driving force for achieving trustworthiness both in autonomic and non-autonomic systems. The International Conference on Trust & Trustworthy Computing (TRUST) and the IEEE International Conference on Trust, Security and Privacy in Computing and Communications (TrustCom) are two major conferences with significant work in the TC domain. In this domain, trust is defined in terms of establishing confidence in the authentication of the identities of parties at both ends of a communication line [143]. Major themes addressed in this domain include access control, privacy, intrusion detection, malicious attack detection and prevention, secure communication, authentication, etc.

[Within the Trusted Computing domain, trust is defined in terms of establishing confidence in the authentication of the identities of parties at both ends of a communication line.]

The TC paradigm focuses mainly on addressing security issues and concerns posed by spiralling security attacks and susceptibilities. The prime concern here is developing computing systems that would be more rugged in dealing with security issues than the current ones. TAC on the other hand focuses on trustworthiness in autonomic environments – with unique and dynamic variabilities. There is a careful consideration of the environmental conditions in which these systems operate. The primary concern here is not how a system operates to achieve a result but how dependable is that result from the user's perspective. The question here is how do we show that a system is capable of achieving a desired and dependable result under expected range of contexts and environmental conditions and beyond? This implies that trustworthiness in autonomic computing should be result orientated and not process orientated. This is necessary for self-managing systems to mitigate the threat of losing control and confidence.

While TC covers general computing, it does not address the dynamic contextual characteristics in which autonomic systems operate. For example, TC seeks trusted interactions and interoperability between parties and platforms. But having a trusted third party or platform does not entirely suggest trustworthiness at the user's end. While this assures security and privacy, it does not assure reliability of results in terms of the degree of assuredness of the system's dependability in the face of any performance tuning. In self-managing systems, decisions are 'made on the fly' to address runtime changes and TAC will ensure that these decisions do not affect the system negatively. TAC will nonetheless benefit from the TC concept. Table 4.1 is a summary of some points that distinguish the TC paradigm (as it is) from the required TAC solution. This in a way explains what will be needed for a TAC solution.

Trusted Computing Paradigm	**Trustworthy Autonomic Computing Solution**
Trust is defined in terms of establishing confidence in the authentication of the identities of parties at both ends of a communication line	The primary concern here is not how a system operates to achieve a result but how dependable is that result from the user's perspective

Table 4.1 An overview of TC vs TAC

	TC Paradigm	**TAC Solution**
Result	Predefined	Could be dynamic
Validation	Design-time	Requires runtime consideration
Orientation	Process orientated	Result orientated
Main Focus	Security focused	Dependability focused

While the introduction of the TC paradigm has led to discussions about *trustworthy computing*, there is as yet no defined and widely accepted trustworthy concept, methodology or architecture specifically targeting autonomic systems. There is, therefore, a need for a context based trustworthy autonomic solution.

4.3 Trustworthy autonomic architecture

The autonomic architecture as originally presented in the autonomic computing blueprint has been widely accepted and deployed across an ever-widening spectrum of autonomic system designs and implementations. This has predominantly focused on the architecture's basic Monitor-Analyse-Plan-Execute control loop. However, several implementation variations of this control loop have been promoted. Despite the progress made, the traditional autonomic architecture and its variations are not sophisticated enough to produce trustworthy autonomic systems. A new approach with inbuilt mechanisms and instrumentation to support trustworthiness was required.

At the core of system trustworthiness is validation and this has to satisfy runtime requirements. In large systems with very wide behavioural space and many dimensions of freedom, it is close to impossible to comprehensively predict possible outcomes at the design stage. So, it becomes highly complex to ensure that or determine whether the autonomic manager's decision(s) are in the overall interest and good of the system. There is a vital need, then, to dynamically validate the runtime decisions of the autonomic manager to avoid the system '*shooting itself in the foot*' through control brevity, i.e., either too loose or too tight control leading to unresponsive or unstable systems, respectively. The traditional autonomic architecture does not explicitly and integrally support runtime self-validation; a common practice is to treat validation and other needed capabilities as add-ons. One of the earlier solutions was an extension of the traditional architecture to accommodate validation by including a *test* activity [18] – see section 4.2.1. The main point of this solution is to integrate a self-test activity into the autonomic architecture to provide a runtime self-validation of autonomic manager decision-making processes. But the concern remains whether validation alone can guarantee trustworthiness.

> ***[The ultimate goal of the new approach is not just to achieve self-management but also to achieve consistency and reliability of results through self-management.]***

The need for trustworthiness in the face of the peculiar nature of autonomic systems (e.g., context dynamism) comes with unique and complex challenges that validation alone cannot sufficiently address. Take, for instance, if an autonomic manager erratically changes its decision, it ends up introducing noise to the system rather than smoothly steering the system. In that instance, a typical validation check will pass each correct decision (following a particular logic or rule) but this could lead to oscillation in the system resulting in instability and inconsistent output which could emerge at a different logical level or time scale. A typical example could be an autonomic manager that follows a set of rules to decide when to move a server to or from a pool of servers. As long as the conditions of the rules are met, the autonomic manager will move servers around not minding the frequency of changes in the conditions. An erratic change of decision (high rate of moving servers around) will cause undesirable oscillations that ultimately detriment the system. What is required is a kind of intelligence that enables the manager to smartly carry out a change only when it is safe and efficient to do so – within a particular (defined) safety margin. A higher level of self-monitoring to achieve, e.g., stability over longer time frames, is absent in the traditional autonomic architectures. This is why autonomic systems need a different approach. The ultimate goal of the new approach is not just to achieve self-management but also to achieve consistency and reliability of results through self-management. These are the core values of the proposed architecture in this chapter.

[What is required is a kind of intelligence that enables the manager to smartly carry out a change only when it is safe and efficient to do so – within a particular (defined) safety margin.]

We have looked at some proposed trustworthy architectures and some isolated pieces of work that could contribute to TAC in section 4.2.1. We have also established the case for the consideration of trustworthiness as an integral part of the system's architecture. What is missing is the capability of addressing issues beyond system validation. As important as validation capability is, also crucial is the capability to ensure that any 'validated' process does not lead to oscillation and/or instability in the system resulting in undesirable results.

This section presents a new architecture for trustworthy autonomic systems. This new architecture differs from the traditional autonomic computing architecture and includes mechanisms and instrumentation to explicitly support runtime self-validation and trustworthiness. The traditional architecture does not lend itself robustly enough to support trustworthiness and system dependability. For example, despite validating the system's decisions within a logical boundary set for the system, there is the possibility of overall erratic behaviour or inconsistency in the system emerging, e.g., at a different logical level or on a different time scale. So, a more thorough and holistic approach, with a higher level of checking, is presented here to convincingly address the dependability and trustworthy concerns. In the new approach presented here, validation and trustworthiness are designed-in and integral at the architectural level.

First, the new TrAArch is introduced. This would represent the stage of sophistication in the autonomic architecture life-cycle denoted by level (v) in Figure 2.2 and shown in Figure 4.2. Next, the components of the new architecture are each discussed in full details. The components themselves are not hardwired – underlying logic are application dependent.

4.3.1 TrAArch framework

TrAArch is a new architecture for trustworthy autonomic computing. This section presents a general view of the architecture followed by a detailed explanation of its components. Figure 4.3 shows the components of the autonomic framework that embody self-management, self-validation and dependability provisions. The architecture builds on the traditional autonomic solution, denoted as the *AutonomicController* (AC) component. Other components include *ValidationCheck* (VC) and *DependabilityCheck* (DC). The VC component is integrated with the decision-making object of the controller to validate all the AC decisions, while the DC component guarantees stability and reliability after validation. The DC component works at a different time scale, thus overseas the finer-grained sequence of decisions made by the AC and VC components.

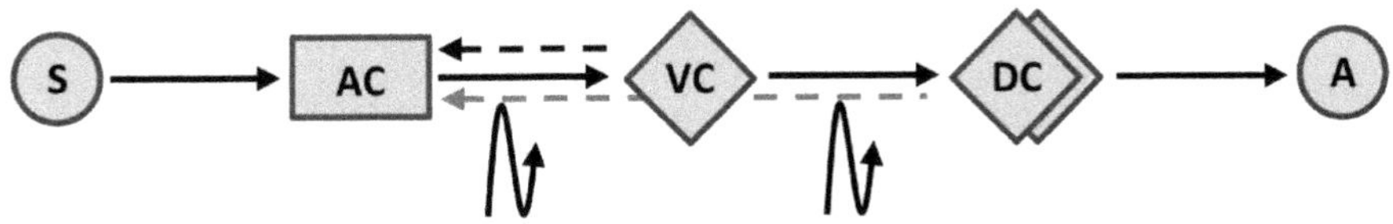

Figure 4.2 *Autonomic architecture life-cycle stage denoting trustworthy autonomics. The sensor (S) receives inputs (context information) into the system, the autonomic controller (AC) analyses these inputs and based on the outcome of the analysis decides on an adaptation action, the validation check (VC) validates the decided action and returns feedback if validation fails, the dependability check (DC) monitors the behaviour of the system over time and compares that with the general goal of the system and may inhibit the actuator (A) that executes the adaptation decision*

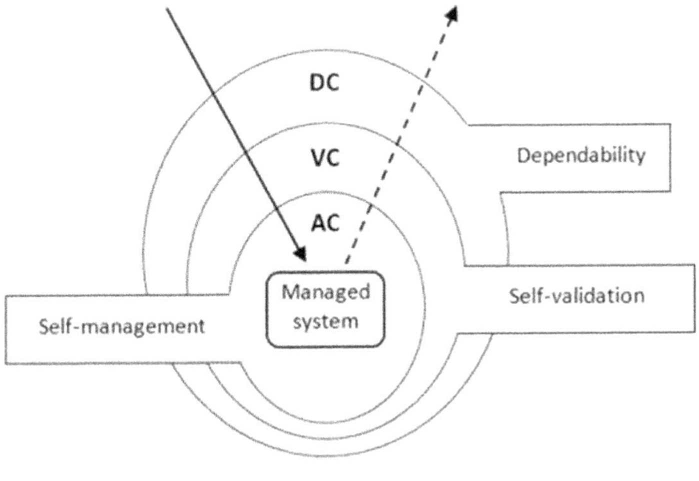

Figure 4.3 *High-level view of the TrAArch*

The AC component (based on, e.g., **M**onitor-**A**nalyse-**P**lan-**E**xecute logic, Intelligent Machine Design framework [11], etc.) monitors the managed system for context information and takes decisions for action based on this information. Initially, the system's goal is defined using policies. The line of action decided by the AC component is then validated against the policies/rules defining the system's goal by the VC component before execution. If, e.g., there is a policy violation, meaning that the validation fails, the VC reports back to the AC otherwise the DC is called to ensure that the outcome does not lead to, e.g., instability in the system.

The DC component comprises of other sub-components that make it adaptable to address different challenges. This feature makes TrAArch generic and suitable for addressing evolving autonomic capability requirements. Take, for instance, as in Chapter 6, TrAArch can be adapted to address interoperability challenges in complex interactions in multi-agent scenarios. Predictive component is one example of the DC sub-components that allows it to predict the outcome of the system based on the validated decision. The DC either prevents execution and sends feedback, e.g., some calibration parameters, to the AC or calls the actuator to execute the validated decision.

4.3.2 *Overview of the TrAArch architecture components*

Let us start by representing the TrAArch architecture in progressive stages of increasing level of detail. First, the self-management process is defined as a *Sense–Manage–Actuate* loop, where *Sense* and *Actuate* define *touchpoints,* and *Manage* is the embodiment of the actual autonomic self-management. The touchpoints are the autonomic manager's interfaces with the managed system. Figure 4.4 is a detailed representation of the architectural framework.

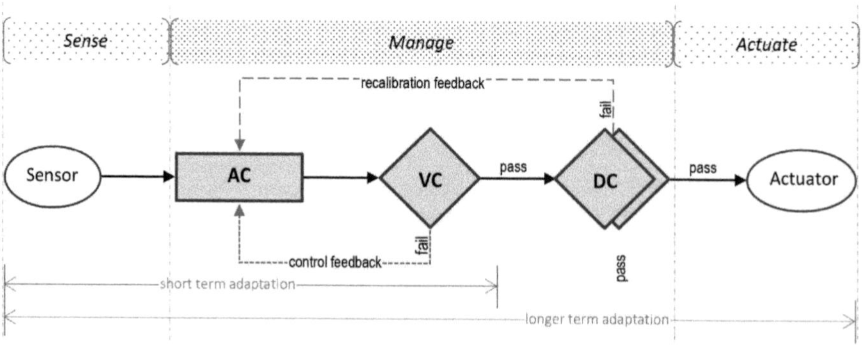

Figure 4.4 TrAArch framework. The AC analyses inputs from the sensor and decides the adaptation action to take. The VC performs runtime validation of the adaptation decision. The DC performs a longer-term validation while the actuator executes the adaptation actions

Traditionally, the AC senses context information, decides on what action to take, following some predefined rules or policies, and then executes the decided action. This is the basic routine of any autonomic manager and it is at the core of most of the autonomic architectures in use today. At this level, it matters that there is an autonomic unit. However, the content of that unit does not matter much – that is, it does not matter what autonomic control logic is employed so long as it provides the desired autonomic functionalities. This means that the AC component can be configured according to any autonomic control logic of choice, making the framework generic as it is not tied to any one control logic. However, the choice of the autonomic control logic will contribute to the eventual Level of Autonoimicity rating of the system – see LoA in Chapter 7.

[The AC component of the TrAArch framework provides designers the platform to express rules that govern target goal and policies that drive decisions on context information for system adaptation to achieve the target goal.]

Basically, the AC component introduces some smartness into the system by intelligently controlling the decision-making of the system. Once an action is decided, following a detailed analysis of context information, the decision is passed on for execution. This is at the level of sophistication defined by the autonomic architecture life-cycle level 1 (Figure 2.2 (i) and (ii) – section 4.1). So, the AC component of the TrAArch framework provides designers the platform to express rules that govern the target goal and policies that drive decisions on context information for system adaptation to achieve the target goal.

There is one significant concern that is unique to autonomic systems: input variables, also known as context information, are dynamic and most times unpredictable. Although rules and policies are carefully and robustly constructed, sensors (data sources) sometimes do inject rogue variables that are capable of thwarting process and policy deliberations. In addition, the operating environment itself can have varying volatility – causing the controller to become unstable in some circumstances. Thus, a mechanism was needed to mitigate behavioural and structural anomalies. Examples of behavioural anomalies include contradiction between two policies, goal distortion, etc., while examples of structural anomalies include illegal structure not conforming to requirement, division by zero, etc. This is where the VC component comes in. It should be noted that AC will always decide on action(s) no matter what the input variable is. Once the AC reaches a decision, it passes control to the VC, which then validates the decision and passes it on for execution. For example, the VC checks to ensure that no system policy is violated as a result of any behavioural and/or structural anomalies. If the check fails, VC sends control feedback (CF) to AC while retaining previous passed decisions. A CF is more of an inhibition command that controls what actions are and are not allowed by the manager. This can be configured according to deployment requirements.

The overview of the VC is that while it focuses on the goal of the system, it deploys self-validation mechanisms to continuously perform self-validation of the autonomic manager's behaviour and configuration against its behavioural goals and also reflects on the quality of the manager's adaptation behaviour. The nature and level of test, and how it is configured, are entirely user-defined. So, the VC is a higher-level mechanism that oversees the activities of the AC to keep the system's goal in check and on track. The ultimate concern here is to maintain the system goal whilst adhering to defined rules and policies, i.e., adding a level of trust by ensuring that the target goal is reached only within the boundaries of specified rules. It is then left for designers to define what constitute validation 'pass' and validation 'fail'. Actual component logics is application specific but some examples in literature include fuzzy logic [47], reinforcement learning [144], policy autonomics, etc. This is at the level of sophistication defined by the autonomic architecture life-cycle level 2 (Figure 2.2 (iii) and (iv) – section 4.1).

In real life however, we understand that despite the autonomic manager taking legitimate decisions within the boundaries of specified rules, it is still possible to have overall system behavioural inconsistencies, that is, a situation where each individual decision could be correct, by logic, and yet the overall behaviour is wrong. A situation where the autonomic manager erratically, though legally, changes its mind, thereby injecting oscillation into the system, could be a major concern especially in large scale and sensitive systems. This is beyond the level of consideration in the state-of-the-art shown in Figure 2.2 (i-iv). Therefore, it is necessary to find a way of enabling the autonomic manager to avoid unnecessary and inefficient change of decisions that could lead to oscillation. This task is handled by the *DC* component.

The DC allows the autonomic manager to change its decision (i.e., adapt) only when it is necessary and safe to do so. Consider a simple example of a room temperature controller, in which it is necessary to track a dynamic goal – a dynamic target room temperature, which depends on inter alia weather conditions. The autonomic manager is configured to maintain the target temperature by complying with the following logic and automatically switching heating ON or OFF:

IF RoomTemperature < TargetTemperature THEN ON_Heating
ELSE IF RoomTemperature > TargetTemperature THEN OFF_Heating

The VC would allow any decision or action that complies with the above basic logic. With the lag in adjusting the temperature, the system may decide to switch ON or OFF heating at every slight tick of the gauge below or above the target, when room temperature is sufficiently close to the target temperature. This may in turn cause oscillation, which can lead to undesirable effects. The effects are more pronounced in more sensitive and critical systems, where such changes come at some cost. For example, a data centre management system that erratically switches servers between pools at every slight fluctuation in demand load is cost ineffective. Actual component and sub-component logic of the DC are user-defined.

One powerful logic example for implementing the DC component is the Dead-Zone (DZ) Logic. A DZ logic is a mechanism to prevent unnecessary, inefficient and ineffective control brevity when the system is sufficiently close to its target value. In simple terms, the logic helps to manage inconsistent and erratic adaptation. It is implemented using an object known as Tolerance-Range-Check (TRC) that encapsulates the logic and a three-way decision fork that flags which action (left, null or right) to take depending on the rules specified [20]. The DZ can be dynamically adjusted to suit changes in environmental volatility. A mechanism to automatically monitor the stability of an autonomic component, in terms of the rate the component changes its decision, e.g., when close to a threshold tipping point, is presented in Reference 43. Dead zone logic allows the system to monitor itself and take action if it detects instability at a higher level than the actual decision-making activity – this means that a system has to exceed a boundary by a *minimum* amount before action is taken. The DZ Logic is explained in Chapter 3 and implemented in Chapter 5.

The DC component may also implement other sub-components like Prediction, Learning, etc. This enables it to predict the outcome of the system and to decide whether it is safe to allow a particular decision or not. An example sub-component logic is Trend Analysis logic, which identifies patterns within streams of information supplied directly from different sources (e.g., sensors). By identifying trends and patterns within a particular information, e.g., spikes in signal strength, fluctuation in stock price, rising/falling trends, etc., the logic enables the autonomic manager to make more-informed control decisions. This has the potential of reducing the number of control adjustments and can improve overall efficiency and stability. The analysis of recent trends enables a more accurate prediction of the future – so with Trend Analysis logics, autonomic managers can base decisions on a more complete view of system behaviour.

So, after validation phase, the DC is called to check, based on specified rules, for dependability. DC avoids unnecessary and inefficient control inputs to maintain stability. If the check passes, control is passed to the Actuator otherwise a recalibration feedback (RF) is sent to the AC component. An example of a RF is dynamically adjusting (or retuning) the *dead zone width* of the DZ logic as appropriate. The RF enables the autonomic manager to adjust its behaviour to maintain the level of required trust.

So, while VC looks at the immediate actions, DC takes a longer-term view of the autonomic manager's behaviour over a certain defined time interval. A particular aspect of concern, though, is that for dynamic systems, the boundary definition of the DZ may itself be context dependent – that is, in some circumstances it may be appropriate to allow some level of changes that under different circumstances may be considered destabilising. This concern is taken into consideration when defining such boundaries (the *DZ width*).

> ***[An autonomic system, no matter the context of deployment, is truly trustworthy when its actions are continuously validated (i.e., at run time) to satisfy set requirements (system goal) and results produced are dependable and not misleading.]***

So, the traditional autonomic architecture suffices for short-term adaptation. To handle longer-term frame adaptation, e.g., cases where continuous validation fails to guarantee stability and reliability, requires a robust autonomic approach. This robust autonomic approach is what the proposed TrAArch offers. Consider the whole TrAArch as a nested control loop (Figure 4.5) with AC as the core control loop while VC and DC are intermediate and outer control loops, respectively. In summary, a system, no matter the context of deployment, is truly trustworthy when its actions are continuously validated (i.e., at run time) to satisfy set requirements (system goal) and results produced are dependable and not misleading.

There are issues that may need further investigation. The three (AC, VC and DC) TrAArch components allow the autonomic system designer to specify individual controls and processes that will guide the system to reach stated goals – that is, the system's goal state or expectations. However, it is possible for the system to struggle to or never be able to reach that goal state. The DC component, in particular, has the capacity to dynamically and continuously modify the general system behaviour until the goal state is reached. But, if the system is not able to ever reach the goal state, it will then be appropriate to modify the design of the components starting with the DC component as it inhibits the behaviour of VC and AC components. There is no element of time in TrAArch solution – there is no specified time limit before the system is considered unable to converge to goal state. A time element will depend on the goal of the system and could be learnt over time for a specific application or could be determined at design.

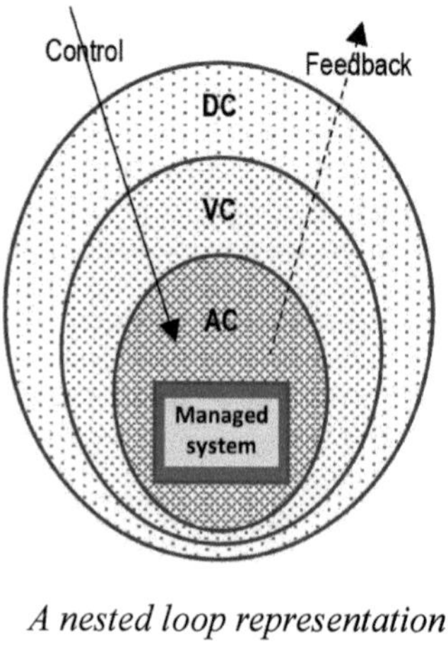

Figure 4.5 A nested loop representation of TrAArch

It is also important to note that, as a limitation, the success of the TrAArch is largely dependent on the way that the system goals are stated. For example, the checks carried out by VC and DC components are in conformity with the system's stated goals. So, the behaviour of these components and, in general, the output of the system will be affected if there is a problem in the rules defining the system goals or if the goals are ambiguous. Although the DC component can be configured to dynamically detect and address some levels of anomalies, this will be to the extent of the component logic used.

4.3.3 Other relevant [early] architectures

Additional area of relevance is the architectures from the Robotics research such as Rodney Brooks' Subsumption Architecture [145] and William Ashby's Ultrastable Systems [146]. Both architectures are selected because of their close relevance to the proposed TrAArch. The subsumption architecture is in some way related to TrAArch in terms of the control techniques employed – for example, layered and multi-loop control techniques. Ultrastable systems relate to TrAArch in the aspect of stability and reliability. In a way, TrAArch may be seen as containing a hybrid of the Subsumption and Ultrastable architectures.

The subsumption architecture is a reactive behaviour-based robotic architecture. As an alternative to the traditional artificial intelligence behaviour guidance through symbolic mental representations of the world, the architecture uses a *sense-decide-action* control to guide robotic behaviour. Generally, the architecture uses the approach of decomposing a problem into several units, solving the sub-problems for each unit and then composing the solutions [145]. In this approach, based on the complete desired behaviour for a robot, the architecture decomposes the desired behaviour into a hierarchy of layered sub-behaviours with corresponding levels of competence. A level of competence is a specification of all the behaviours expected of a robot. Each of the layers is responsible for implementing a particular level of behaviour competence and higher layers are able to subsume (i.e., suppress or inhibit) lower layers. All the layers receive sensor information and then generate decisions that are passed on to actuators.

4.3.3.1 The subsumption architecture and TrAArch

In terms of layered control, the controls in the subsumption architecture are based on the desired behaviour and environment for the robot while the controls in TrAArch, specified within the AC, VC and DC components, are based on the stated goals of the system with additional capacity to handle unexpected environmental conditions. In terms of multi-loop control, higher levels of control in both architectures are able to inhibit lower levels of control. In subsumption architecture, however, higher levels of competence include, as subsets, lower levels of competence. For example, if a robot encounters a task requiring a level of behaviour competence at level '2', the layer of control at level '2' will inhibit the controls at levels '1' and '0' while the controls from level '3' up will not be activated. With this approach, the system gets more complex as the level of competence grows. In TrAArch, on the other hand, a higher control inhibits a lower control only when the lower control '*operates outside the system stated goals*'. Whereas sensor information is fed into all the layers (both active and inactive) in the subsumption architecture at the same time, only the first layer, the AC, in TrAArch receives sensor information. For the subsumption architecture, feeding sensor information to all the layers has memory implications and also leads to redundancy, as all layers do not use the information at the same time. In TrAArch, the sensor information is fed into the AC component that makes control decisions after analysing the sensed information. In actual sense, the output of the AC component is passed as input to the VC component and the output of the VC component is passed as input to the DC component.

4.3.3.2 The ultrastable system architecture and TrAArch

The Ashby's ultrastable system architecture [146] defines adaptive behaviour that is aimed at achieving stability in the same way and manner the human autonomic nervous system aims to achieve survivability. The whole idea of the ultrastable system is to maintain the subsystems in a state of stable equilibrium. Parashar and Hariri [147] give a detailed description of Ashby's ultrastable system within the framework of the autonomic nervous system (ANS). ANS is an independent control mechanism within the human body that monitors body changes and affects appropriate regulatory responses to ensure survival amongst other things. To achieve this, the ANS autonomically regulates a number of parameters within 'predetermined' safe or operational limits. These parameters have a bearing on survivability and examples include blood-glucose concentration, blood pressure, heartbeat rate, pressure of heat on the skin, and so on. However, all parameters are not uniformly related to lethality. To survive, all essential parameters must be kept within their defined safe limits. Ashby has described those parameters that are closely linked to survival and are also closely linked to each other such that changes in one lead to changes in others as essential parameters [146]. Observing that the human internal mechanisms, by working together, continuously maintain the body's essential parameters within their safe limits, Ashby concludes that a system is adaptive only if it maintains its essential parameters within the bounds required for '*survival*'. The term '*survival*' is relative and, in ultrastable systems, means a state of 'stable equilibrium'.

The ultrastable system architecture builds on two principles: (1) the goal of the adaptive behaviour and the survivability of the system are directly linked and (2) the system will always work towards returning to its original equilibrium state if the environment pushes it out of its state of stable equilibrium [147]. The ultrastable system architecture consists of two feedback loops: one that operates frequently and makes small corrections to control small disturbances and a second that operates infrequently and changes the structure of the system when the essential parameters are pushed outside the survival boundary – the later handles longer disturbances. The two feedback loops allow the system to continuously interact with the environment and be able to self-adapt to maintain a stable state of equilibrium.

Ashby's ultrastable system is an excellent technique for achieving stability within the frameworks of a predefined state of stable equilibrium. This overlaps with the stability aspect of TrAArch. Although in TrAArch, the boundary that defines state of stability could be dynamic which the system is able to track over time. Also, within the frameworks of stability as defined in TrAArch, the rate at which the ultrastable system architecture returns a system to stable equilibrium could itself have a bearing on instability.

4.4 Conclusion

In this chapter, I have analysed the differences between TAC and Trusted (or Trustworthy) Computing. I note that, although a *trustworthy system* has been defined as one that *'does what people expect it to do – and nothing more – despite any form of disruption*', the peculiarity of context dynamism in autonomic computing places unique and different challenges on trustworthiness for autonomic systems. So appropriate measures need to be put in place – for example, runtime based self-validation and self-monitoring capability that guarantees stability over longer-term time frames.

I have also analysed the traditional autonomic architecture, with its variations, and have found that it is not sophisticated enough to guarantee the level of trustworthiness required for autonomic systems. A new architecture for trustworthy autonomic systems that is different from the traditional architecture and that includes instrumentation to explicitly support runtime self-validation and trustworthiness has also been presented. The new architecture is termed TrAArch. The definitive goal of this new approach is not just to achieve self-management but also to achieve consistency and reliability of results through self-management. Other relevant architectures have also been discussed.

The Monitor-Analyse-Plan-Execute (MAPE) control loop forms the building blocks of the traditional autonomic architecture. With wide acceptance, many autonomic studies and implementations are predominantly based on this architecture's control loop. I admit that while successes have been achieved using this architecture, it remains vague and limited in offerings as already identified. For example, the MAPE-based architecture does not integrally support runtime self-validation that is a prerequisite for trustworthiness; a common practice is to treat validation and other needed capabilities as add-ons. It is important to note that these capabilities cannot be reliably retro-fitted to systems.

> **[*A trustworthy system* has been defined as one which *does what users expect it to do – and nothing more – despite any form of disruption*. However, the peculiarity of context fluidity in autonomic computing places unique challenges on trustworthiness for autonomic systems.]**

It is also important to note that validation alone does not always guarantee trustworthiness as each individual decision could be logically correct but overall system may be unreliable. Take, for instance, a system that makes decisions based on binary conditions will be validated as long as such conditions are met, regardless of how close to the margins. But it could be undesirable and distractingly annoying to human users if the system changes its decision at every slight deviation from the margins – in this case, the actions of the controller may be validated but at the same time lead to unstable and undesirable conditions. So, it is important to consider situations beyond the level of validation where logical processes/actions could sometimes lead to overall system instability. Such a situation, capable of injecting oscillation into the system, is a major concern especially in large scale and sensitive systems. Consequently, a new approach is required in which validation and support for trustworthiness are not treated as add-ons. The TrAArch design guarantees self-monitoring over shorter and longer time frames. To demonstrate the feasibility and practicability of the proposed approach, empirical analysis case example scenarios have been presented in this book (see Chapters 5 and 6).

Chapter 5

Trustworthy autonomic architecture implementations

The traditional autonomic architecture has been shown in Chapter 2 not to explicitly and integrally support runtime self-validation that is a prerequisite for trustworthiness. The practice of treating required capabilities, e.g. for trustworthiness, as retrofitted add-ons are unscalable and unsustainable. A new trustworthy autonomic architecture (TrAArch) with inbuilt mechanisms and instrumentation to support trustworthiness is proposed in Chapter 4. This chapter provides an implementation and empirical analysis of the new architecture.

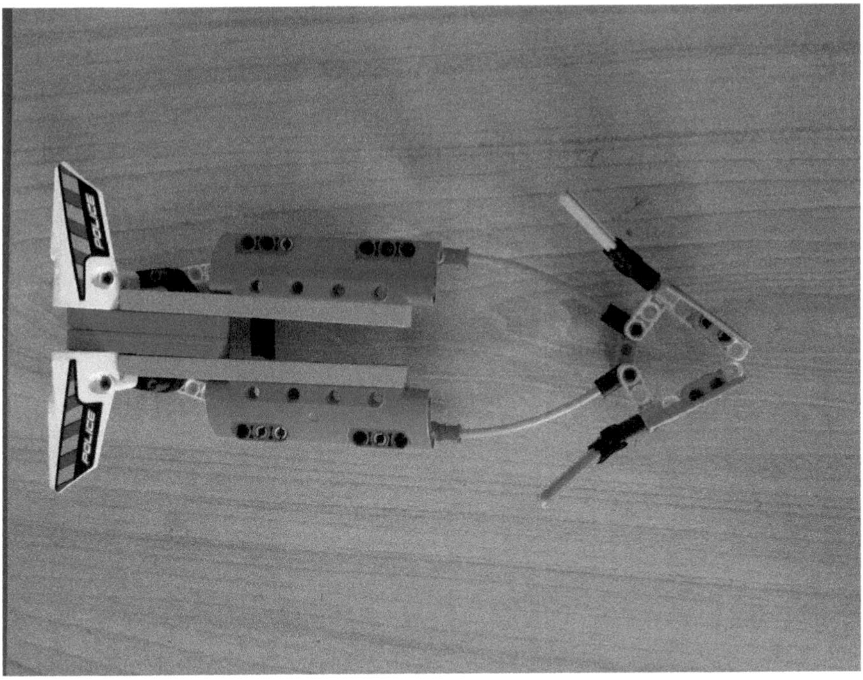

In this chapter, you will:

- learn the workings of TrAArch
- understand how to adapt, implement and use the new architecture
- appreciate the attributes of trustworthy autonomics
- understand the differences between stability and optimality in the context of autonomic computing

This chapter provides an implementation and empirical analysis of the new architecture. Two experimental demonstrations – an easy-to-understand autonomic marketing scenario and a more complex self-adapting datacentre resource request and allocation management case scenario – are used. The first case scenario demonstrates how the new architecture can maximise cost and improve trustability and efficient target marketing in a company-centric autonomic marketing system that has many dimensions of freedom and which is sensitive to a number of contextual volatilities. The second case example scenario, which is an implementation of a datacentre resource request and allocation management, is a more complex experimental analysis designed to analyse the performance of the proposed TrAArch architecture.

To demonstrate the attributes of the new architecture, this chapter presents an implementation and simulation analysis of the TrAArch architecture. Two case example scenarios are examined. The first case example is a deployment of the architecture to an envisioned autonomic marketing system that has many dimensions of freedom and which is sensitive to a number of contextual volatilities. An autonomic marketing system, equipped with autonomic functionalities, monitors the market in real time to formulate, using real-time market information, appropriate marketing strategies for dynamic, adaptive and effective target marketing. This scenario is chosen because autonomic marketing offers a simple, easy-to-understand and yet robust platform for expressing autonomic systems according to discrete levels of autonomic capabilities. In the second example, the architecture is demonstrated in a resource allocation scenario, modelling basic datacentre resource allocation management. This is a more complex and robust implementation of TrAArch. Since datacentres have many dimensions of complexities, arising from their scale, large number of tuning parameters, etc., they provide a rich domain in which to evaluate a wide range of techniques, tools and frameworks for autonomic computing. However, the implementation here focuses on resource request and allocation.

In both examples, detailed experiments are designed to analyse the performance of three different systems, based on three different autonomic architectures. The first system (***SysA***) is based on the traditional autonomic architecture, represented by the basic ***M****onitor–****A****nalyse–****P****lan–****E****xecute* logic. The second system (***SysB***) is an upgraded version of the traditional autonomic architecture that includes a *test* element, represented by ***M****onitor–****A****nalyse–****P****lan–****V****alidate–****E****xecute* logic. The third system (***SysC***) is based on TrAArch, represented by a nested ***M****onitor–****A****nalyse–****P****lan–****V****alidate–****D****ependabilityCheck–****E****xecute* logic. The *DependabilityCheck*

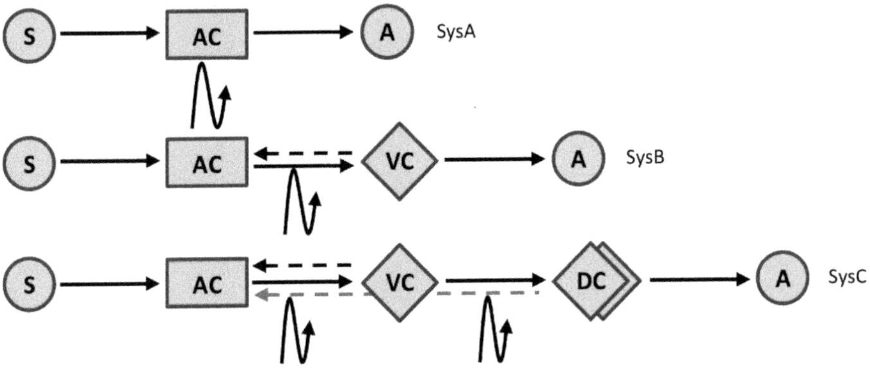

Figure 5.1 *Representation of systems for the experiment. SysA is based on the traditional autonomic architecture, while SysB is an upgraded version of the traditional autonomic architecture that includes a test element and SysC is based on TrAArch.*

component incorporates the dead-zone logic (see Chapter 3). Note that *SysB* does everything *SysA* can do and more and *SysC* does everything *SysB* can do plus more (see Figure 5.1).

Key for Figure 5.1:

- **S** – Sensor for monitoring context information
- **AC** – Autonomic Controller, comprising the analyse and plan elements of the MAPE loop
- **VC** – Validation Check, for testing/validating the decision taken by the AC
- **DC** – Dependability check, a longer-term check on the validated decision to ensure output is trustworthy
- **A** – for actuating/executing the overall/eventual decision

5.1 Case example scenario 1: autonomic marketing system

The scenario here is that of targeted television advertising during a live sports game. A company wishes to run an adaptable marketing campaign on television with different adverts (of different products), appealing to audiences (fans) of different demographics. For example, to be aired at different times, in two countries, during a live World Cup match between the two nations. There are four adverts (Ad1, Ad2, Ad3 and Ad4) to be run and the choice of an ad will be influenced by, amongst other things, viewer demographics, time of ad (local time, time in game, e.g. half time, TV peak/off-peak time, etc.), length of ad (time constraint), cost of ad, who is winning in the match, etc. The ad choice, amongst other things, would have to meet business goals and also appeal to viewers. The autonomic manager is expected, within the boundaries of the system's set rules and goal (see excerpt in Rule 5.1), to dynamically decide on which ad to run. So, at every decision instance, the autonomic marketing system collects context information (e.g. viewer demographics, ad constraints, who is winning in the game, etc.) and makes decisions based on the analysis of the information collected.

Rule 5.1: Example rule defining system goal

---

1. Extract external variables (decision parameters) at defined time interval and decide on action
2. Send Trap and change action (advert) if <condition> is met, otherwise retain previous ad
3. <condition> should meet the measure of success below
4. If current action is same as previous action, do not send Trap and do not change action
5. <<<snip>>>

================Measure of Success================

6. Cost of action change (total ad run) must fall within <budget>
7. <budget> is set at the beginning
8. Rate of change should be considerably reasonable
9. Turnover should justify cost
10. <<<snip>>>

The idea is to dynamically and yet efficiently run localised market campaigns that are sensitive to fans' setting while the match lasts. This is a typical example of a system with many dimensions of freedom and very wide behaviour space. For brevity, the behaviour space is divided into four different zones (Zones A–D) and expressed along two dimensions of freedom (*Mood* and *CostImplication*) as shown in Figure 5.2.

The two dimensions of freedom represent a collation of all possible decision influencers (context information) into two key external variables – *Mood* and *CostImplication*. Mood is defined by many variables (e.g., *MatchScore*, i.e., information about who is winning, and *WeatherInfo*), while CostImplication is defined by other variables like *TimeOfAd* and *LengthOfAd*. An action (in this case, RunAd1 or RunAd2 or RunAd3 or RunAd4) is defined for each zone. Each action (ad run) is thus activated only in its allocated zone, following specified policy (excerpt shown in Rule 5.2). The policy analyses the context information fed into the system and throws up a decision for an action – which ad to run. If the behaviour of the system, for example, falls within the zone defined by low mood and low costimplication (Zone C), the autonomic manager activates RunAd1 – in this case, Ad1 is run. Various design-time specified internal variables, e.g., **L**_BenchMarkMatchScore and **U**_BenchMarkTimeOfAd, are used to define decision benchmarks, **L**ower and **U**pper limits, respectively. The fixed logic in the policy (Rule 5.2) enables the manager to make specific decisions based on the dynamic environmental information (external variables).

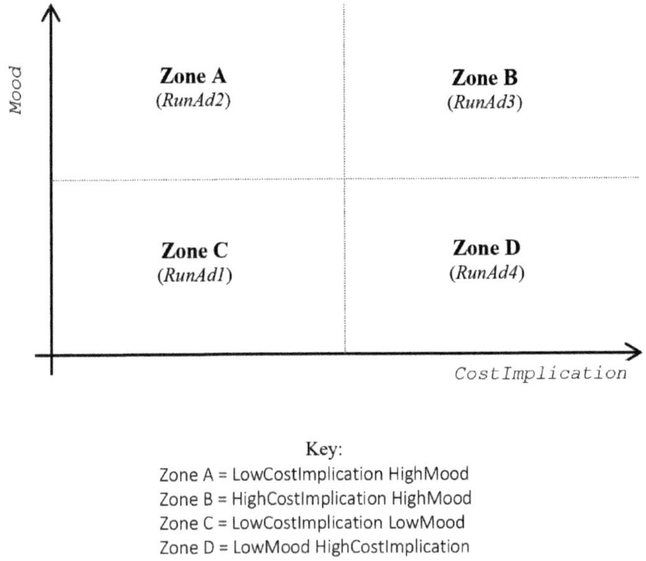

Figure 5.2 System behaviour space

Rule 5. 2: Excerpt of decision policy

```
If MatchScore < L_BenchMarkMatchScore And WeatherInfo <
      L_BenchMarkWeatherInfo Then
         Mood = "LowMood"
  ElseIf MatchScore > U_BenchMarkMatchScore And WeatherInfo >
      U_BenchMarkWeatherInfo Then
          Mood = "HighMood"
    Else: Mood = "Null"
End If
If TimeOfAd < L_BenchMarkTimeOfAd And LengthOfAd <
      L_BenchMarkLengthOfAd Or TimeOfAd > U_BenchMarkTimeOfAd And
      LengthOfAd > U_BenchMarkLengthOfAd Then
         CostImplication = "LowCostImplication"
    ElseIf TimeOfAd > U_BenchMarkTimeOfAd And LengthOfAd >
      M_BenchMarkLengthOfAd Then
         CostImplication = "HighCostImplication"
    Else: CostImplication = "Null"
End If

Select Case DecisionParameter
      Case "LowMoodLowCostImplication"
              CurrentAction(CurrentActionCounter) = "RunAd1"
      Case "LowCostImplicationHighMood"
              CurrentAction(CurrentActionCounter) = "RunAd2"
      Case "HighMoodHighCostImplication"
              CurrentAction(CurrentActionCounter) = "RunAd3"
      Case Else
              CurrentAction(CurrentActionCounter) = "RunAd4"
 End Select
```

5.1.1 Experimental environment

The system goal is defined by a set of rules (Rule 5.1) that the autonomic manager must adhere to in making decisions. A decision here is whether to change a running ad to another one or not. Basically, SysA is concerned with making decisions within the boundaries of the rules, while in SysB, those decisions are validated for conformity with the rules. SysC verifies that the measure of success is achieved. SysC also improves reliability by instilling stability in the system. This is done by implementing a dead-zone logic that introduces dead-zone boundaries (Figure 5.3) to the boundaries of the behaviour zones defined in Figure 5.2.

Within the dead-zone boundaries, no change of action is allowed – in this case, a running ad is not changed. So, take, for instance, in Figure 5.3, the action for Zone A (*RunAd2*) is usually activated within the area defined by (*x*) and when the system behaviour falls outside, this area another action is activated. With dead-zone logic implemented, this boundary is dynamically extended to the area defined by (*y*). So, in this case, the action for Zone A (*RunAd2*) is persisted until the (*y*) boundary is breached. As soon as the system behaviour moves beyond the area of (*y*) *to the right, the action for Zone B (RunAd3*) is activated. This action, likewise, is persisted until system behaviour moves beyond the area defined by (*z*). The gap, (*i*), between the new boundaries (represented by the double-edged arrow lines) can be dynamically adjusted. This technique is implemented by the DC component of SysC and helps to avoid erratic and unnecessary changes. Although the size of the boundaries can be dynamically adjusted to suit real-time changes, it is initially design-time specified. See Chapter 3 for full details of the dead-zone logic.

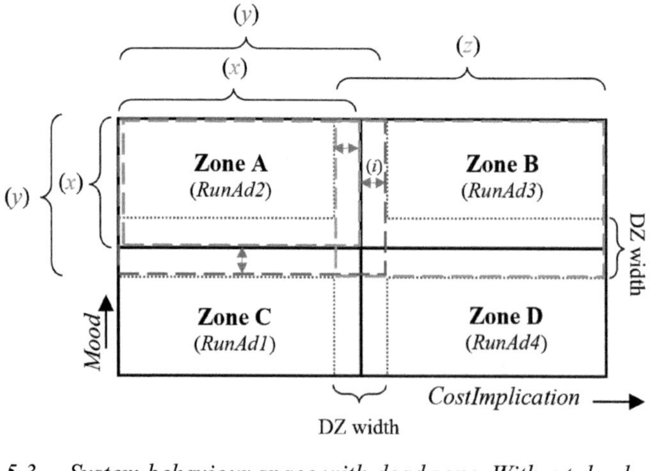

Figure 5.3 System behaviour space with dead zone. Without dead zone, Ad2 would be activated whenever the system behaviour falls within the area defined by x, but with dead zone, Ad2 is extended to the area defined by y.

The runtime context for this application arises from collecting and analysing samples of context information. The AC component (available in SysA, SysB and SysC) will, at every sample collection, decide (using the policy in Rule 5.2) which ad to run and then sends a trap message (notice of change of ad). Since it is wired to make a fresh decision at every policy execution, it is bound to send a trap message at every sample collection or decision instance. But before that decision is implemented, the VC component (available in SysB and SysC) validates it for *pass/fail*. It is important to define what pass/fail means in this context: for example, if the decided action is the same as the previous action (current ad), the VC component returns *fail* (then no trap is sent and no change is made) and passes control back to the AC component while retaining the previous action. The VC component also returns *fail* if the policy is violated in decision making, i.e., decision must be within the boundaries of specified benchmarks (e.g., a 'Null' return should not influence action change). Control is passed to the DC component each time VC returns a *pass*. The DC component (available only in SysC) is concerned with the measure of success aspect of the rule. In this case, a Tolerance Range Check is implemented: DC returns *fail* if *ActionChange is more than one within the first five sample collections and subsequently if action changes at every sample instance*. So, the DC component maintains action change at maximum of one within the first five sample collections and subsequently maximum of two in any three sample instances. This will help calm any erratic behaviour that could arise. Take, for instance, the fact that there could be a 360° change in '*Mood*' within a short space of time (e.g., a team's status in a game could change from winning→losing→winning within a very short space of time), which is capable of adversely affecting the choice of an ad.

Rule 5.3: Excerpts of SysB and SysC managers

```
If Mood < > "Null" And CostImplication < > "Null" Then
          DecisionContainer(IntervalCounter) = Mood & CostImplication
          DecisionParameter = DecisionContainer(IntervalCounter)
       <<<snip>>>
End if                                                                  (a)
If CurrentAction(CurrentActionCounter) = CurrentAction_
(CurrentActionCounter - 1) Then
      CurrentAction = CurrentAction(CurrentActionCounter - 1)
```

```
If IntervalCounter - IntervalCounterSysC(Interval - 1) > 4 Then
       ActionChangeCounterSysC = ActionChangeCounterSysC + 1            (b)
      <<<snip>>>
End if
```

Rules 5.3 (a) and (b) show excerpts of managers of SysB and SysC, respectively. This shows the conditions under which the managers change their actions. 'Action' in this case refers to 'Ad' – so 'CurrentAction' refers to currently running ad or new ad to run, while 'CurrentActionCounter – 1' refers to the previous ad. The need for a new and different approach is reinforced by the capabilities exhibited in SysC. It addresses situations where it is possible for the overall system to fail despite process (in terms of structural, legal, syntactical, etc.) correctness.

The experiments presented here simulate the performances of three autonomic systems (SysA, SysB and SysC) for the defined autonomic marketing scenario. Four external variables, now referred to as context samples (MatchScore, WeatherInfo, TimeOfAd and LengthOfAd), are fed into the autonomic managers of the systems (SysA, SysB and SysC) at every sample collection instance. Sample collection instances are defined by a set time interval that can be fixed (design-time specific) or dynamically tuned. Based on the policies (Rule 5.2), the managers decide how, when and which ad to change/run. The simulation was run for a total duration of 50 sample collection instances. During this simulation, the managers are analysed for the total number of ad changes and the distributions of those changes. For accurate analysis and comparison, the same samples at the same time instance and interval are fed into the managers concurrently. This is because samples may (most likely) change at every time instance and separately feeding these to the managers will lead to unbalanced judgment. Table 5.1 shows the main parameters used for the experiments.

It is important to note that the external variables hold values representing dynamic context information fed into the system. The computation of these values according to the policy in Rule 5.2 results in decision parameters with which the manager decides on what action to take. Also, several internal variables are used to specify boundaries as decision benchmarks. The metrics for analysis are explained as follows:

- No. of action (ad) change: the number of times actions change in any given sample collection interval. The lower value of action change means the better performance of the autonomic manager.
- Rate of action change: the rate at which actions change, measured as the number of action changes per sample collection (no. of action change/simulation time). This illustrates the level of stability in the system. A lower value means better performance.
- Rate of action run: the rate at which ads were run. This calculates the ratio of ad run to number of sample collections. Value of 1 indicates that the manager runs a different ad at every sample collection which means the manager is highly unstable.

Table 5.1 Main experimental parameters

Parameter	Value
Autonomic systems	SysA, SysB and SysC
Simulation time	50 sample collections
Metrics	No. of action (ad) change, rate of action change, rate of action run, no. of action run, action run distribution and no. of samples per time
Sample interval	Five samples
External variables	*MatchScore*, *WeatherInfo*, *TimeOfAd* and *LengthOfAd*

- No. of action runs: the cumulative number of individual action runs. This is the summation of the number of runs for each ad. This metric illustrates the sensitivity of the manager to the configuration of the behaviour space. This value does not directly, on its own, translate to level of performance. However, it validates the action distribution metric.
- Action run distribution: the distributed number of action runs. This gives the breakdown of the total action run. Nature of action run distribution illustrates the performance of the manager in terms of cost management.
- No. of samples per time: a constant (in this case, 50) spread across a defined time interval (in this case, five samples).

5.1.2 Results and evaluation

The results presented are for a simulation of 50 sample collections. All three autonomic managers (for SysA, SysB and SysC) are analysed based on the number of ad changes and number of ad distributions. Table 5.2 shows the results of 10 simulation runs for each of 50 sample collections.

Table 5.2 is a high-level view of the systems' performances. Figures 5.4 and 5.5 are a closer inspection and analysis of the system's performances. There is a clear indication of the stability and autonomic efficiency in SysC.

As a benchmark to compare against, it is difficult to say exactly what a perfect performance would be as that is context- and application-dependent. However, it is quite easy to say what a poor performance would be. For 'no. of ad change', a very poor performing (non-autonomic) system would have 50 ad changes in 50 sample collections. 'No. of ad run' wouldn't have a benchmark as the distribution of individual ad run is dependent on decision parameters (i.e., the combination of real-time context information). Value of '1' for 'rate of ad change' indicates that the manager is rapidly changing its mind which shows instability and lack of self-optimisation. So, the higher the 'rate of ad change' is, the lower the performance of the system. For 'rate of ad run', the performance of the system is very poor if value is '1' – this indicates that the manager runs a different ad at every sample collection and collectively runs all ads almost the same number of times. A quick glance at the results (Table 5.2) reveals that there is a significant performance gap between SysC and the other two systems. Also, the lower standard deviation in SysC gives more confidence in the spread of the results of the 10 simulation runs.

The optimisation of the TrAArch (SysC) in this autonomic marketing scenario is in terms of achieving a balance between efficient just-in-time target-marketing decision and cost effectiveness (savings maximisation) while maintaining improved trustability and dependability in the process. Figure 5.5 shows the behaviour of the systems in 50 sample collections in a game duration in which SysC shows significant gain in stability, efficiency and cost savings. It is clearly seen, for example, how SysC smoothened the high fluctuation rate (high adaptability frequency) experienced

Table 5.2 Results of 10 simulation runs

Runs	**No. of ad changes (x)**			**No. of ad runs (y)**			**Rate of ad change (x/50)**			**Rate of ad run (y/50)**		
	SysA	**SysB**	**SysC**	**SysA**	**SysB**	**SysC**	**SysA**	**SysB**	**SysC**	**SysA**	**SysB**	**SysC**
1	12	12	7	7	7	5	0.24	0.24	0.14	0.14	0.14	0.1
2	8	6	3	7	5	3	0.16	0.12	0.06	0.14	0.1	0.06
3	15	11	8	12	8	6	0.3	0.22	0.16	0.24	0.16	0.12
4	10	7	6	7	7	5	0.2	0.14	0.12	0.14	0.14	0.1
5	15	12	9	10	9	7	0.3	0.24	0.18	0.2	0.18	0.14
6	10	9	8	9	9	8	0.2	0.18	0.16	0.18	0.18	0.16
7	13	10	6	12	9	6	0.26	0.2	0.12	0.24	0.18	0.12
8	11	11	7	7	7	5	0.22	0.22	0.14	0.14	0.14	0.1
9	11	9	7	10	9	7	0.22	0.18	0.14	0.2	0.18	0.14
10	11	9	7	9	7	6	0.22	0.18	0.14	0.18	0.14	0.12
Avg	**11.6**	**9.6**	**6.8**	**9**	**7.7**	**5.8**	**0.232**	**0.192**	**0.136**	**0.18**	**0.154**	**0.116**
SD	**2.2**	**2**	**1.6**									

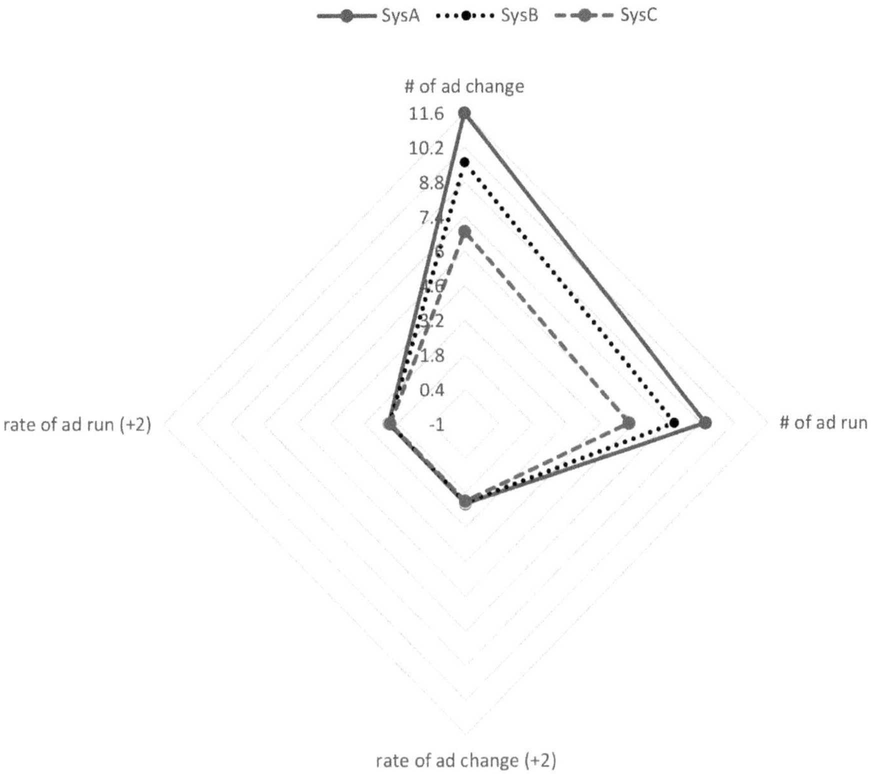

Figure 5.4 *Graphical representation of the results of 10 simulation runs (note that the values for rate of ad change/run have been scaled up by 2 to improve graph visibility)*

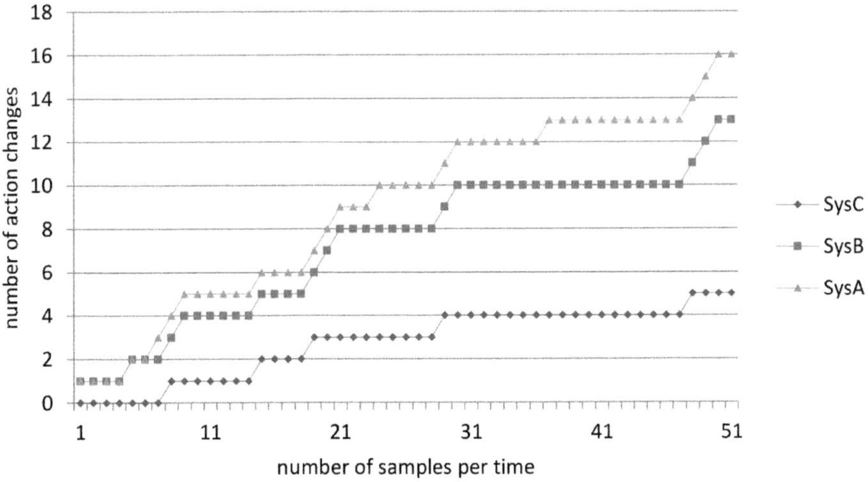

Figure 5.5 *An instance of systems' behaviour in a 50-sample collection*

between the 5th and 25th sample collections. In general, the average ad change ratio of about one change in three samples (1:3) is reduced to one change in ten samples (1:10), representing an overall gain of about 68.75 per cent in terms of stability and cost efficiency.

Figure 5.6 shows the distribution of ads across the 50-sample duration. '*NullActions*', i.e., 'run no ad', are not shown. This also corroborates the significant gain made by the SysC manager. For example, the SysC autonomic manager runs only one Ad3 and two Ad2, while SysB runs four Ad3 and Ad2 in both cases. This directly translates to adaptive cost savings by SysC. Recall from Figure 5.2 that Ad2 is run when *Mood* is high and *CostImplication* is low (best value for money), while Ad3 is run when *Mood* and *CostImplication* are both high (when it costs more to run an Ad). SysC runs more of Ad2 (best value for money).

While it has been shown that the TrAArch (SysC) is capable of maintaining reliability by reducing inefficient adaptation (cutting off unnecessary adaptations), it should be noted that reduction alone is not the answer. If the rate is very low, it will not be right either. For example, if the rate of change is too low, it could indicate that the manager is almost inactive (or not making decisions frequently enough). For every application, it is necessary to determine which rate is appropriate or cost effective in the long run. The proposed approach in this book provides a way for tuning this (e.g., through dynamically adjusting the width of the dead zone). There is a cost associated with bad or over-frequent changes and also a cost with not making frequent enough changes. Success is measured by striking a balance between the two.

5.2 Case example scenario 2: self-adapting resource allocation

In case example scenario 2, a more complex experimental analysis is designed to analyse the performance of the proposed TrAArch architecture over existing autonomic architectures. The experimental analysis is an implementation of a datacentre resource request and allocation management scenario. Although the demonstration of the proposed architecture uses a datacentre scenario, which though offers a way of efficiently managing complex datacentres, the application of the architecture can be widespread. In other words, although a datacentre is used to demonstrate the functionalities of the proposed architecture, it is not limited to this scenario. The datacentre model represents a very simple datacentre scenario where the simulation focuses on the efficiency and dependability of resource request and allocation management rather than other vast areas of datacentre, e.g., security, power, cooling, etc. So, the purpose of the experiments is to demonstrate the applicability and performance of the proposed architecture and not to investigate datacentres themselves. However, the datacentre is chosen as the implementation scenario because its many dimensions of complexity and large number of tuning parameters offer a rich domain in which to evaluate a wide range of techniques, tools and frameworks.

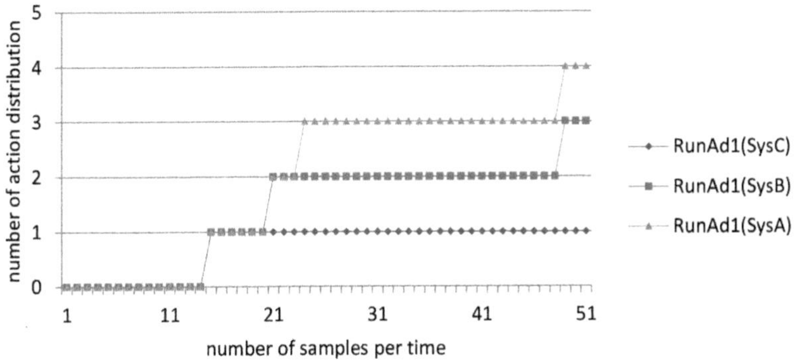

(a)

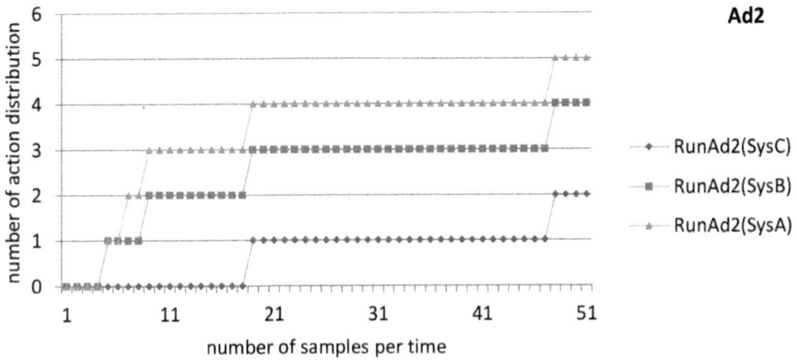

(b)

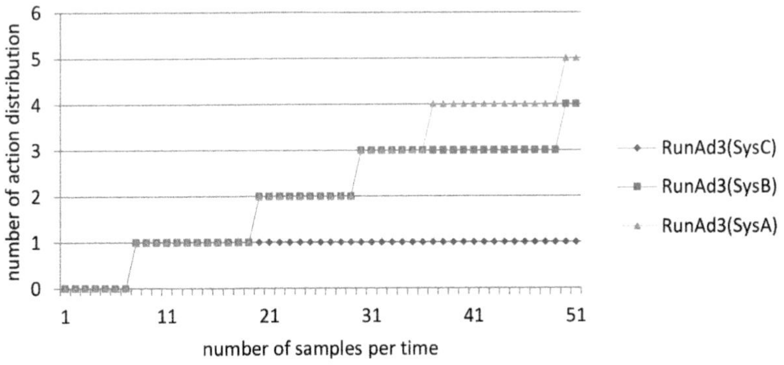

(c)

Figure 5.6 A distribution of the ads (Ad1, Ad2 and Ad3). (a) Distribution of Ad1. (b) Distribution of Ad2. (c) Distribution of Ad3.

Several research works, e.g. References 148–150, have proposed scheduling algorithms that optimise the performance of datacentres. In a utility function-based approach, Das *et al.* [148] are able to quantify and manage trade-offs between competing goals such as performance and energy consumption. Their approach reduced datacentre power consumption by up to 14 per cent. Other works that have resulted in improved performance and resource utilisation by proposing new scheduling algorithms include Reference 149, which focuses on the allocation of virtual machines in datacentre nodes, and Reference 150, which uses a 'greedy resource allocation algorithm' that allows distributing a web workload among different servers assigned to each service. This book, on the other hand, does not propose any new scheduling algorithm for efficient utilisation of datacentre resources; instead, it uses the basic resource allocation technique to model the performance of datacentre autonomic managers in terms of the effectiveness of resource request and allocation management.

5.2.1 TrAArch simulator

Note: It is important to first go through the experiments presented in this book before attempting to use this application. This will ensure that the user fully understands how the application works so that it can be used properly and efficiently. This will also help the user understand the parameters properly.

The TrAArch simulator is an application developed in C# for simulating autonomic managers for datacentres. This is a direct demonstration of the TrAArch presented in Chapter 4. The simulator can be used to evaluate the performance of three autonomic managers – SysA (represented by AC), SysB (represented by VC) and SysC (represented by DC). The application supports two experiments '*Normal Simulation*' and '*Interoperability*' – example normal simulation is presented here while interoperability is presented in Chapter 6. Figure 5.7 shows the front end of the simulator.

The simulator is available via **Downloadable material**. To use the application, follow these steps:

- Select the type of simulation you want – *Normal Simulation* or *Interoperability*. Selecting *Normal Simulation* gives the options of simulating the individual autonomic managers (AC, VC or DC) separately or concurrently (AC+VC+DC) for performance analysis of the three systems. The *Interoperability* option allows for the analysis and comparison of two autonomic managers – one with interoperability capability and the other without.
- Set the resource parameters. The application supports a maximum of four applications and 1000 servers. Select these from the drop-down lists. The size of the applications can be changed before or during the simulation via the *Change App Size* button.

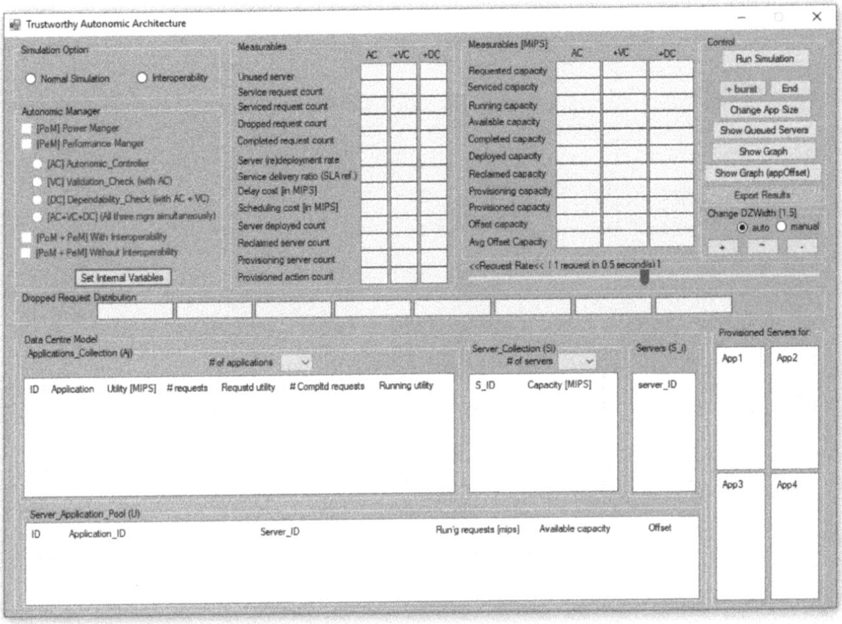

Figure 5.7 *TrAArch simulator*

- Set additional parameters – the internal and external variables. Clicking on *Set Internal Variables* button allows the user to see the default values and to change any variable of choice. Description of these variables can be accessed via the *Info* button and in section 5.2.2.2. Note that these variables cannot be changed once the simulation starts. The rate at which service requests are received can be adjusted via the *Request Rate* control. The dead zone width (*DZWidth*) is set to *auto* by default and can be changed to *manual*.
- *Run Simulation* will start the simulation.
- Once the simulation starts, the user can inject burst into the system via *+burst*, change the size of each application and add or remove applications and servers. The user can also view the servers that are on the queue and the applications they are prepared to service via *Show Queued Servers*. The application is designed to print selected graphs of the simulation results in real time, and these can be viewed via *Show Graph* and *Show Graph (appOffset)*. The entire simulation result can be exported to Microsoft Excel at the end of the simulation via *Export Results*. Also, the *Simulation Speed* parameter is used to configure and track *Request Rate* – i.e., the number of requests per time.

The *Export Results* and *Show Graph* are two unique features of this application. The export results feature allows for the entire simulation result (according to metrics) to be exported to Microsoft Excel at the end of the simulation while the show graph feature allows for real-time graph plotting of the results. Below are C# code implementations of the three features and *SysC*:

Export Results: This example is for only six metrics – more can be added as required.

```
using System;
using System.Collections.Generic;
using System.ComponentModel;
using System.Data;
using System.Drawing;
using System.Linq;
using System.Text;
using System.Windows.Forms;
using Microsoft.VisualBasic;
using System.Windows.Forms.DataVisualization.Charting;
using System.Diagnostics;
using Microsoft.Office.Interop.Excel;
using System.Collections;
//these are required libraries for both features

private void buttonExportResults_Click(object sender, EventArgs e)
{
    Microsoft.Office.Interop.Excel.Application xla = new
Microsoft.Office.Interop.Excel.Application();
    Workbook wb = xla.Workbooks.Add(XlSheetType.xlWorksheet);
    Worksheet ws = (Worksheet)xla.ActiveSheet;

    if (timerPeM_AC.Enabled == true) //implementing within a timer class gives greater control
    {
        for (int i = 0; i < simulationTime + 1; i++)
        {
            ws.Cells[1, 1] = "SimulationTime"; ws.Cells[1, 2] = "UnusedServerCountAC";
ws.Cells[1, 3] = "serviceRequestCountAC"; ws.Cells[1, 4] = "ServicedRequestCountAC";
            ws.Cells[1, 5] = "DroppedRequestCountAC"; ws.Cells[1, 6] = "slaAC";

            ws.Cells[i + 2, 1] = i;
            ws.Cells[i + 2, 2] = UnusedServerCountACList[i + 1];
            ws.Cells[i + 2, 3] = serviceRequestCountACList[i + 1];
            ws.Cells[i + 2, 4] = ServicedRequestCountACList[i + 1];
            ws.Cells[i + 2, 5] = DroppedRequestCountACList[i + 1];
            ws.Cells[i + 2, 6] = slaACList[i + 1];
        }
        xla.Visible = true;
    }
}
```

Show Graph: This example plots graphs of selected metrics for all three systems (AC, VC and DC).

```
formGraphAvgMetrics.PlotGraphAvgACVCDC(); //calls the PlotGraphAvgACVCDC() method

public void PlotGraphAvgACVCDC()
{
    Form1 mainform = ((Form1)this.Owner);

    //chart1_______________________________________
    chart1.Series["SysAC"].ChartType = SeriesChartType.FastLine;
    chart1.Series["SysAC"].Points.AddXY(mainform.simulationTime, mainform.AverageOffsetAC);

    chart1.Series["SysVC"].ChartType = SeriesChartType.FastLine;
    chart1.Series["SysVC"].Points.AddXY(mainform.simulationTime, mainform.AverageOffsetVC);
    chart1.Series["SysDC"].ChartType = SeriesChartType.FastLine;
    chart1.Series["SysDC"].Points.AddXY(mainform.simulationTime, mainform.AverageOffsetDC);

    //chart2_______________________________________
    chart2.Series["SysAC"].ChartType = SeriesChartType.FastLine;
    chart2.Series["SysAC"].Points.AddXY(mainform.simulationTime, mainform.DelayCostAC);
```

```
    chart2.Series["SysVC"].ChartType = SeriesChartType.FastLine;
    chart2.Series["SysVC"].Points.AddXY(mainform.simulationTime, mainform.DelayCostVC);

    chart2.Series["SysDC"].ChartType = SeriesChartType.FastLine;
    chart2.Series["SysDC"].Points.AddXY(mainform.simulationTime, mainform.DelayCostDC);

    //chart3_________________________________
    chart3.Series["SysAC"].ChartType = SeriesChartType.FastLine;
    chart3.Series["SysAC"].Points.AddXY(mainform.simulationTime, mainform.SchedulingCostAC);

    chart3.Series["SysVC"].ChartType = SeriesChartType.FastLine;
    chart3.Series["SysVC"].Points.AddXY(mainform.simulationTime, mainform.SchedulingCostVC);

    chart3.Series["SysDC"].ChartType = SeriesChartType.FastLine;
    chart3.Series["SysDC"].Points.AddXY(mainform.simulationTime, mainform.SchedulingCostDC);

    //chart4_________________________________
    chart4.Series["SysAC"].ChartType = SeriesChartType.FastLine;
    chart4.Series["SysAC"].Points.AddXY(mainform.simulationTime, mainform.DeploymentRateAC);

    chart4.Series["SysVC"].ChartType = SeriesChartType.FastLine;
    chart4.Series["SysVC"].Points.AddXY(mainform.simulationTime, mainform.DeploymentRateVC);

    chart4.Series["SysDC"].ChartType = SeriesChartType.FastLine;
    chart4.Series["SysDC"].Points.AddXY(mainform.simulationTime, mainform.DeploymentRateDC);

    //chart5_________________________________
    chart5.Series["SysAC"].ChartType = SeriesChartType.FastLine;
    chart5.Series["SysAC"].Points.AddXY(mainform.simulationTime, mainform.slaAC);

    chart5.Series["SysVC"].ChartType = SeriesChartType.FastLine;
    chart5.Series["SysVC"].Points.AddXY(mainform.simulationTime, mainform.slaVC);

    chart5.Series["SysDC"].ChartType = SeriesChartType.FastLine;
    chart5.Series["SysDC"].Points.AddXY(mainform.simulationTime, mainform.slaDC);

    chart5.Series["DZ_Width"].ChartType = SeriesChartType.FastLine;
    chart5.Series["DZ_Width"].Points.AddXY(mainform.simulationTime, mainform.DZConst);

    chart5.Series["reference point"].ChartType = SeriesChartType.FastLine;
    chart5.Series["reference point"].Points.AddXY(mainform.simulationTime, 1);
}
```

Simulation Speed: The user can adjust the simulation speed by increasing or reducing the request rate in real time. The request rate measures the number of requests received per time – minimum of one request per second. This feature is implemented using a TrackBar. The track bar also shows the request rate in real time. Here is the code for the implementation:

```
private void trackBarsimspeed_Scroll(object sender, EventArgs e)
{
    if (radioButtonInteroperability.Checked==false && radioButtonNormalSim.Checked==false )
    {
        MessageBox.Show("Select Simulation Option first",
            "Info"); comboServerNumber.Focus();
    }
    groupBoxSimulationSpeed.Text = "<<Request Rate<<  " + "[ 1 request in " +
((Convert.ToDouble(trackBarsimspeed.Value * RequestRateParam) / 1000)).ToString() + " second(s)
]";

    if (radioButtonNormalSim.Checked == true)
    {//this allows the simulation to continue even if trackBarsimspeed.Value = 0
        if (trackBarsimspeed.Value == 0)
        {
            trackBarsimspeed.Value = 1;
            groupBoxSimulationSpeed.Text = "<<Request Rate<<  " + "[ 1 request in " +
```

```
((Convert.ToDouble(trackBarsimspeed.Value * RequestRateParam) / 1000)).ToString() + " second(s)
]";
        }
    }
    if (radioButtonInteroperability.Checked == true)
    {//the interoperability simulation can't cope with request rate under 10
        if (trackBarsimspeed.Value < 10)
        {
            trackBarsimspeed.Value = 10;
            groupBoxSimulationSpeed.Text = "<<Request Rate<<  " + "[ 1 request in " +
((Convert.ToDouble(trackBarsimspeed.Value * RequestRateParam) / 1000)).ToString() + " second(s)
]";
        }
    }
}
```

***SysC (DC)*:** This is the system represented as DC in the simulator and the autonomic manager is denoted as *PeM_DC* (Performance Manager DC). Note that three systems (autonomic managers – AC, VC and DC) are simulated and whose performances can be analysed individually (as [AC], [VC] or [DC]) or collectively (as [AC+VC+DC]). Below is the code implementation of *SysC* also known as *PeM_DC*:

*When the user clicks on 'Run Simulation', internal variables (which are set or selected before the simulation starts) are fetched (*Figure 5.8*), the 'Set Internal Variables' button is disabled to prevent the change of internal variables in real time, some validations are carried out, and then the PeM_DC object is called.*

```
private void buttonRunSim_Click(object sender, EventArgs e)
{ //Gets the set internal variables values and then disables the 'Set Internal Variables' button
    SimulationRun = "IsActive";
    GetInternalVariables();
    formchangeInternalVariables.DisableVariableChange();

    if (radioButtonNormalSim.Checked == true)
    { //ensures that server & application numbers are set and that a manager is selected
        if (comboServerNumber.Text != "" && comboAppNumber.Text != "" &&
checkBoxPerformanceMgr.Checked != false)
        {//… this is only showing code for DC (SysC). Full code contains that of AC, VC, ACVCDC
            if (radioButtonDC.Checked)
            { //calls the timer object for DC - PeM_DC (Performance Manager DC)
                timerPeM_DC.Enabled = true; buttonRunSim.Enabled = false;
                this.Text = "Trustworthy Autonomic Architecture  [Normal Simulation, DC]";
            }
        }
    }
}
```

PeM_DC, and all major aspects of the simulator, are implemented as Timer objects with different settings. This helps to synchronise and manage the entire system and all its parts in real time. The simulator works on the basis of provisioning servers to service application requests. Application requests is simulated using a random number generator – every instance of the random number generation represents an application request for app1, app2, app3 or app4.

```
private void timerPeM_DC_Tick(object sender, EventArgs e) // the beginning of timerPeM_DC
{ // returns trackBarsimspeed.Value * RequestRateParam as timer-interval to be used globally for
controlled simulation speed
    TimerIntervalPublic = trackBarsimspeed.Value * RequestRateParam;
    timerGeneral.Enabled = true;
    if (listViewServer.Items.Count != 0)
    {
        timerPeM_DC.Interval = TimerIntervalPublic;

        int num = randomAppGen.Next(1, app.appNumber + 1); // random number generator used to
generate app request

        serviceRequestCountDC += 1;

        if (serviceRequestCountDC > (RetrieveRequestParam * (server.sNumber)))
        {
            timerAppRetrieveDC.Interval = TimerIntervalPublic * RetrieveRate;
            timerAppRetrieveDC.Enabled = true;    // App request starts to drop as soon as (20%
of number of servers) app requests are generated
        }

        PeM_DC = "Enabled";
        switch (num - 1)
        {
            case 0:                // App1 request generated
                RequestedCapacityDC += app1.appCapacity;
                app1RequestedCapacityDC += app1.appCapacity;
                if (app1DCOffset > (0 - app1.appCapacity))
                {
                    ServicedRequestCountDC += 1;
                    app1DCCount += 1;
                    app1DCTotalCapacity += app1.appCapacity;
                    app1DCRunningCapacity = app1DCTotalCapacity - (app1DCCompletedRequestCount *
app1.appCapacity);
                    listViewApp.Items[0].SubItems[3].Text = app1DCCount.ToString();
                    listViewApp.Items[0].SubItems[2].Text = app1.appCapacity.ToString();
                    listViewApp.Items[0].SubItems[4].Text = app1DCTotalCapacity.ToString();
                    listViewApp.Items[0].SubItems[6].Text = app1DCRunningCapacity.ToString();

                    listViewPool.Items[0].SubItems[3].Text = app1DCRunningCapacity.ToString();
                    app1DCOffset = app1DCAvailableCapacity - app1DCRunningCapacity;
                    listViewPool.Items[0].SubItems[5].Text = app1DCOffset.ToString();

                    App1.DZUpperBound = (app1.appCapacity + (app1.appCapacity * DZ.DZConst));
                    App1.DZLowerBound = (app1.appCapacity - (app1.appCapacity * DZ.DZConst));

                    if (app1DCCount < 6)
                    {
                        if (app1DCOffset < app1.appCapacity)
                        { App1.SystemBehaviour = "IsInDeployZone"; }
                        else
                        { App1.SystemBehaviour = "IsNotInDeployZone"; }
                    }
                    if (app1DCCount >= 6)
                    {
                        if (app1DCOffset >= app1.appCapacity)
                        { App1.SystemBehaviour = "IsNotInDeployZone"; }

                        if ((App1.SystemBehaviour == "IsInDeployZone") && (app1DCOffset <
App1.DZUpperBound))
                        { App1.SystemBehaviour = "IsInDeployZone"; }
                        else { App1.SystemBehaviour = "IsNotInDeployZone"; }
```

```
                    if ((App1.SystemBehaviour == "IsNotInDeployZone") && (app1DCOffset >
App1.DZLowerBound))
                    { App1.SystemBehaviour = "IsNotInDeployZone"; }
                    else { App1.SystemBehaviour = "IsInDeployZone"; }
                }

                if (App1.SystemBehaviour == "IsInDeployZone")
                {
                    if (listViewServer.Items.Count != 0)
                    {//this populates App1 queued server list. so this is queuing servers
                        this.formQS.QSApp1 = listViewServer.Items[0].SubItems[0].Text;
                        ProvisioningServerCountDC += 1;
                        ProvisioningCapacityDC += server.sCapacity;
                        ServerDeployedCountDC += 1;
                        DeployedCapacityDC += server.sCapacity;
                        app1DeployedCapacityDC += server.sCapacity;
                        listViewServer.Items.Remove(listViewServer.Items[0]);
                        this.formQS.EnableTimerDelayQS_App1DC();
                    }
                }
            }
            else if (app1DCOffset <= (0 - app1.appCapacity))
            {
                DroppedRequestCountDC += 1;
            }
            break;

        case 1:                         // App2 request generated
            RequestedCapacityDC += app2.appCapacity;
            app2RequestedCapacityDC += app2.appCapacity;
            if (app2DCOffset > (0 - app2.appCapacity))
            {
                ServicedRequestCountDC += 1;
                app2DCCount += 1;
                app2DCTotalCapacity += app2.appCapacity;
                app2DCRunningCapacity = app2DCTotalCapacity - (app2DCCompletedRequestCount *
app2.appCapacity);
                listViewApp.Items[1].SubItems[3].Text = app2DCCount.ToString();
                listViewApp.Items[1].SubItems[2].Text = app2.appCapacity.ToString();
                listViewApp.Items[1].SubItems[4].Text = app2DCTotalCapacity.ToString();
                listViewApp.Items[1].SubItems[6].Text = app2DCRunningCapacity.ToString();

                listViewPool.Items[1].SubItems[3].Text = app2DCRunningCapacity.ToString();
                app2DCOffset = app2DCAvailableCapacity - app2DCRunningCapacity;
                listViewPool.Items[1].SubItems[5].Text = app2DCOffset.ToString();

                App2.DZUpperBound = (app2.appCapacity + (app2.appCapacity * DZ.DZConst));
                App2.DZLowerBound = (app2.appCapacity - (app2.appCapacity * DZ.DZConst));

                if (app2DCCount < 6)
                {
                    if (app2DCOffset < app2.appCapacity)
                    { App2.SystemBehaviour = "IsInDeployZone"; }
                    else
                    { App2.SystemBehaviour = "IsNotInDeployZone"; }
                }
                if (app2DCCount >= 6)
                {
                    if (app2DCOffset >= app2.appCapacity)
                    { App2.SystemBehaviour = "IsNotInDeployZone"; }

                    if ((App2.SystemBehaviour == "IsInDeployZone") && (app2DCOffset <
App2.DZUpperBound))
                    { App2.SystemBehaviour = "IsInDeployZone"; }
                    else { App2.SystemBehaviour = "IsNotInDeployZone"; }

                    if ((App2.SystemBehaviour == "IsNotInDeployZone") && (app2DCOffset >
App2.DZLowerBound))
                    { App2.SystemBehaviour = "IsNotInDeployZone"; }
                    else { App2.SystemBehaviour = "IsInDeployZone"; }
```

```
                }
                if (App2.SystemBehaviour == "IsInDeployZone")
                {
                    if (listViewServer.Items.Count != 0)
                    {
                        this.formQS.QSApp2 = listViewServer.Items[0].SubItems[0].Text;
//this populates App2 queued server list. so this is queuing servers
                        ProvisioningServerCountDC += 1;
                        ProvisioningCapacityDC += server.sCapacity;
                        ServerDeployedCountDC += 1;
                        DeployedCapacityDC += server.sCapacity;
                        app2DeployedCapacityDC += server.sCapacity;
                        listViewServer.Items.Remove(listViewServer.Items[0]);
                        this.formQS.EnableTimerDelayQS_App2DC();
                    }
                }
            }
            else if (app2DCOffset <= (0 - app2.appCapacity))
            { DroppedRequestCountDC += 1; }

            break;

        case 2:                         // App3 request generated
            RequestedCapacityDC += app3.appCapacity;
            app3RequestedCapacityDC += app3.appCapacity;
            if (app3DCOffset > (0 - app3.appCapacity))
            {
                ServicedRequestCountDC += 1;
                app3DCCount += 1;
                app3DCTotalCapacity += app3.appCapacity;
                app3DCRunningCapacity = app3DCTotalCapacity - (app3DCCompletedRequestCount *
app3.appCapacity);
                listViewApp.Items[2].SubItems[3].Text = app3DCCount.ToString();
                listViewApp.Items[2].SubItems[2].Text = app3.appCapacity.ToString();
                listViewApp.Items[2].SubItems[4].Text = app3DCTotalCapacity.ToString();
                listViewApp.Items[2].SubItems[6].Text = app3DCRunningCapacity.ToString();

                listViewPool.Items[2].SubItems[3].Text = app3DCRunningCapacity.ToString();
                app3DCOffset = app3DCAvailableCapacity - app3DCRunningCapacity;
                listViewPool.Items[2].SubItems[5].Text = app3DCOffset.ToString();

                App3.DZUpperBound = (app3.appCapacity + (app3.appCapacity * DZ.DZConst));
                App3.DZLowerBound = (app3.appCapacity - (app3.appCapacity * DZ.DZConst));

                if (app3DCCount < 6)
                {
                    if (app3DCOffset < app3.appCapacity)
                    { App3.SystemBehaviour = "IsInDeployZone"; }
                    else
                    { App3.SystemBehaviour = "IsNotInDeployZone"; }
                }
                if (app3DCCount >= 6)
                {
                    if (app3DCOffset >= app3.appCapacity)
                    { App3.SystemBehaviour = "IsNotInDeployZone"; }

                    if ((App3.SystemBehaviour == "IsInDeployZone") && (app3DCOffset <
App3.DZUpperBound))
                    { App3.SystemBehaviour = "IsInDeployZone"; }
                    else { App3.SystemBehaviour = "IsNotInDeployZone"; }

                    if ((App3.SystemBehaviour == "IsNotInDeployZone") && (app3DCOffset >
App3.DZLowerBound))
                    { App3.SystemBehaviour = "IsNotInDeployZone"; }
                    else { App3.SystemBehaviour = "IsInDeployZone"; }
                }

                if (App3.SystemBehaviour == "IsInDeployZone")
                {
```

```
                    if (listViewServer.Items.Count != 0)
                    {
                        this.formQS.QSApp3 = listViewServer.Items[0].SubItems[0].Text;
//this populates App3 queued server list. so this is queuing servers
                        ProvisioningServerCountDC += 1;
                        ProvisioningCapacityDC += server.sCapacity;
                        ServerDeployedCountDC += 1;
                        DeployedCapacityDC += server.sCapacity;
                        app3DeployedCapacityDC += server.sCapacity;
                        listViewServer.Items.Remove(listViewServer.Items[0]);
                        this.formQS.EnableTimerDelayQS_App3DC();
                    }
                }
            }
            else if (app3DCOffset <= (0 - app3.appCapacity))
            {
                DroppedRequestCountDC += 1;
            }
            break;

        case 3:                         // App4 request generated
            RequestedCapacityDC += app4.appCapacity;
            app4RequestedCapacityDC += app4.appCapacity;
            if (app4DCOffset > (0 - app4.appCapacity))
            {
                ServicedRequestCountDC += 1;
                app4DCCount += 1;
                app4DCTotalCapacity += app4.appCapacity;
                app4DCRunningCapacity = app4DCTotalCapacity - (app4DCCompletedRequestCount *
app4.appCapacity);
                listViewApp.Items[3].SubItems[3].Text = app4DCCount.ToString();
                listViewApp.Items[3].SubItems[2].Text = app4.appCapacity.ToString();
                listViewApp.Items[3].SubItems[4].Text = app4DCTotalCapacity.ToString();
                listViewApp.Items[3].SubItems[6].Text = app4DCRunningCapacity.ToString();

                listViewPool.Items[3].SubItems[3].Text = app4DCRunningCapacity.ToString();
                app4DCOffset = app4DCAvailableCapacity - app4DCRunningCapacity;
                listViewPool.Items[3].SubItems[5].Text = app4DCOffset.ToString();

                App4.DZUpperBound = (app4.appCapacity + (app4.appCapacity * DZ.DZConst));
                App4.DZLowerBound = (app4.appCapacity - (app4.appCapacity * DZ.DZConst));

                if (app4DCCount < 6)
                {
                    if (app4DCOffset < app4.appCapacity)
                    { App4.SystemBehaviour = "IsInDeployZone"; }
                    else
                    { App4.SystemBehaviour = "IsNotInDeployZone"; }
                }
                if (app4DCCount >= 6)
                {
                    if (app4DCOffset >= app4.appCapacity)
                    { App4.SystemBehaviour = "IsNotInDeployZone"; }

                    if ((App4.SystemBehaviour == "IsInDeployZone") && (app4DCOffset <
App4.DZUpperBound))
                    { App4.SystemBehaviour = "IsInDeployZone"; }
                    else { App4.SystemBehaviour = "IsNotInDeployZone"; }

                    if ((App4.SystemBehaviour == "IsNotInDeployZone") && (app4DCOffset >
App4.DZLowerBound))
                    { App4.SystemBehaviour = "IsNotInDeployZone"; }
                    else { App4.SystemBehaviour = "IsInDeployZone"; }
                }

                if (App4.SystemBehaviour == "IsInDeployZone")
                {
                    if (listViewServer.Items.Count != 0)
                    {
```

```
                            this.formQS.QSApp4 = listViewServer.Items[0].SubItems[0].Text;
//this populates App4 queued server list. so this is queuing servers
                            ProvisioningServerCountDC += 1;
                            ProvisioningCapacityDC += server.sCapacity;
                            ServerDeployedCountDC += 1;
                            DeployedCapacityDC += server.sCapacity;
                            app4DeployedCapacityDC += server.sCapacity;
                            listViewServer.Items.Remove(listViewServer.Items[0]);
                            this.formQS.EnableTimerDelayQS_App4DC();
                        }
                    }
                }
                else if (app4DCOffset <= (0 - app4.appCapacity))
                {
                    DroppedRequestCountDC += 1;
                }
                break;
            default:
                break;
        }
    }
}       // the end of timerPeM_DC +++++++++++++++++++++++++++++++++++++++++
```

Once an application request is generated, the system provisions a server (or servers, depending on the size of outstanding application requests) for that particular application. Over time, the system is able to forecast application requests using historic data. So, servers are released/loaded and queued in anticipation of the forecast requests. Queued servers are managed by formQS *and can be seen by clicking on the 'Show Queued Servers' button.*

```
// Provisioning For App1
public void ProvisionForApp1DC()      // ProvisionForApp1DC()
{
    if (timerPeM_DC.Enabled == true)
    {
        string S_deployed1 = "";
        listViewPoolApp1.Items.Add(this.formQS.QSapp1DCReadyToProvisionServer);
        app1DCAvailableCapacity += server.sCapacity;

        for (int d = 0; d < listViewPoolApp1.Items.Count; d++)
        {
            S_deployed1 += "[" + listViewPoolApp1.Items[d].Text + "]";
        }
        listViewPool.Items[0].SubItems[2].Text = S_deployed1;
        ProvisionedActionCountDC += 1;
        ProvisionedCapacityDC += server.sCapacity;
        ProvisioningServerCountDC -= 1;
        ProvisioningCapacityDC -= server.sCapacity;

        app1DCRunningCapacity = app1DCTotalCapacity - (app1DCCompletedRequestCount *
app1.appCapacity);
        listViewApp.Items[0].SubItems[6].Text = app1DCRunningCapacity.ToString();
listViewPool.Items[0].SubItems[3].Text = app1DCRunningCapacity.ToString();

        listViewPool.Items[0].SubItems[4].Text = app1DCAvailableCapacity.ToString();
                app1DCOffset = app1DCAvailableCapacity - app1DCRunningCapacity;

        if (app1DCOffset >= (app1.appCapacity * 2.5))
        {
            app1DCAvailableCapacity -= server.sCapacity;

               listViewServer.Items.Add(listViewPoolApp1.Items[0].Text).SubItems.Add(Convert.ToS
               tring(server.sCapacity));
            listViewPoolApp1.Items.Remove(listViewPoolApp1.Items[0]);
            ReclaimedServerCountDC += 1;
            ReclaimedCapacityDC += server.sCapacity;

            for (int d = 0; d < listViewPoolApp1.Items.Count; d++)
```

```
            {
                S_deployed1 += "[" + listViewPoolApp1.Items[d].Text + "]";
            }
            listViewPool.Items[0].SubItems[2].Text = S_deployed1;
        }

        app1DCRunningCapacity = app1DCTotalCapacity - (app1DCCompletedRequestCount *
app1.appCapacity);
        app1DCOffset = app1DCAvailableCapacity - app1DCRunningCapacity;
        listViewPool.Items[0].SubItems[5].Text = app1DCOffset.ToString();
        listViewPool.Items[0].SubItems[4].Text = app1DCAvailableCapacity.ToString();
    }
}
// Provisioning For App2
public void ProvisionForApp2DC()     // ProvisionForApp2DC()
{
    if (timerPeM_DC.Enabled == true)
    {
        string S_deployed2 = "";
        listViewPoolApp2.Items.Add(this.formQS.QSapp2DCReadyToProvisionServer);
        app2DCAvailableCapacity += server.sCapacity;

        for (int d = 0; d < listViewPoolApp2.Items.Count; d++)
        {
            S_deployed2 += "[" + listViewPoolApp2.Items[d].Text + "]";
        }
        listViewPool.Items[1].SubItems[2].Text = S_deployed2;
        ProvisionedActionCountDC += 1;
        ProvisionedCapacityDC += server.sCapacity;
        ProvisioningServerCountDC -= 1;
        ProvisioningCapacityDC -= server.sCapacity;

        app2DCRunningCapacity = app2DCTotalCapacity - (app2DCCompletedRequestCount *
app2.appCapacity);
        listViewApp.Items[1].SubItems[6].Text = app2DCRunningCapacity.ToString();
listViewPool.Items[1].SubItems[3].Text = app2DCRunningCapacity.ToString();

        listViewPool.Items[1].SubItems[4].Text = app2DCAvailableCapacity.ToString();
        app2DCOffset = app2DCAvailableCapacity - app2DCRunningCapacity;

        if (app2DCOffset >= (app2.appCapacity * 2.5))
        {
            app2DCAvailableCapacity -= server.sCapacity;

               listViewServer.Items.Add(listViewPoolApp2.Items[0].Text).SubItems.Add(Convert.ToS
               tring(server.sCapacity));
            listViewPoolApp2.Items.Remove(listViewPoolApp2.Items[0]);
            ReclaimedServerCountDC += 1;
            ReclaimedCapacityDC += server.sCapacity;

            for (int d = 0; d < listViewPoolApp2.Items.Count; d++)
            {
                S_deployed2 += "[" + listViewPoolApp2.Items[d].Text + "]";
            }
            listViewPool.Items[1].SubItems[2].Text = S_deployed2;
        }

        app2DCRunningCapacity = app2DCTotalCapacity - (app2DCCompletedRequestCount *
app2.appCapacity);
        app2DCOffset = app2DCAvailableCapacity - app2DCRunningCapacity;
        listViewPool.Items[1].SubItems[5].Text = app2DCOffset.ToString();
        listViewPool.Items[1].SubItems[4].Text = app2DCAvailableCapacity.ToString();
    }
}
// Provisioning For App3
public void ProvisionForApp3DC()   // ProvisionForApp3DC()
{
    if (timerPeM_DC.Enabled == true)
    {
        string S_deployed3 = "";
```

```
        listViewPoolApp3.Items.Add(this.formQS.QSapp3DCReadyToProvisionServer);
        app3DCAvailableCapacity += server.sCapacity;

        for (int d = 0; d < listViewPoolApp3.Items.Count; d++)
        {
            S_deployed3 += "[" + listViewPoolApp3.Items[d].Text + "]";
        }
        listViewPool.Items[2].SubItems[2].Text = S_deployed3;
        ProvisionedActionCountDC += 1;
        ProvisionedCapacityDC += server.sCapacity;
        ProvisioningServerCountDC -= 1;
        ProvisioningCapacityDC -= server.sCapacity;

        app3DCRunningCapacity = app3DCTotalCapacity - (app3DCCompletedRequestCount *
app3.appCapacity);
        listViewApp.Items[2].SubItems[6].Text = app3DCRunningCapacity.ToString();
listViewPool.Items[2].SubItems[3].Text = app3DCRunningCapacity.ToString();

        listViewPool.Items[2].SubItems[4].Text = app3DCAvailableCapacity.ToString();
        app3DCOffset = app3DCAvailableCapacity - app3DCRunningCapacity;

        if (app3DCOffset >= (app3.appCapacity * 2.5))
        {
            app3DCAvailableCapacity -= server.sCapacity;

              listViewServer.Items.Add(listViewPoolApp3.Items[0].Text).SubItems.Add(Convert.ToS
              tring(server.sCapacity));
            listViewPoolApp3.Items.Remove(listViewPoolApp3.Items[0]);
            ReclaimedServerCountDC += 1;
            ReclaimedCapacityDC += server.sCapacity;

            for (int d = 0; d < listViewPoolApp3.Items.Count; d++)
            {
                S_deployed3 += "[" + listViewPoolApp3.Items[d].Text + "]";
            }
            listViewPool.Items[2].SubItems[2].Text = S_deployed3;
        }

        app3DCRunningCapacity = app3DCTotalCapacity - (app3DCCompletedRequestCount *
app3.appCapacity);
        app3DCOffset = app3DCAvailableCapacity - app3DCRunningCapacity;
        listViewPool.Items[2].SubItems[5].Text = app3DCOffset.ToString();
        listViewPool.Items[2].SubItems[4].Text = app3DCAvailableCapacity.ToString();
    }
}
// Provisioning For App4
public void ProvisionForApp4DC()      // ProvisionForApp4DC()
{
    if (timerPeM_DC.Enabled == true)
    {
        string S_deployed4 = "";
        listViewPoolApp4.Items.Add(this.formQS.QSapp4DCReadyToProvisionServer);
        app4DCAvailableCapacity += server.sCapacity;

        for (int d = 0; d < listViewPoolApp4.Items.Count; d++)
        {
            S_deployed4 += "[" + listViewPoolApp4.Items[d].Text + "]";
        }
        listViewPool.Items[3].SubItems[2].Text = S_deployed4;
        ProvisionedActionCountDC += 1;
        ProvisionedCapacityDC += server.sCapacity;
        ProvisioningServerCountDC -= 1;
        ProvisioningCapacityDC -= server.sCapacity;

        app4DCRunningCapacity = app4DCTotalCapacity - (app4DCCompletedRequestCount *
app4.appCapacity);
        listViewApp.Items[3].SubItems[6].Text = app4DCRunningCapacity.ToString();
        listViewPool.Items[3].SubItems[3].Text = app4DCRunningCapacity.ToString();

        listViewPool.Items[3].SubItems[4].Text = app4DCAvailableCapacity.ToString();
```

```
        app4DCOffset = app4DCAvailableCapacity - app4DCRunningCapacity;

        if (app4DCOffset >= (app4.appCapacity * 2.5))
        {
            app4DCAvailableCapacity -= server.sCapacity;

                listViewServer.Items.Add(listViewPoolApp4.Items[0].Text).SubItems.Add(Convert.ToS
                tring(server.sCapacity));
            listViewPoolApp4.Items.Remove(listViewPoolApp4.Items[0]);
            ReclaimedServerCountDC += 1;
            ReclaimedCapacityDC += server.sCapacity;

            for (int d = 0; d < listViewPoolApp4.Items.Count; d++)
            {
                S_deployed4 += "[" + listViewPoolApp4.Items[d].Text + "]";
            }
            listViewPool.Items[3].SubItems[2].Text = S_deployed4;
        }

        app4DCRunningCapacity = app4DCTotalCapacity - (app4DCCompletedRequestCount *
app4.appCapacity);
        app4DCOffset = app4DCAvailableCapacity - app4DCRunningCapacity;
        listViewPool.Items[3].SubItems[5].Text = app4DCOffset.ToString();
        listViewPool.Items[3].SubItems[4].Text = app4DCAvailableCapacity.ToString();
    }
}
```

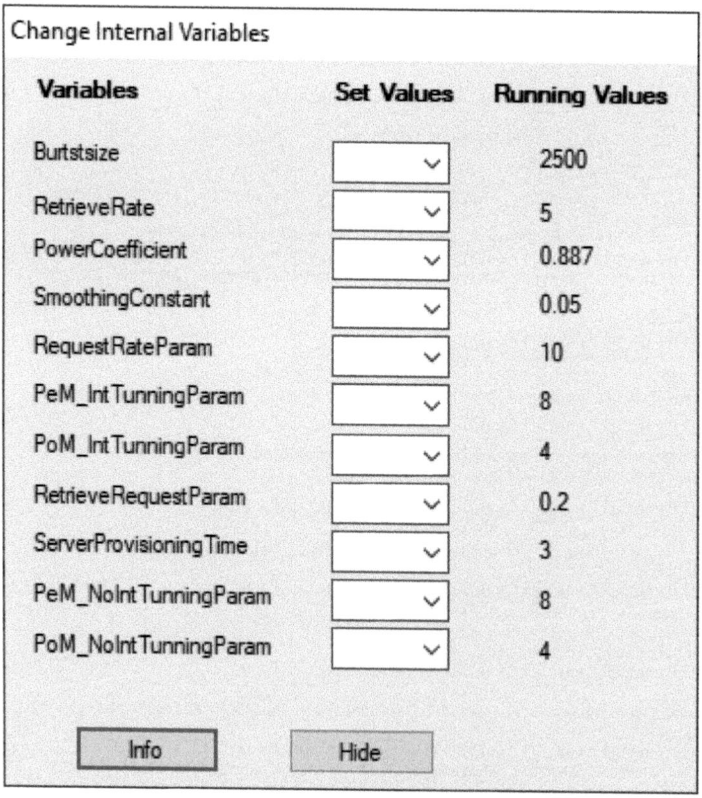

Figure 5.8 *TrAArch simulator: set internal variables. This shows default simulation variables and enables the user to change them as desired.*

5.2.2 *Experimental environment*

The experiments are designed and implemented using the TrAArch simulator (section 5.2.1) developed in C# programming. The scope of the experiments focuses on the performance of datacentre autonomic managers in resource request and allocation management activities under varying workloads. Although some workload parameters are sourced from experimental results of other research, e.g., References 151-153, the designed experiments allow for the tailoring of all parameters (internal and external variables) according to user preferences. Simulations are designed to model several options of real datacentre scenarios. So, depending on what is being investigated, the user can design individual scenarios and set workloads according to specific requirements.

5.2.2.1 Scheduling and resource allocation

Let us consider the model of the datacentre used in this experimentation in detail – in terms of scheduling and request services. The datacentre model comprises a pool of resources S_i (live servers), a pool of shutdown servers $\check{S}_i$ (ready to be powered and restored to S_i as need be), a list of applications A_j, a pool of services $\underset{..}{U}$ (a combination of applications and their provisioning servers) and an autonomic manager (performance manager, denoted *PeM*) that optimises the entire system. A_j and S_i are, respectively, a collection of applications supported (as services) by the datacentre and a collection of servers available to the manager (*PeM*) for provisioning (or scheduling) available services according to request. As service requests arrive, *PeM* dynamically populates $\underset{..}{U}$ to service the requests. $\underset{..}{U}$ is defined
by (5.1)

$$\underset{..}{U}=\begin{cases} A_1\colon (S_{11}, S_{12}, S_{13}, \ldots, S_{1i}) \\ A_2\colon (S_{21}, S_{22}, S_{23}, \ldots, S_{2i}) \\ \ldots \; \ldots \; \ldots \; \ldots \; \ldots \; \ldots \\ A_n\colon (S_{n1}, S_{n2}, S_{n3}, \ldots, S) \end{cases} \tag{5.1}$$

where $A_1\colon (S_{11}, S_{12}, S_{13}, \ldots, S_{1i})$ means that $(S_{11}, S_{12}, S_{13}, \ldots, S_{1i})$ servers are currently allocated to Application A_1 and A_n is the number of application entries into $\underset{..}{U}$. Equation (5.1) indicates that a server can be (re)deployed for different applications. All the servers in S_i are up and running (constantly available – or so desired by *PeM*) waiting for (re)deployment. The primary performance goal of *PeM* is to minimise oscillation and maximise stability [including just-in-time service delivery to meet service level achievement (SLA) target], while the secondary performance goal is to maximise the throughput.

Service (application) requests arrive and are queued. If there are enough resources to service a particular request, then it is serviced otherwise it remains in the queue (or may eventually be dropped). The autonomic manager checks for resource availability and deploys server(s) according to the size of the request. The size of application requests and the capacity of servers are defined in million instructions per second (MIPS). In this book, '*size*' and '*capacity*' are used interchangeably and mostly would refer to MIPS, i.e., the extent of its processing requirement. When a server is deployed, it is placed in a queue (Figure 5.9) for a time defined by the variable *ProvisioningTime*. This queue simulates the time (delay) it takes to load or configure a server with necessary application before provisioning.

Recall from (5.1) that any server can be (re)configured for different applications, and so servers are not pre-configured. Servers are then '*Provisioned*' after spending *ProvisioningTime* in the queue (Figure 5.9). The provisioning pool is constantly populated as requests arrive. Now as a result of the lag between provisioning time and the rate of request arrival or as a result of some unforeseen process disruptions, some servers do overshoot their provisioning time and thereby are left redundant in the queue. This can be addressed by the autonomic manager, depending on configuration, to reduce the impact on the whole system. As requests are fully serviced (completed) servers are released into the server pool and redeployed as may be needed. Note that SLA is calculated based on accepted requests. Rejected or dropped requests are not considered in calculating SLA. The essence of the request queue is to allow the autonomic manager to accept requests only when it has enough resources to service them. The service contract is entered only when requests are accepted. So, the manager could look at its capacity, in terms of available resources,

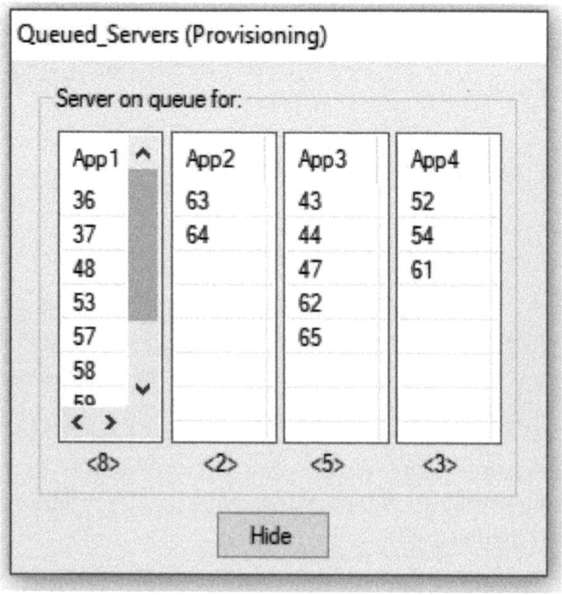

Figure 5.9 TrAArch simulator showing queued servers

compare that with the capacity requested and say '*sorry I haven't got enough resources*' and reject or drop the request. This whole process goes on and the manager manages the system to the level of its sophistication.

A basic system without any form of smartness can barely go far before the whole system is clogged due to inefficient and unstructured resource management. The level to which any autonomic manager can successfully and efficiently manage the process defined above depends on its level of sophistication. For me, this largely depends on how each manager is wired (in terms of architecture) and not necessarily the scheduling algorithm or actual component logic used. For example, two autonomic managers, differently wired, may employ the same scheduling algorithm but achieve different results. Results here may be looked at in terms of, say, '*with such level of available resources how many requests were successfully serviced over a period of time?*'. These are the kinds of considerations in the following experiments where three differently wired autonomic managers are analysed.

5.2.2.2 Workload and simulation parameters

The result of every simulation analysis is relative to the set of workload or parameter set used that configures the specific application instance. The parameter set used for the datacentre model analysis is classified into internal and external variables. *Internal variables* are those variables that do not change during runtime, e.g., the capacity of a server. *External variables*, on the other hand, are those that can change in the course of the simulation, e.g., the rate at which requests arrive. External variables are usually system generated and are always unpredictable. The experimental design has the capacity for heterogeneous workload representation. This means that even the internal variables can be reset before the simulation begins, thereby offering the possibility of scaling to high/low load to suit user preferences . The range of value options for most of the variables reflects the experimental results of other research, especially References 151–153. Note that the following variables are used with the C#-based TrAArch simulator.

- **Internal variables**

Below is the list of internal variables used in this experiment. Some of the variables used are specific to this experiment while some are general datacentre variables.

- *SmoothingConstant*

This variable is the smoothing constant (α) for calculating simple exponential smoothing used to forecast the size (capacity) of expected/arriving requests. This, as used in this experiment, enables the autonomic manager to decide safe boundaries at which it is no longer safe to allow server shutdown. Alpha (α) is a number between

0 and 1. The experiments in this book use experimental results for three values of α (0.05, 0.15 and 0.25) to justify the choice of alpha. It is important to choose an α value that will not result in exponential smoothed average that is very close to the actual data as that will not smoothen the system's behaviour. See Chapter 3 for more details about the exponential smoothing average technology used in experiments in this book.

- *server.sCapacity*

This represents the service capacity of each server and for the purposes of the experiments here all servers are assumed to be of equal capacity – 40 000 MIPS. Server capacity (size) is measured in MIPS.

- *RetrieveRequestParam*

The tuning parameter indicating when to start shutting services (this simulates service request completion) – at which point some running requests are closed as completed. This value is measured as percentage of number of servers in use and has been restricted to a value between 0.1 and 0.3. The margin 0.1–0.3 (representing 10–30 per cent) is used because experiments show that it is the safest margin within which accurate results can be guaranteed. The datacentre is not completely settled below 10 per cent, and beyond 30 per cent, scenarios with a low number of servers will yield inaccurate results. The higher the value of *RetrieveRequestParam,* the earlier the start of request completion.

- *RetrieveRate*

This indicates the rate at which requests are completed once simulation for service request completion is initiated. Value is relative to the rate of request arrival – e.g., if value is 5, then it means service request completion is five times slower than the rate of service request.

- *Burtsize*

This indicates how long the user wants the burst (injected disturbance) to last. This value is measured in milliseconds. Burst is a disturbance introduced by the user to cause disruption in the system. This alters the smooth running of the system and autonomic managers react to it differently. Often, injecting a burst disorientates the system. The nature of this disruption is usually in the form of sudden burst or significant shift in the rate of service request.

- *ServerProvisioningTime*

This indicates how long it takes to load or configure a server with an application. This is relative to the rate of request arrival – it is measured as half the rate of request arrival, e.g., the value of 3 will translate to 1.5 of the rate of request arrival.

- *ServerOnTime*

This indicates how long it takes a server to power on. This is relative to the rate of request arrival – it is *ServerProvisioningTime* + 1.

- *RequestRateParam*

This constant is used to adjust the possible range of request arrival rate. The user of the TrAArch Application can set the request rate according to preference, but this preference may not be accommodated within the available rate range. For example, if the least available rate is 1 request/second and the user wishes to use 2 requests/second, the *RequestRateParam* parameter can be used to extend the available range. A higher value increases the range for a lower rate of request arrival.

- **External variables**

Below is the list of external variables used in this experiment. Recall that external variables, also known as dynamic variables, are those variables that are fed into the system during runtime either as system generated (dynamic sensitivity to contextual changes) or human input (through external touch-points). Some of the variables used are specific to this experiment while some are general datacentre variables.

- *DZConst*

This variable is the tuning parameter that the autonomic manager uses to dynamically adjust dead zone boundaries. Because this variable has a significant effect on the system, it is suggested that the initial value be set at 1.5. The autonomic manager usually adjusts this value dynamically, and there is also a provision to manually adjust the value during run time.

- *AppSize*

This variable represents the size or capacity of a service request (request for an application). In the experiments that follow, except otherwise changed, all applications are initially assumed to be of the same size. There are touch-points to dynamically change this value. The application size variable is measured in MIPS.

- *RequestRate*

This variable, also referred to as rate of service request or rate of request arrival, is the measure of the frequency of service request. This is in terms of the number of requests recorded per unit of time. In real systems, this can be calculated as an average for all services (applications) or for individual services. In Reference 151, for example, *RequestRate* values are calculated for each service and are presented in requests/day. The experiments in this book take an average of *RequestRate* for all services and represent values as requests/second.

- *BurstInterval*

This variable defines the interval at which bursts are injected into the system during the simulation. This is specific to the experimental application and is dependent on what the user wants to investigate. Usually, bursts are introduced once at a specific time or several at random times.

The experimental workload is flexible in that all variables can be scaled to suit user's workload (high or low) requirements. Every experiment has a detailed workload outline used, as shown in the following experiments.

5.2.3 Simulation

The purpose of this simulation is not to investigate datacentres but to analyse the performance of three autonomic manager architectures based on varying datacentre model scenarios to investigate their level of dependability and robustness. The three systems here are the same as in section 5.1. The first system (***SysA***) is based on the traditional autonomic architecture, represented by the basic ***M****onitor*–***A****nalyse*–***P****lan*–***E****xecute* logic. The second system (***SysB***) is an upgraded version of the traditional autonomic architecture that includes a *test* element, represented by ***M****onitor*–***A****nalyse*–***P****lan*–***V****alidate*–***E****xecute* logic. The third system (***SysC***) is based on TrAArch, represented by a nested ***M****onitor*–***A****nalyse*–***P****lan*–***V****alidate*–***D****ependabilityCheck*-***E****xecute* logic. The *DependabilityCheck* component incorporates the dead-zone logic (see Chapter 3). Note that *SysB* does everything *SysA* can do and more and *SysC* does everything *SysB* can do plus more (see Figure 5.1).

The primary goal of the autonomic manager, in this case also referred to as the performance manager – PeM, is to ensure that the system remains stable under almost all perceivable operating and contextual circumstances and is capable of achieving desired and dependable results within such circumstances (i.e., over the expected range of contexts and environmental conditions and beyond). The secondary goal is to maximise the throughput.

5.2.3.1 Autonomic manager logic

The autonomic manager logic describes the individual control logic employed by each of the autonomic managers in order to achieve the performance goal. This explains the logical composition of each autonomic manager.

- *SysA*

This autonomic manager implements the basic autonomic control logic. Structurally based on Figure 5.10, the manager receives requests and allocates

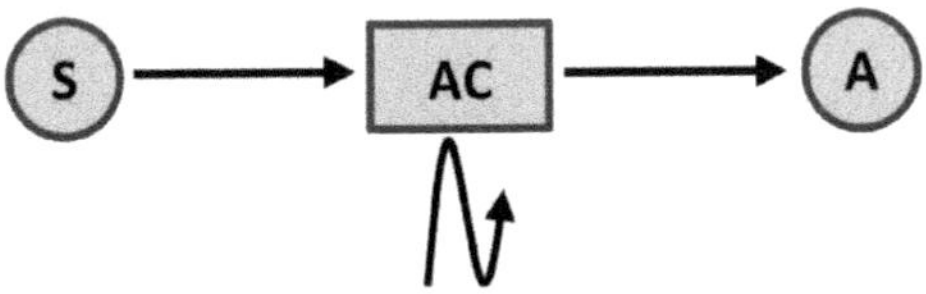

Figure 5.10 *Structural representation of SysA*

resources accordingly. The basic allocation logic here is to deploy a server whenever capacity offset (i.e., excess capacity of running servers – these are used to service new requests) is less than the current capacity of a single request. This is known as the *DecisionBoundary*. This is depicted, for example, as:

```
if (app1SysAOffset < app1.appCapacity)
  {      <...deploy server...>    }
```

Where

```
app1SysAOffset = app1SysAAvailableCapacity - app1SysARunningCapacity;
```

SysA has no additional intelligence. For example, decisions are not validated and the manager does not consider the rate at which system behaviour crosses the *DecisionBoundary*. As long as boundary conditions are met, the autonomic manager executes appropriate decisions.

Figure 5.10 is a representation of the early stages of autonomic architecture life-cycle presented in section 2.2.

- ***SysB***

This autonomic manager shows a higher level of intelligence than SysA. One aspect of validation here is to check the performance of the manager in terms of correctness. The manager does not start a job that cannot be completed – i.e., at every *DecisionBoundary,* the manager checks to make sure that it has enough resources to service a request. Where this is not the case, meaning the check has failed, the manager rejects the request and updates itself. The manager has a limit to which it can allow capacity deficit which is expressed as:

```
else if (app1SysBOffset <= (0 - app1.appCapacity))
{
    DroppedRequestCountSysB += 1;
}
```

So, in addition to the basic control and resource allocation logic of SysA, SysB carries out a validation of every allocation decision. Validation here is in terms of behavioural (e.g., starting a job only when there is enough capacity to complete it) and structural (e.g., avoiding initiating provisioning when server pool is empty, i.e., listViewServer.Items.Count = 0) correctness.

Figure 5.11 is a representation of the current stages of autonomic architecture life-cycle presented in Section 2.2. Beyond the level of validation, SysB exhibits no further intelligence.

- **SysC**

SysC performs all the activities of the *SysA* and SysB autonomic managers with additional intelligence. The manager looks at the balance of cost over longer term and retunes its configuration to ensure a balanced performance. For example, the autonomic manager implements dead-zone logic on decision boundaries. First, the dead-zone boundaries (upper and lower bounds), for example, are calculated as follows:

```
App1.DZUpperBound = (app1.appCapacity + (app1.appCapacity * DZ.DZConst));
App1.DZLowerBound = (app1.appCapacity - (app1.appCapacity * DZ.DZConst));
```

Note: *DZConst* is a tuning parameter used to adjust the dead-zone width. The size of dead-zone width depends on the nature of the system and data being processed. For example, in fine-grained data instance, where small shifts from the target can easily tip decisions, sometimes leading to erratic behaviour, the dead-zone width is expected to be small and closely tracked to the target value.

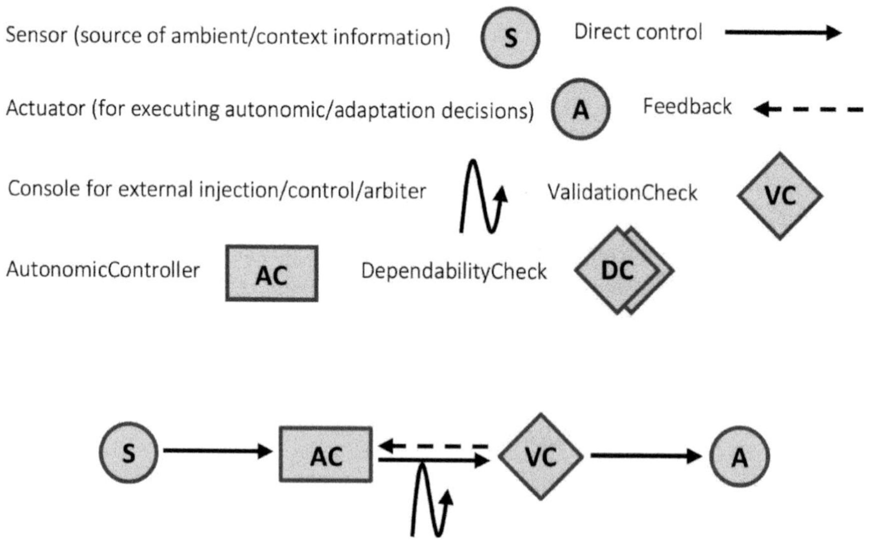

Figure 5.11 Structural representation of SysB

However, in other cases as in this experiment, the dead-zone width cannot be as closely tracked to the target value. Here the target value (*DecisionBoundary*) is defined by capacity Offset (see later) and this is used by the autonomic manager to decide whether or not to deploy a server. Also, because Offset is populated in *serverCapacity* and depleted in *appCapacity*, any movement across the decision boundary, either on the positive side or on the negative side, is in excess of *appCapacity*. This means that fluctuations around the decision boundary are usually in multiples of *appCapacity,* and to handle erratic behaviour around DecisionBoundary, the manager will need to take *appCapacity* into consideration when calculating dead-zone boundaries. This explains the boundary size calculation of App1.DZUpperBound and App1.DZLowerBound above. Offset is positive when there is excess capacity and negative when there is a shortfall. Also, sample simulation results show that smaller sizes of dead-zone width have no effect on the system behaviour.

Second, the zone areas are defined as follows (two zones are defined with one on either side of the *DecisionBoundary* – see Figure 5.12):

```
if (app1SysCOffset < app1.appCapacity)
{
App1.SystemBehaviour = "IsInDeployZone";
}
else
{ App1.SystemBehaviour = "IsNotInDeployZone"; }
```

Then stability is maintained by persisting the behaviour (*DecisionBoundary* outcome) of the system across the zones as follows:

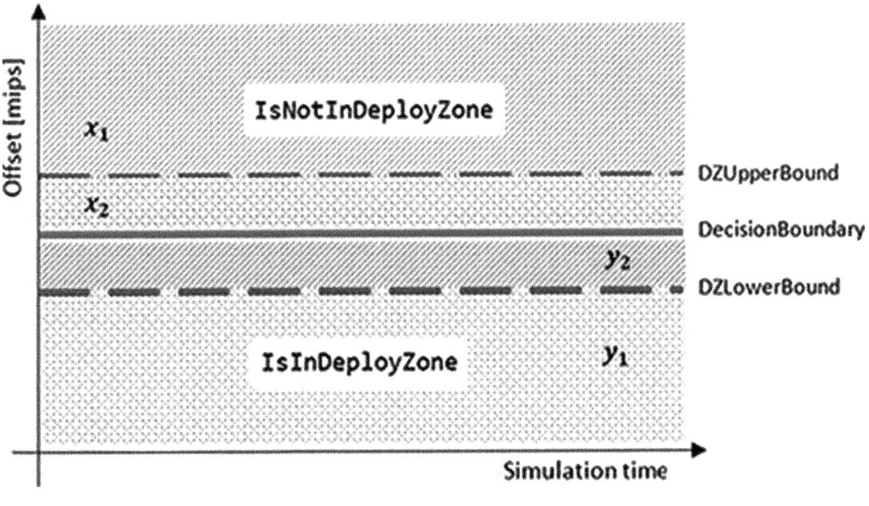

Figure 5.12 Dead-zone logic implemented by SysC

```
if (app1SysCOffset >= app1.appCapacity)
{ App1.SystemBehaviour = "IsNotInDeployZone"; }

if ((App1.SystemBehaviour == "IsInDeployZone") && (app1SysCOffset <
App1.DZUpperBound))
{ App1.SystemBehaviour = "IsInDeployZone"; }
else
{ App1.SystemBehaviour = "IsNotInDeployZone"; }

if ((App1.SystemBehaviour == "IsNotInDeployZone") && (app1SysCOffset >
App1.DZLowerBound))
{ App1.SystemBehaviour = "IsNotInDeployZone"; }
else
{ App1.SystemBehaviour = "IsInDeployZone"; }
```

Thus, the *DecisionBoundary* in SysA, which would be (app1SysCOffset < app1.appCapacity) becomes (App1.SystemBehaviour == "IsInDeployZone") in *SysC*. The manager dynamically changes the DZ.DZConst value between three values of 1, 1.5 and 2. By doing this, the manager is sensitive to its own behaviour and pro-actively regulates (retunes) its decision pattern to maintain stability and reliability.

In Figure 5.12, the area denoted y (y_1 and y_2 represents the 'IsInDeployZone', which means the autonomic manager should deploy a server, while the area denoted x (x_1 and x_2 represents the 'IsNotInDeployZone', which means the manager should not deploy a server. Likewise, the dotted shade pattern (y_1) represents the 'IsInDeployZone', while the diagonal shade pattern (y_2) represents the 'IsNotInDeployZone' when dead-zone logic is applied. As shown, if, for example, the system behaviour falls within the 'IsNotInDeployZone' area, the manager will persist the action associated to the 'IsNotInDeployZone' area until the system behaviour falls below the 'DZLowerBound' boundary at which point the action associated to the 'IsInDeployZone' area is activated. This way the autonomic manager is able to maintain reliability and efficiency. The autonomic manager also retunes its behaviour (as explained earlier) by adjusting the DZ Width (i.e., dynamically changing the size of DZConst as appropriate) if fluctuation is not reduced to an acceptable level. Thus, three behaviour regions, in which different actions are activated, are defined:

- 'Upper Region' (IsNotInDeployZone) with 'DO NOT DEPLOY SERVER' action,
- 'Lower Region' (IsInDeployZone) with 'DEPLOY SERVER' action
- 'In DZ' (x_2 and y_2 – within the DZ Width) with either of the two actions above.

It is important to note, as shown in Figure 5.12, that within the DZ boundary (x_2 and y_2) i.e., the 'In DZ' region, either of the actions associated to 'IsInDeployZone' and 'IsNotInDeployZone' areas could be maintained depending on the 'current action' prior to deviation into the 'In DZ' region. So actions activated in the 'Upper Region' and 'Lower Region' are, respectively, persisted in the 'In DZ' region. This is further explained in Figure 5.13 which shows the resultant effect of the DZ logic in terms of what zone action is activated per time.

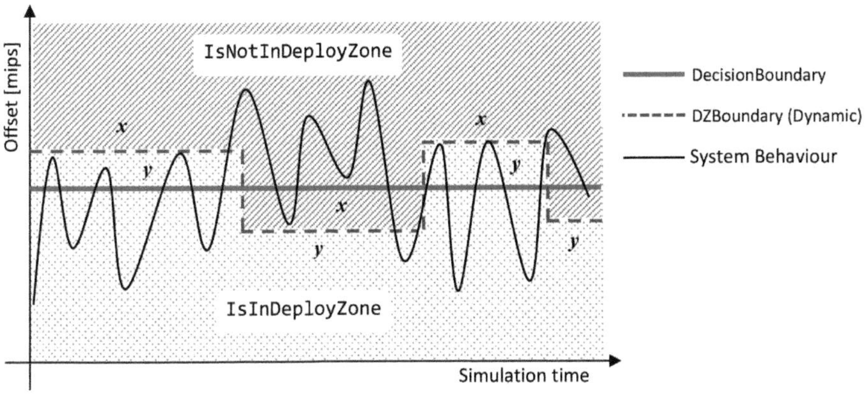

Figure 5.13 Illustration explaining the actual performance effect of dead-zone logic

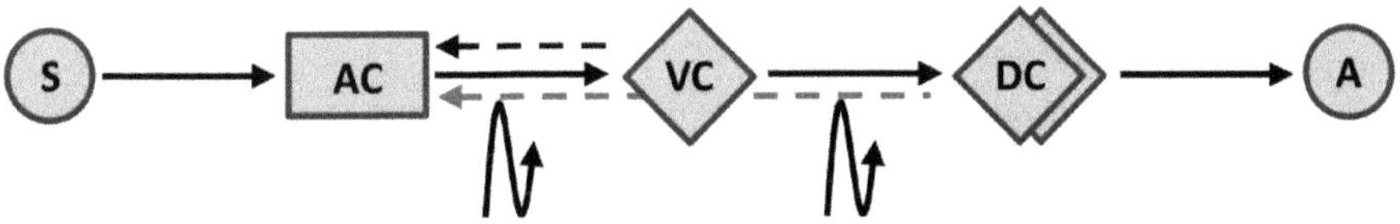

Figure 5.14 Structural representation of SysC

Figure 5.13 explains what happens in Figure 5.12. As system behaviour fluctuates around the decision boundary, the autonomic manager dynamically adjusts the DZBoundary to mitigate erratic adaptation. As shown, minor deviations across the DecisionBoundary do not result in decision (or action) change. In this case (Figure 5.13), actions for IsInDeployZone and IsNotInDeployZone are persisted at states '*x*' and '*y*', respectively, despite system behaviour crossing the DecisionBoundary at those state points.

Figure 5.14 is a representation of the next level of sophistication in autonomic architecture life cycle required to ensure dependability. This also represents the internal structure of TrAArch proposed in this book. See an illustration of the operation of the dead-zone logic in Chapter 3.

5.2.3.2 Simulation scenarios

In the following simulations to analyse the performances of the three systems (SysA, SysB and SysC), four simulation scenarios are used. The scenarios are presented in Table 5.3. The user of the TrAArch application can define further scenarios as required – see section 5.2.1 for details.

Scenario 1: In this scenario, all parameters are kept constant except those (e.g., DZConst) that may need dynamic tuning by the autonomic manager as the need

Table 5.3 Self-adapting resource allocation simulation scenarios

Scenario	Description	Metrics
Scenario 1	Basic case: uniform request rate and application size	SLA Server deployment rate
Scenario 2	Medium case: uniform request rate and varying application sizes	Optimum provisioning (Offset analysis)
Scenario 3	Complex case: varying application sizes with inconsistent request rate	

arises. This scenario gives a default view of the behaviour of the autonomic managers under normal conditions. Under this scenario of normal conditions, it is expected that all autonomic managers will behave significantly closely.

Scenario 2: This scenario creates a condition where the managers will have to deal with irregular sizes of service request. This leads to contention between applications – huge applications will demand huge resources thereby starving smaller applications. Performance analysis here will include individual application analysis. Request rate is kept constant so that the effect of varying application sizes could be better analysed.

Scenario 3: This is the most complex scenario, with resource contention and several instances of burst injected at chosen SimulationTimes in the simulation. The impact of the burst is relative to the size of the burst (BurstSize). This scenario creates a tough operating situation for the autonomic manager. Request sizes vary leading to resource contention, and request rate is highly erratic. Inconsistent request rate can also lead to '*flooding*' which is also a kind of burst. *Flooding* is a situation where the system is inundated with requests at a disproportionate rate.

5.2.4 Results and Analysis

This section presents the analysis of the experimental results. Results will be presented according to simulation scenarios, and in doing this, the metrics listed in Table 5.3 will be used. A detailed description of the metrics is presented below, followed by the simulation results.

5.2.4.1 Metrics

All metrics are mathematically defined, giving the reader a clear picture of the definition criteria should they wish to replicate this experiment.

SLA: SLA is the ratio of provided service to requested service. It measures the system's level of success in meeting request needs. Note that requests and services are not time bound, so the time it takes to complete a request does not count in this regard. The metric is defined as (5.2):

$$\mathrm{SLA}=\begin{cases}\dfrac{ProvisionedCapacity}{RequestedCapacity} & (i)\\ \dfrac{AvailableCapacity}{RunningCapacity} & (ii)\end{cases} \tag{5.2}$$

where *ProvisionedCapacity* is the total deployed server capacity (excluding those in the queue and including those already reclaimed back to the pool) and *RequestedCapacity* is the total size of request (including completed requests). *AvailableCapacity* is *ProvisionedCapacity* minus capacity of reclaimed servers (*ReclaimedCapacity*), while *RunningCapacity* is the total size of request (excluding completed requests). In (5.2), (i) is more of a whole picture consideration – considering the entire capacity activities of the system, while (ii) takes a real-time view of the system – tracking to the minute details of the system with delay, completed requests and reclaimed server effects all considered. The reference value for SLA is 1 indicating 100 per cent. Any value above 1 indicates over-provisioning while values under 1 indicate shortfall. Optimum provisioning is achieved at close proximity to 1.

Deployment rate: Server deployment or redeployment rate is the ratio of server deployment to service request. It measures the frequency at which autonomic managers deploy servers with regard to the nature of requests. This is mathematically represented as (5.3):

$$DeploymentRate = \frac{DeployedCapacity}{(RequestedCapacity - CompletedCapacity)} \tag{5.3}$$

The lower value of deployment rate means the better performance of the system translating to better maximisation of throughput.

Optimum provisioning: This metric is also an offset analysis. It indicates whether and when the autonomic manager is over- or under-provisioning. This is also known as efficiency calculation. Offset is calculated as shown in (5.4):

$$Offset = AvailableCapacity - RunningCapacity \tag{5.4}$$

In ideal circumstances, average offset is not expected to fall below zero. The system is optimally provisioning when offset falls between zero and the average capacity of all applications. The closer to zero the offset value is, the better the performance of the system is.

Note that, for all metrics, low or high values do not always necessarily translate to better performance. It is not usually realistic for the supposed better autonomic manager to always outperform the other managers. There are times when the manager underperforms and usually there may be a trade-off of some kind that explains the situation.

5.2.4.2 Additional metrics

For the simulations in this book, only the metrics identified above will be used. For class exercises or if the reader wishes to explore further, additional metrics may be defined for more studies. Note that as well as real-time graph printing, the provided simulator also outputs raw simulation results to a Spreadsheet for further tailored analysis. Two examples of additional metrics are provided below.

Delay cost: Delay cost can be calculated in many different ways as the cost can be influenced by many delay contributors. In this instance, delay cost is defined as the cost (in capacity) as a result of the delay experienced by the servers. This delay affects the completion time of service requests. This is mathematically represented as follows:

$$DeployCost = \frac{DeployedCapacity - ProvisionedCapacity}{DeployedCapacity} = \frac{ProvisioningCapacity}{DeployedCapacity}$$

ProvisioningCapacity is the capacity of servers in the queue, while *DeployedCapacity* is the total capacity of all deployed servers. The lower value of delay cost means the better performance of the system.

Scheduling cost: This is the capacity cost of servicing each request, i.e., the unnecessary capacity consumed in scheduling resources for individual requests. So, it measures the cost in excess of capacity (MIPS) for servicing each request and is represented as follows:

$$SchedulingCost = \frac{DeployedCapacity - RunningCapacity}{RequestedCapacity}$$

The lower value of scheduling cost means the better performance of the system.

5.2.4.3 Scenarios and result analysis

Results are presented and analysed according to simulation scenarios. It is important to note the workload and parameters used for individual simulations as results will largely depend on those.

5.2.4.3.1 Scenario 1: basic case: uniform request rate and application size

Table 5.4 is a collection of the major parameters used in this scenario. For precise results, ten different simulations of scenario 1 are performed and the results presented are based on average of these ten simulations. For each of the ten simulations, the same parameter set as in Table 5.4 is used. However, the number of requests and the distribution of those requests amongst the four applications will differ as they are dynamically generated and unpredictable. This does not distort the results as analysis is based on system-wide performance and not on individual application performance.

In every simulation, there are 400 servers of 40 000 MIPS capacity each. This means there is a total of initial 16 000 000 MIPS available to share between

Table 5.4 Scenario 1 simulation parameters

Parameter		Value
No. of servers		400
No. of applications		4
Request rate		1 req/s
Application capacity (MIPS)		20 000
Server capacity (MIPS)		40 000
Internal variables	RetrieveRate	5x
	RequestRateParam	10
	RetrieveRequestParam	0.2
	ServerProvisioningTime	3 (1.5 sec)
Autonomic Managers (PeM – Performance Manager)		*SysA*, *SysB* & *SysC*)
DZConst		1.5

requests for four applications (App1, App2, App3 and App4). *Reclaimed servers* are later added to this available capacity. If the total requested capacity is higher than the total provisioned capacity, the unused server list will be empty (leaving the autonomic manager with a deficit of outstanding requests without resources to service them) and the datacentre is overloaded. So the simulation stops whenever any autonomic manager runs out of resources – i.e., when the unused server list of any manager becomes empty. It is necessary to stop the simulation at this point because as soon as the unused server list of a particular manager becomes empty, the *RequestedCapacity* for that manager starts piling up while *AvailableCapacity* remains at zero, which leads to continuously increasing negative Offset. This will lead to an inaccurate assessment of the three managers (recall that all three managers are compared concurrently and it is safer to do this, while all three managers are active). Also, usually at this point, other managers may have outstanding resources and this will mean better efficiency.

Table 5.5 is a number distribution of requests and services for ten simulation runs of scenario 1. The values shown are collected at the end of each simulation, for example, it can be seen that the manager of SysA has no servers left in each of the simulations, while SysB has a few and SysC even more. Though SysA and SysB are able to service almost the same number of requests, SysB has outstanding server capacity ($9.3 * 40\,000 = 372\,000 mips$) and could service about $\frac{372\,000}{20\,000} = 19$ more requests. However, the additional smartness of SysB does not always translate to better performance as highlighted in Table 5.5 (this is an example of manager interference leading to overcompensation). SysC clearly outperformed the others with an average of about 46 outstanding servers out of 400 initial plus *Reclaimed* servers. This means that SysC could still service about 92 more requests. Figures 5.15–5.17 give a breakdown of the performances against the metrics in Table 5.3 for the three autonomic managers.

Table 5.5 High-level performance analysis of managers over ten simulation runs of scenario 1

Sim.	**Unused server**			**Serviced request**			**Dropped/queued request**			**Deployed server**		
	SysA	**SysB**	**SysC**	**SysA**	**SysB**	**SysC**	**SysA**	**SysB**	**SysC**	**SysA**	**SysB**	**SysC**
1	0	29	30	706	699	687	0	7	19	459	439	405
2	0	8	45	725	719	697	0	6	28	465	467	392
3	0	4	46	735	729	711	0	6	24	470	465	386
4	0	1	35	732	726	701	0	6	31	462	469	394
5	0	13	59	702	695	674	0	7	28	456	447	368
6	0	3	51	708	706	681	0	2	27	460	455	374
7	0	14	48	706	702	684	0	4	22	468	443	369
8	0	12	59	701	694	675	0	7	26	457	453	369
9	0	7	51	710	705	686	0	5	24	462	462	386
10	0	2	31	759	756	733	0	3	26	472	479	400
Avg	**0**	**9.3**	**45.5**	**718.4**	**713.1**	**692.9**	**0**	**5.3**	**25.5**	**463.1**	**457.9**	**384.3**

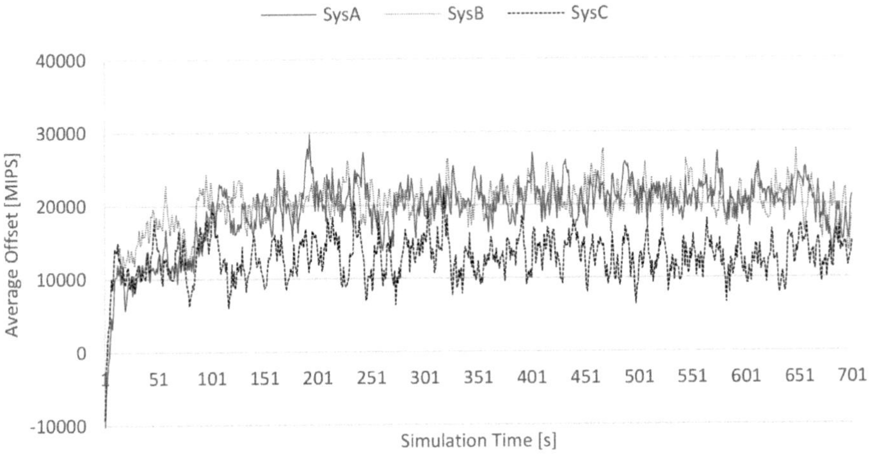

Figure 5.15 Offset = AvailableCapacity – RunningCapacity: provisioning analysis for scenario 1

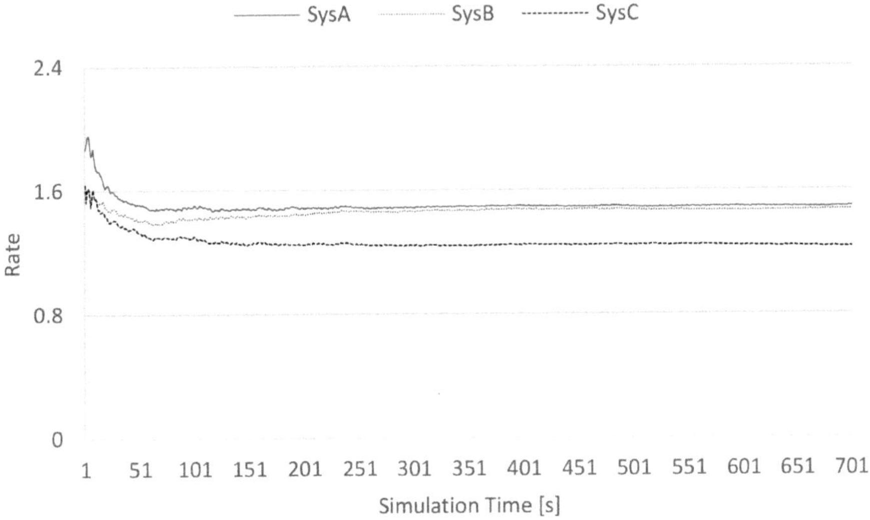

Figure 5.16 Server deployment rate for scenario 1

The difference between requested capacity and provisioned capacity (or in real time analysis, running capacity and available capacity) is known as *Offset*. Where offset is close to zero, the difference with respect to running and available MIPS is low and the autonomic manager is therefore very efficient. That means that the closer to zero the offset value is, the better the performance of the autonomic manager is. When offset is much greater than or much less than zero, the autonomic manager is over-provisioning or under-provisioning respectively and is very inefficient.

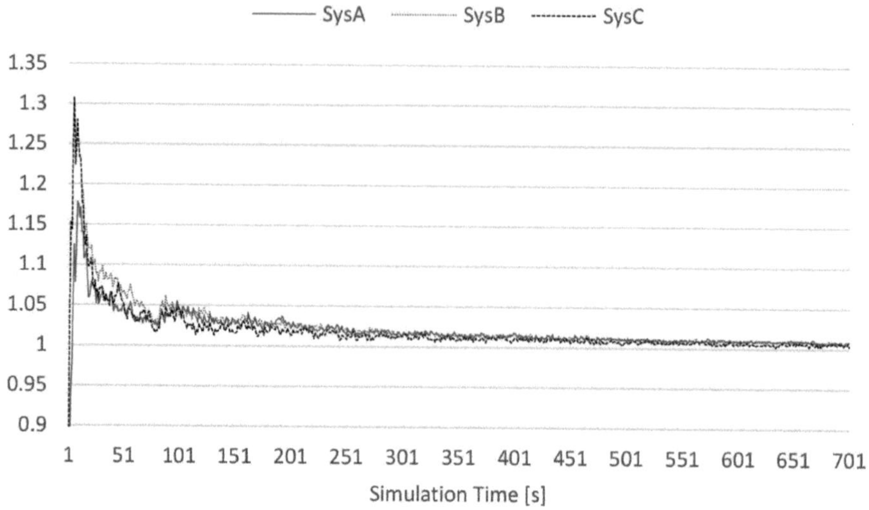

Figure 5.17 Service level achievement analysis for scenario 1

The autonomic managers are designed to have a window of *optimum provisioning* defined by the interval ($0 \leq Offset \leq AvgAppCapacity$), which means that the managers are configured to maintain *AvailableCapacity* of up to average *appCapacity* for just-in-time provisioning. However, manager efficiency is defined by its ability to maintain *Offset* as close as possible to zero. Figure 5.15 shows the efficiency analysis of the three autonomic managers in terms of maximising resources. This shows the average performances of the three autonomic managers over ten simulation runs. This means that the same scenario was run for ten times and then the average result was calculated in order to obtain a clearer and more accurate analysis of manager performance.

Figure 5.15 shows that, in terms of efficiency, SysA performed significantly similar to SysB with offset at about 20 000 MIPS. There are a couple of instances where SysA also performed better than SysB. This is as a result of overcompensation introduced by the extra level of smartness in SysB. The *validation check* of SysB gives it an advantage over SysA, but it sometimes leads to overcompensation. For example, though SysB checks to ensure resource availability against resource requests, it is not adequately sensitive to erratic request fluctuation. High level of erratic request fluctuation disorientates SysB (as can be seen in scenarios 3 where burst is injected), but this effect is naturally and dynamically handled by SysC. SysC, with a trustworthiness component (*DependabilityCheck*), takes a longer-term look at the self-management effect on the datacentre and retunes its self-management behaviour.

The rate at which the autonomic managers change decision (which can indicate erratic behaviour) is indicated by the gap between the crests and troughs of the graph in Figure 5.15. A smaller gap indicates an erratic change of decision, while a bigger gap indicates a more persisted decision. As can be clearly seen, SysC has significantly more persisted decisions and this allows it to more adequately track resource availability against resource requests, which leads to more efficient performance as can be seen. Recall that optimum provisioning is defined by the ($0 \leq Offset \leq AvgAppCapacity$) interval that in this case is between 0 and 20 000 MIPS. SysC clearly falls within this range, though a bit towards the 20 000 border, while SysA and SysB revolve around the upper bound, significantly away from 0. This means that while SysA and SysB try to maintain *AvailableCapacity* of up to 20 000 MIPS for just-in-time provisioning, SysC efficiently depletes this reserve to maximise resources while at the same time maintaining the same level of performance and even better compared to the other two. This is evidently seen in the following deployment rate and SLA metrics analyses.

Figure 5.16 shows the rate at which the three autonomic managers deploy servers as requests arrive. With the same rate of request arrival, the managers deployed servers differently. While SysA deployed the most servers (average of 1.5 servers per service request), closely followed by SysB, SysC deployed the least servers (average of 1.2 servers per service request). Whereas the difference might seem small, this is actually significant in this context – it means an increase in scheduling, delay and power costs. This explains why SysA easily runs out of servers followed by SysB, while SysC still retains a number of unused servers (Table 5.5). Interestingly, this does not negatively affect the performance of SysC and when SysC underperforms in one aspect there is usually compensation, say trade-off, in another aspect. The lower server deployment rate of SysC resulted in a slightly lower SLA value of SysC when compared to SysA and SysB – Figure 5.17. But this only keeps the value very close to the optimum value of 1, which also indicates high efficiency. It is important to note even though SysC does not significantly outperform the others for SLA, it has far more *unused servers,* which means it services more requests under the same condition.

Figure 5.17 depicts the service levels of the three autonomic managers. As expected, following the result trend above, SysA and SysB performed quite similarly, with each outperforming the other in some places. SysC on the other hand keeps SLA as close as possible to the target goal of 1 – a perfect system would keep SLA at 1. SysC has the ability to dynamically scale down unnecessary and inefficient provisioning by proactively throttling oscillation. This capability also leads to cost savings. The high level of deployment rate (i.e. deploying more MIPS than required) for SysA and SysB (Figure 5.16) leads to high cost (in terms of excess MIPS) of servicing individual requests. Also, this means that the rate at which servers enter the *provisioning queue* is much higher than the rate they leave the queue. This results in an increasing number of redundant servers in the queue, which contributes to delay cost.

The results analyses of scenario 1 indicate that the proposed TrAArch (represented by SysC) has significant performance improvement over existing architectures. This assertion is further tested in the following scenarios.

5.2.4.3.2 Scenario 2: medium case: uniform request rate and varying application sizes

Table 5.6 is a collection of the major parameters used in this scenario. As in scenario 1, ten different simulations are conducted and the results presented are based on average of these ten simulations.

In every simulation of this scenario, there are 400 servers of 40 000 capacity each to be shared amongst two applications (App1 and App2). This means there is a total of initial 16 000 000 MIPS to share between requests for App1 with 10 000 MIPS and App2 with 30 000 MIPS. The capacity gap between the two applications is so wide that it may naturally lead to contention with App2 demanding more resources than App1. In this kind of situation, where it is easy to underserve one application because of the contention, it is left for the datacentre autonomic managers to decide how best to efficiently allocate resources. Results show that while SysA maintained a proportionate resource allocation (in terms of applications) for the two applications, SysB and SysC prioritised provisioning for App2 with much higher MIPS request. One disadvantage of proportionate provisioning is that it treats requests according to applications (in this case two applications) and not according to capacity (in this case 10 000 versus 30 000). When this happens, the high capacity application (App2) will be heavily under-provisioned, while the low capacity application (App1) will be adequately provisioned (and sometimes over-provisioned) compared to the level of provisioning for App2 as shown in Figure 5.18(a) for SysA Offset analysis. Also, this amounts to inefficiency and explains why SysA easily exhausts its resources as shown in Table 5.7 – the results of requests distribution amongst the three autonomic managers.

The 'dropped/queued request' column shows that in prioritising App2, SysB and SysC dropped more of App1 requests, while SysA, which does not drop any application, struggled to cope with the capacity imbalance. For a clearer picture,

Table 5.6 Scenario 2 simulation parameters

Parameter		Value
No. of servers		400
No. of applications		2
App capacity (MIPS)	App1	10 000
	App2	30 000
Request rate		1 req/s
Server capacity (MIPS)		40 000
Internal variables	RetrieveRate	5x
	RequestRateParam	10
	RetrieveRequestParam	0.2
	ServerProvisioningTime	3 (1.5 s)
Autonomic managers (PeM – performance manager)		*SysA*, *SysB* and *SysC*
DZConst		1.5

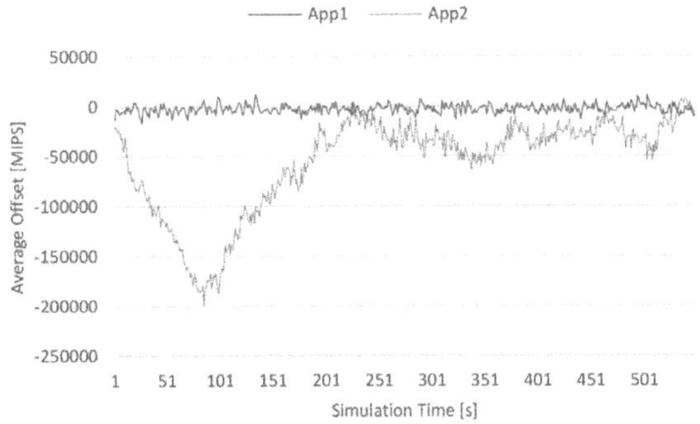

(a)

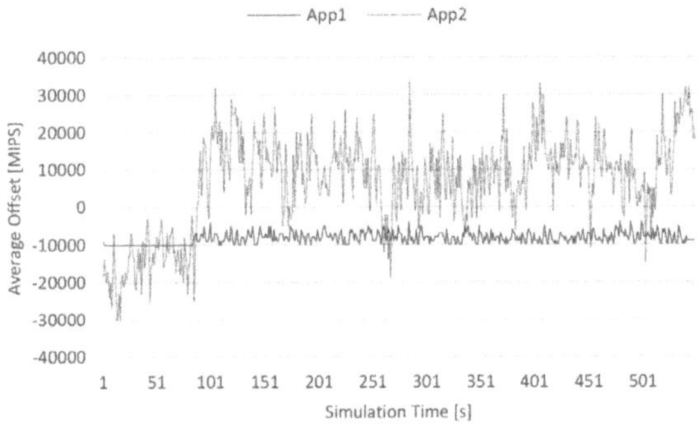

(b)

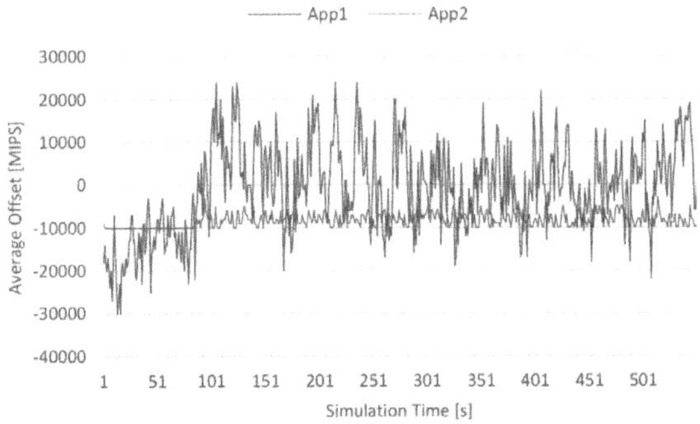

(c)

Figure 5.18 Individual autonomic manager offset analysis for scenario 2. (a) SysA Offset analysis for App1 and App2. App1 is about adequately provisioned (i.e. Offset ≈ 0), while App2 is heavily under-provisioned. (b) SysB Offset analysis for App1 and App2. App1 is about adequately provisioned while App2 is over-provisioned (well above the optimal provisioning mark which is defined by 0 ≤ Offset ≤ AvgAppCapacity). (c) SysC Offset analysis for App1 and App2. App1 is about adequately provisioned while App2 is slightly over-provisioned (slightly above the optimal provisioning mark which is defined by 0 ≤ Offset ≤ AvgAppCapacity).

Table 5.7 High-level performance analysis of managers over ten simulation runs of scenario 2

Sim.	Unused server			Serviced request			Dropped/Queued request					Deployed server		
	SysA	SysB	SysC	SysA	SysB	SysC	SysA	SysB		SysC		SysA	SysB	SysC
								app1	app2	app1	app2			
1	0	165	171	559	312	309	0	236	11	236	14	492	287	281
2	0	161	174	572	322	315	0	237	13	239	18	499	285	271
3	0	161	166	579	329	323	0	237	13	234	22	497	289	286
4	0	169	180	574	318	309	0	240	17	242	24	500	285	269
5	0	164	180	566	318	308	0	238	10	242	16	492	291	270
6	0	160	151	559	320	326	0	222	17	215	18	492	281	295
7	0	162	192	612	334	316	0	266	12	272	24	509	297	258
8	0	172	171	550	309	306	0	224	17	223	21	487	275	276
9	0	179	188	583	310	306	0	258	15	256	21	492	271	264
10	0	164	172	575	324	315	0	236	15	240	20	497	293	279
Avg	**0**	**165.7**	**174.5**	**572.9**	**319.6**	**313.3**	**0**	**239.4**	**14**	**239.9**	**19.8**	**495.7**	**285.4**	**274.9**

Figure 5.19 shows how SysB and SysC prioritised App2 over App1. As can be seen, there is a consistent trend of high rate of dropped App1 requests. This means that more resources were allocated to App2, thereby starving App1. As this contention continued, it led to more App1 requests being dropped as there were limited resources per time to service App2 requests. Also noticeable is the smoothness of provisioning for App2 compared to the bumpiness of provisioning for App1 – this is further explained in the offset analysis that follows.

SysA on the other hand did not drop any request and trying to evenly joggle resources between the highly imbalanced MIPS requests for the two applications meant that more resources per time than necessary are used. This explains why SysA exhausted its resources quite early in the simulation while the other managers have hundreds of servers still unused (Table 5.7). Figure 5.18(a) shows that while App1 is about adequately provisioned, App2 is heavily under-provisioned. This is because SysA evenly provisioned for the two applications, thereby starving App2 that has very high MIPS requests. So by accepting all requests despite low resource availability, SysA under-provisioned for App2 far more than it did for App1 because of the large size of App2 requests. There is no check in SysA to ensure resource availability before requests are accepted.

In Figure 5.18, App1 average offset is maintained at about (−17 000 ≤ 12 000 MIPS) by SysA, (−10 000 ≤ −4 000 MIPS) by SysB and (−10 000 ≤ −3 000 MIPS) by SysC. Also, App2 offset ranges between (7 000 and −200 000 MIPS) for SysA, (−30 000 and 34 000 MIPS) for SysB and (−30 000 and 24 000 MIPS) for SysC. This shows that while SysA treats requests according to applications (i.e., by trying to evenly provision for both applications), SysB and SysC are sensitive

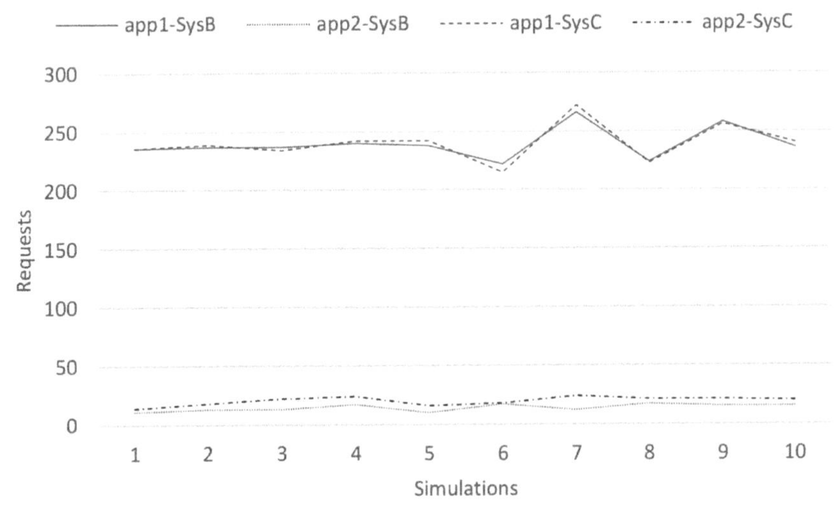

Figure 5.19 Dropped and queued request analysis for scenario 2

to the individual size of requests. As a result, by taking on all requests and attempting an even distribution of resources for both applications, SysA heavily under-provisions for App2 but performed well for App1. SysB and SysC on the other hand maintained more balanced resource allocation for both applications in terms of request capacity with SysC showing higher efficiency than SysB. Note that a positive *Offset* above the optimal provisioning mark amounts to over-provisioning while a negative *Offset* amounts to under-provisioning. Recall that optimal provisioning mark is defined by the interval ($0 \leq Offset \leq AvgAppCapacity$) which in this case is ($0 \leq Offset \leq ((10000 + 30000)/2)$) – i.e., between 0 and 20 000 MIPS. Figure 5.20 shows the average manager efficiency analysis for all three systems.

On average, SysA did not stand up to the complex provisioning condition of scenario 2 as did the other systems. Figure 5.20 shows that SysA could not efficiently cope with the level of resource contention experienced between App1 and App2. SysB and SysC show almost the same level of autonomic sophistication; however, SysC is shown to be more efficient. Although both systems have a similar level of under-provisioning, SysB has a higher level of over-provisioning – significantly above the optimal provisioning mark. This indicates that SysC is efficiently more sophisticated in handling complex resource allocation scenarios that would ordinarily prove difficult for traditional autonomic managers (SysA and SysB) to handle. For example, this increased efficiency arises from the fact that the *DependabilityCheck* sub-component of SysC enables it to go beyond dropping requests, if there are insufficient resources, to deploying resources only when it is necessary and efficient to do so. Also, the SLA analysis (Figure 5.21) corroborates the above results. While SysA performed just below the SLA reference point of one '1', SysC performed very close to the reference point indicating very high efficiency.

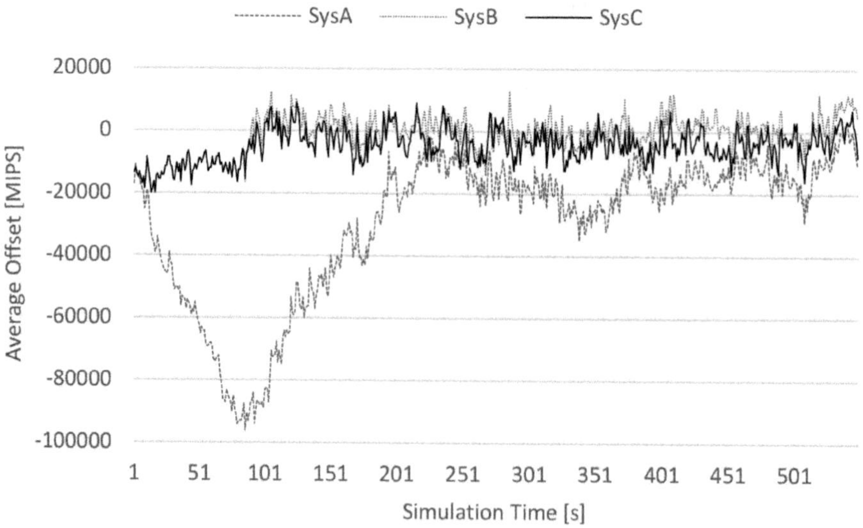

Figure 5.20 Autonomic manager efficiency analysis for scenario 2

The results analyses of scenario 2 is a further corroboration of the assertion that the proposed TrAArch (represented by SysC) has significant performance improvement over the existing architectures. There is one more complex simulation scenario to further test this assertion.

5.2.4.3.3 Scenario 3: complex case: varying application sizes with inconsistent request rate

This is the most complex scenario with a combined effect of the previous scenarios. The complexity presented by this scenario (i.e., a combined effect of resource contention and two injected disruptions) allows us to further test the robustness of these systems by stretching their capabilities to extremes. Table 5.8 is a collection of the major parameters used in this scenario. As in previous scenarios, the results presented are based on the average of ten different simulation runs.

In every simulation of this scenario, there are 400 servers of 40 000 MIPS each to be shared amongst two applications (App1 and App2). This means there is a total of initial 16 000 000 MIPS to share between requests for App1 with 5 000 MIPS and App2 with 20 000 MIPS. Table 5.9 shows a distribution of requests and services for ten simulation runs of scenario 3.

Results reveal that SysA is not adequately robust in such complex situations as in scenario 3. The system is heavily inefficient in handling this type of situation [Figure 5.22, Figure 5.22(a)]. Its algorithm, which maintains proportionate provisioning with respect to number of applications as against capacity of requests, was disorientated by the level of contention and disruption experienced.

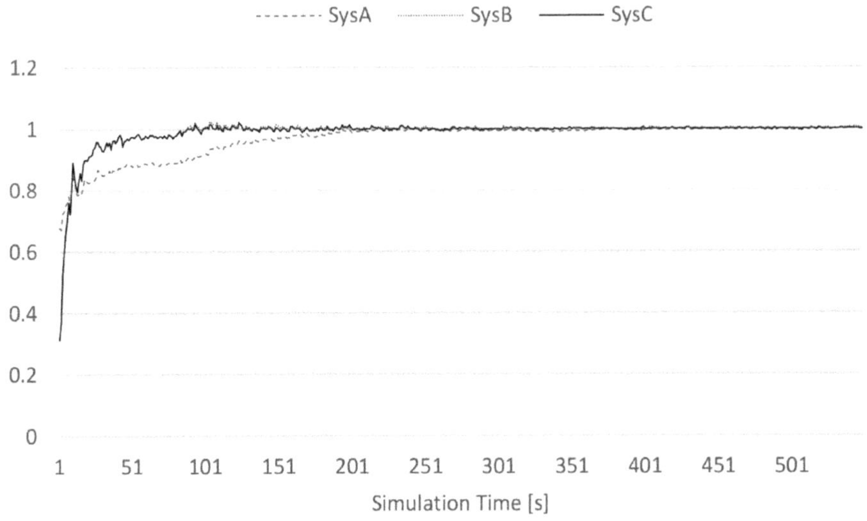

Figure 5.21 SLA analysis for scenario 2

Table 5.8 Scenario 3 simulation parameters

Parameter		Value
No. of servers		400
No. of applications		2
App capacity (MIPS)	App1	5 000
	App2	20 000
Request rate (initial)		1 req/s
Server capacity (MIPS)		40 000
Internal variables	RetrieveRate	5x
	RequestRateParam	10
	RetrieveRequestParam	0.2
	BurstSize	1 500 ms
	ServerProvisioningTime	3 (1.5 s)
Autonomic managers (PeM – performance manager)		*SysA*, *SysB* and *SysC*)
DZConst (initial)		1.5

As shown in Figure 5.22, the first burst was injected at about 120s, while the second was injected at 300s. SysA is limited in its ability to handle complex situations and so cannot be relied upon to operate large-scale and complex datacentres. SysB and SysC both have a wide range of operability in complex situations. However, a closer look at SysB and SysC [Figure 5.22(b)] in this scenario reveals a unique change in the expected (as observed in scenario 1) trend. Under a more normal situation, like in scenario 1, SysC is expected to drop significantly (about five times) more servers than SysB. Table 5.9 shows that SysC dropped only a few more servers than SysB. This was also noticed in scenario 2, which is a bit more complex than scenario 1. In this scenario 3 situation, the level of disturbance (as a result of resource contention and erratic request disorder) in the datacentre led to instability in SysB which caused it to overreact by inefficiently dropping requests. This instability reveals a weakness in design because in real-life datacentres, such disturbances (like sudden request spikes) do occur and autonomic managers are expected to adequately stabilise the entire system under such circumstances. SysC, on the other hand, with the capability of a longer-term view of the entire system, was able to take on more requests. It can be seen that SysC is slightly more efficient with performance a bit closer to the optimal provisioning mark.

(a) Autonomic manager efficiency analysis of all three systems

However, this achievement comes with an associated trade-off in delay cost. This shows that SysC is more sensitive to the relationship between the requested MIPS and available MIPS. For example, in a situation where SysB dropped a number of requests following a fixed decision boundary (when there is lack of immediate available resources to handle incoming requests), SysC used a dynamic decision boundary to accommodate more requests allowing it to efficiently use up its available

Table 5.9 High level performance analysis of managers over ten simulation runs of Scenario 3

	unused server			**serviced request**			**dropped/queued request**			**deployed server**		
	SysA	**SysB**	**SysC**	**SysA**	**SysB**	**SysC**	**SysA**	**SysB**	**SysC**	**SysA**	**SysB**	**SysC**
1	0	259	271	584	265	257	0	319	327	521	178	168
2	0	250	264	587	276	279	0	311	308	523	189	185
3	0	256	271	572	264	257	0	308	415	511	180	165
4	0	162	155	460	340	349	0	120	111	432	289	276
5	0	262	265	585	264	256	0	321	329	519	182	176
6	0	246	278	575	272	253	0	303	322	512	198	153
7	0	242	247	574	292	284	0	282	290	514	201	197
8	0	246	271	611	287	272	0	324	339	531	204	171
9	0	235	252	578	292	287	0	286	291	516	202	188
10	0	252	272	565	270	261	0	295	304	506	192	159
Avg	**0**	**241**	**254.6**	**569.1**	**282.2**	**275.5**	**0**	**286.9**	**303.6**	**508.5**	**201.5**	**183.8**

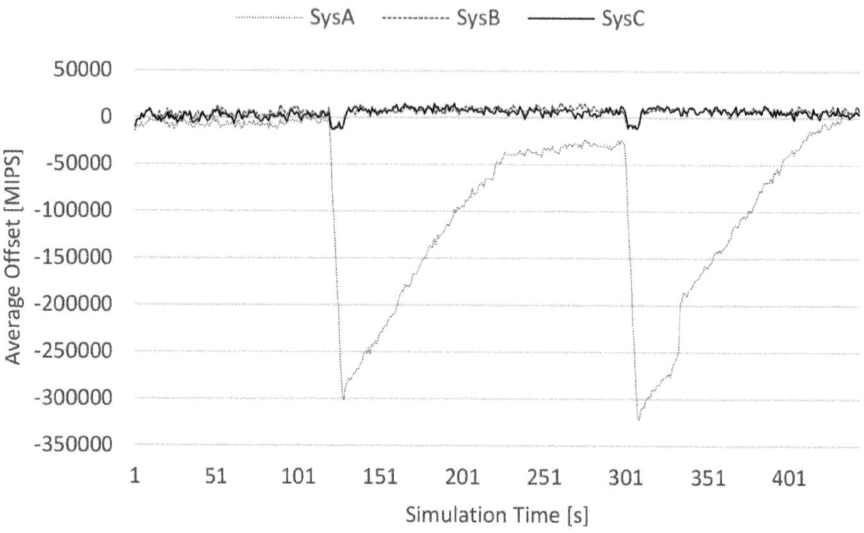

(a)

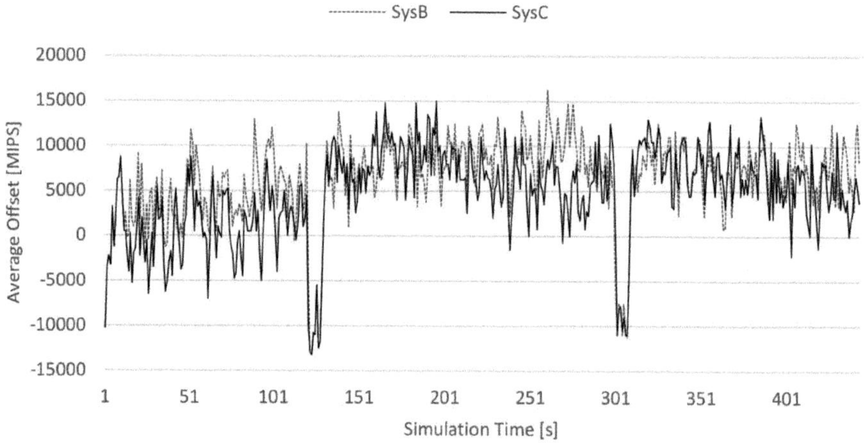

(b)

Figure 5.22 Autonomic manager efficiency analysis for scenario 3. Bursts were introduced at 120 s and 300 s time frames. (a) Autonomic manager efficiency analysis of all three systems. (b) Autonomic manager efficiency analysis of SysB and SysC.

resources. By taking on more requests, SysC trades off scheduling cost by a very tiny margin. See section 5.2.4.2 for how to calculate delay and scheduling costs. Interestingly, the efficiency level is not affected – Figure 5.22(b) shows that efficiency performance is even slightly better in SysC. So, we have a situation where,

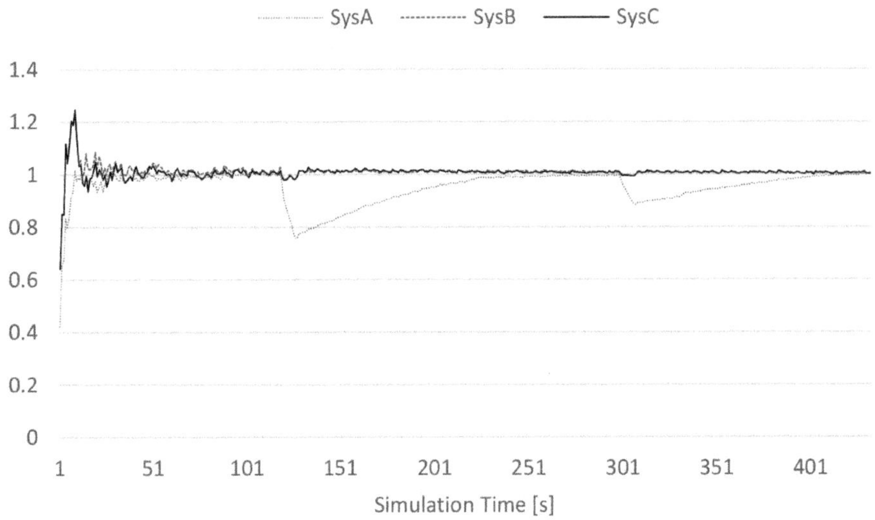

Figure 5.23 SLA analysis for scenario 3

on average, SysC utilised significantly fewer resources (servers) to serve slightly higher number of requests than SysB and still maintains approximately same level of SLA (Figure 5.23), delay cost, scheduling cost and efficiency achievements with SysB.

There is consistent corroboration of the fact that SysA is limited in the range of its operational scope when it comes to complex situations. Scenario 3 results show that it is highly expensive, inefficient and unreliable to operate complex datacentres with autonomic managers based on SysA. However, SysA-based managers may suffice for simple and basic datacentres. On the other hand, SysC has shown consistent reliability in all tested scenarios. The level of robustness exhibited in this scenario by SysC is a clear indication that it is not a hard-wired one-directional self-managing system. For example, in this scenario, we have seen that SysC does not only act when SysB is taking more actions than necessary but also when it is taking fewer actions than necessary. So, it can be said that SysC is capable of reducing inefficient adaptation (e.g., when SysB's decisions are erratic) as well as increasing adaptation when it is necessary and efficient to (e.g., when SysB is not making decisions frequently enough). This capability of increased adaptation has been shown in scenarios 2 and 3 – SysC is able to maximise resources while achieving the same level of performance as SysB.

From the results of the three experimental scenarios presented above, we can conclude that SysA has a narrow envelope of operational conditions in which it is both self-managing and returns satisfactory behaviour. On the other hand, SysB tends towards a wider operational envelope with increased efficiency and satisfactory behaviour, but once the limits of that envelope are reached, the efficiency and reliability of the system drop. In moderate operational complexities, SysB performs adequately efficient but fluctuates rapidly and may need human input to override some decisions that lead to instability in the case of a highly erratic and complex situation, which, for example, SysC can deal with autonomically. Results have shown that SysC is sufficiently sophisticated to operate efficiently and yield satisfactory results under almost all perceivable operating circumstances. So, we can now confidently conclude that the proposed TrAArch (represented by SysC) has significant performance improvement over existing architectures and can be relied upon to operate (or manage) almost all level of datacentre scale and complexity.

Generally, SysC shows significant performance improvement over SysB. However, the extent of this improvement is application and context dependent. Results show that there are circumstances in which performance improvement is evident from SysC as well as circumstances in which improvement is not evident. Complex applications with the possibility of unexpected behaviour patterns, e.g., large-scale datacentres with complex algorithms, will usually experience improvement with SysC. Also, applications that are sensitive to fluctuating environmental inputs (i.e., depend on volatile environmental information for decision-making), for example, auto stock trading systems are expected to see greater benefit from SysC. On the other hand, there are applications that are not expected to see any benefit. Example includes small-scale datacentres with predefined request rate and request capacity.

5.3 Stability versus optimality

This subsection provides a further discussion on system stability and performance. Up to this point in this book, stability has been used as a metric for measuring system performance and it may wrongly seem that high stability is always synonymous to optimality. While it has been shown, from experimental results so far, that stability contributes to optimality and reliability, it is important to note that stability and optimality are not necessarily always mutually inclusive. That is, a system is not necessarily performing optimally because it is stable. The definition of stability, on its own, is dependent on the context and goal of the system. For example, there are situations where it may be suitable to allow some level of fluctuation and decision changes which under different situations may be considered destabilising. So, for every system, it is necessary to pre-define an acceptable level of fluctuation.

Naturally, a system that does not make any decisions or rarely changes its decisions is considered to be very stable. However, this is inefficient and would be a wrong generalisation for autonomic systems. A proposed solution in this book is to determine a boundary of the appropriate and efficient level of system behaviour fluctuation for each system and then plug this into the design of the system's autonomic manager. For example, as used in this book, limits of acceptable fluctuation or stability are defined as benchmarks in the system's goals and these are used to configure the decision fork of the tolerance range check object used by the dead-zone logic – see Chapter 3. In essence, stability is defined in the goals of the system (note that systems are designed based on or to meet a set goal) and the system designer implements this through the component logic of the system. For example, as specified in the rule for the experiment in section 3.2.1, for every 10 decision cycles, decision change count of 4 or above is considered unstable, while no decision change is considered inactive. So, the autonomic manager is configured to dynamically throttle the size of the DZ Width to only allow a minimum of 1 and maximum of 3 decision changes in every 10 decision cycles.

5.4 Conclusion

This chapter has presented an implementation and empirical investigation of the proposed trustworthy architecture. Two case examples have been used to demonstrate an implementation of the TrAArch. Experiments are based on different scenarios that replicate real-life systems and operating conditions. The experiments investigate performance differences between the traditional autonomic architecture and the proposed TrAArch. Results show that the proposed architecture has significant performance improvement over the existing architectures and can be relied upon to operate (or manage) almost all levels of autonomic system scale and complexity. The traditional architecture has a narrow envelope of operational conditions in which it is both self-managing and returns satisfactory behaviour, while TrAArch is sufficiently sophisticated to operate efficiently and yield satisfactory results under almost all perceivable operating circumstances. This chapter has also shown the importance of trustworthiness, also referred to as dependability, to autonomic computing and how this can significantly improve the performance of autonomic systems.

The TrAArch simulator has also been presented in Section 5.2.1 with a detailed explanation of how to use it. This is particularly important if the reader wants to recreate the experiments presented in this book or design new ones. To help the reader further understand or demonstrate the effect of trustworthiness, it is advisable to design new simulations of different scenarios and analyse the results following the examples presented here. For the self-adapting resource allocation case example, only three scenarios are used in this book. The reader can study more scenarios for this same case example. This can also help as a guide for studying other case studies of choice.

Chapter 6
Multi-agent interoperability

The concept of autonomic computing was initially envisioned to address the increasing complexity of managing computing systems. Over time, also with improved and new technologies, these systems have continued to grow both in scale and ubiquity, leading to even more and more management complexities. This increase in scale and deployment of multi-agent systems (e.g., datacentres and distributed systems) coupled with heterogeneity of services and platforms means that more autonomic managers (agents) could be integrated to achieve a particular goal. This bringing together of many autonomic managers for a common goal has led to the need for interoperability – managing the unique and complex interactions between the coexisting autonomic managers. Autonomic computing is an aspect of multi-agent system field where autonomic managers act as individual agents.

In this chapter you will

- learn about multi-agent systems coordination
- learn about trustworthy autonomic interoperability
- explore experimental demonstrations of trustworthy autonomic interoperability

6.1 Introduction to multi-agent interoperability

This chapter provides an overview of interoperability solutions and makes case for a proposed solution that is suitable for trustworthy autonomic computing. An implementation and empirical analysis of the proposed solution are presented. This involves an experimental demonstration using a datacentre multi-manager scenario.

Autonomic computing has progressively grown to become a mainstream concept. Many mechanisms and techniques have been successfully explored, and the very success of autonomic systems has inevitably led to situations where multiple autonomic managers need to coexist and/or interact (directly or indirectly) within the same system. This is evident, e.g., in the increasing availability of large-scale datacentres with multiple (heterogeneous) managers (agents), which are independently designed. This increase in scale and size of datacentres coupled with heterogeneity of services and platforms means that more autonomic managers could be integrated to achieve a particular goal, e.g., datacentre optimisation. This has led to the need for interoperability between autonomic managers. Interoperability deals with how to manage multi-manager scenarios, to govern complex interactions between managers and to arbitrate when conflicts arise. Although several researchers have identified interoperability as a key challenge for future autonomic systems, the challenge is already imminent.

Potentially, problems can arise as a result of conflict of interest when these autonomic managers (components/agents) coexist. There is a growing concern that the lack of support for interoperability will become a break issue for future systems. This book presents an architecture-based solution to interoperability. The proposed solution is based on the Trustworthy Autonomic Architecture (presented in Chapter 4), which includes mechanisms and instrumentation to explicitly support interoperability and trustworthiness. Interoperability support should be designed in and integral at the architectural level, and not be treated as an add-on as it cannot be reliably retro-fitted to systems. This chapter analyses the issue of interoperability and presents the proposed approach using a datacentre multi-manager scenario.

6.2 Multi-agent systems and multi-agent coordination

'*Multi-agent systems*' is a generic term referring to systems consisting of different subsystems (agents) that cooperate (interact) with each other in order to achieve a common goal. The idea of a system with several components working together towards a common goal has been applied to an increasing number of domains including distributed systems, autonomic systems, supply chain, networks of networks, etc. Multi-agent coordination deals with the way the subsystems interact with each other in the process of working together to achieve the common goal – and many techniques have been proposed. A detailed survey of multi-agent systems, e.g., is presented in Reference 154. Multi-manager scenario – which is an aspect of multi-agent systems – as described in this book, is a situation requiring the cooperation of different autonomic managers in the same system, and this cooperation is referred to as *interoperability*. Several multi-agent coordination techniques have been proposed in the multi-agent systems community, and this chapter also compares some of the early techniques.

A multi-agent coordination in multi-robot systems is discussed in Reference 155. A multi-robot system is a system of heterogeneous cooperative robots working together to achieve a common goal. The multi-robot coordination discussed in Reference 155 is based on genetic programming. To coordinate a cooperative task between robots, Liu and Iba [155] proposed an approach called evolutionary subsumption arguing that it is inefficient and intractable to directly use genetic programming to generate a controller for complex behaviours. The proposed evolutionary subsumption applies genetic programming to Brooks' subsumption architecture [145]. The subsumption architecture is an early autonomous robotics architecture in which the complete behaviour of a robot is decomposed into sub-behaviours presented as hierarchical layers where higher-level layers can subsume the roles of lower levels. Take for instance, a robot could have '*avoid objects*', '*move around*' and '*explore the room*' layers which are interdependent – in order to explore the room, the robot would need to be able to move around freely and should be able to avoid obstacles. These layers are implemented as separate competences which generate outputs, and the higher-level layers can *subsume* the competences of lower levels by suppressing their outputs.

In a subsumption architecture, as illustrated in Figure 6.1, all layers take input (contextual data) from the sensor and send output (decision, action, etc.) to the actuator. However, *higher* layers can 'inhibit' the outputs of *lower layers and cause theirs to be actuated instead. This is the central idea of the subsumption architecture and can be adapted for multi-agent coordination in which case the layers will represent different agents (autonomic managers).*

Challenge 6.1
The subsumption architecture gives us an idea that can be very useful in autonomic systems interoperability. Try an implementation of two or three autonomic managers working together for a specific goal. Design it in a way that there will be at least one conflict – it could be a case where the output (action) of one manager contradicts the output of another manager and thereby affects the overall goal. Adapting the subsumption

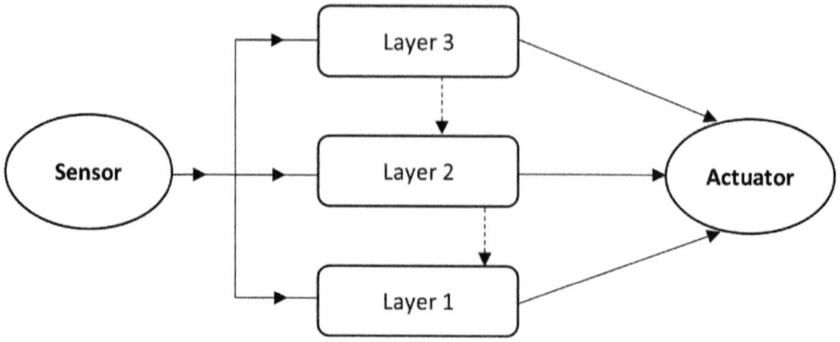

Figure 6.1 Illustration of the subsumption architecture with three layers

architecture, let the autonomic managers act as sublayers in which conflicts can be resolved by higher autonomic managers inhibiting the actions of lower autonomic managers. One of the main issues here would be the algorithm for the conflict resolution – how to decide higher/lower managers (may need to be defined by policy, learning, etc.), how and when to inhibit actions, the direction of communication flow, etc. To keep things simple, limit the autonomic functionalities of the managers to any or all of the four self-managing functionalities.

Stigmergy is another promising concept for autonomic interoperability. The potential of utilising stigmergy by software agents to interact with each other and to collectively solve a common task is presented in Reference 132. Stigmergy, which is found among social insects (e.g., ant colony), is the indirect communication among coexisting individuals through their environment. O'Reilly and Ehlerspresent a methodology of mimicking stigmergy into a software system positing that many software projects are deemed failures due to the inability of the software systems to adapt to changing business environments. A multi-agent stigmergic coordination in manufacturing control system has been presented in References 133 and 156. Coordination among the agents in the manufacturing control system is a direct reflection of the pheromone-based stigmergy in ant colony. In this approach, the control system consists of agents (e.g., resource, product and order) that distribute pheromones (e.g., agents' connections, location and general info) within the environment (cyber world) in which they reside. Sharing such global information on a collective environment (the cyber world) reduces design cycle, products' time to market and order lead times and also facilitates flexibility [133]. Stigmergy-based coordination is a rich and wide area of research that can be explored in many forms, and this is just one aspect. The principle of stigmergy is explained in Chapter 3.

However, in these and many other approaches, the agents are logically (and in some approaches, physically) connected together which, in actual sense, indicates that the agents are aware of the existence of others. This is not always the case in real-life systems. In some real-life environment, multi-agent systems are made up of agents by different vendors which are designed to perform in environments where they are not necessarily aware of the existence of other agents. In the stigmergic approach presented in this chapter, the agents do not need to be aware of the existence of other agents. The agents have a sense of operating in '*isolation*' and simply respond to changes in the environment (in the form of process conflicts, unexpected disturbance, etc.) – see the office share example in section 6.3. Trend analysis (TA) logic enables agents to easily infer the presence of other 'agents' by the kind (or nature) of environmental changes experienced. In this approach, an external adjustment of some parameters (by a human user) – which by the way may be correctly or erroneously applied – is considered an agent action by other agents. One sophistication of the stigmergic interoperability approach is that, no matter the conflict or disturbance, agents (in this case autonomic managers) are designed to react (e.g., by self-retuning) within the boundaries of the system's stated goals. This is because the agents are designed using the trustworthy autonomic architecture (TrAArch).

6.3 A review of autonomic interoperability solutions

The challenge of multi-manager interactions can be understandably enormous. This stems from the fact that, e.g., components (and indeed autonomic managers) could be multi-vendor supplied, upgrades in one manager could trigger unfamiliar events, increasing scale can introduce bottlenecks, one manager may be unaware of the existence of another and managers, though tested and perfected in isolation, may not have been wired at design to coexist with other managers. Multi-manager coexistence leads to potential conflicts. A typical example is illustrated with a multi-manager datacentre scenario – Figure 6.2.

Consider a figurative datacentre with three independent autonomic managers working together (unaware of each other) to optimise the datacentre as in Figure 6.2. The autonomic managers have direct control and management of certain aspects of the datacentre – they pass control signals (solid arrow) to the datacentre and receive feedback (dotted arrow) on the impact of their actions. The performance manager optimises resource provisioning to maintain service-level achievement (SLA). It does this, e.g., by dynamically (re)allocating resources and maintaining a pool of idle servers to ensure high responsiveness to high-priority applications. The power manager seeks to optimise power usage (as power is one of the major cost overheads of datacentres) by shutting down servers that have been idle for a certain length of time. The cooling manager ensures that the temperature of the datacentre is maintained within a certain range of degrees. Although each manager performs brilliantly in isolation, by coexisting, the success of one manager may defeat the goal of another. In this scenario, one can identify two sources of conflict:

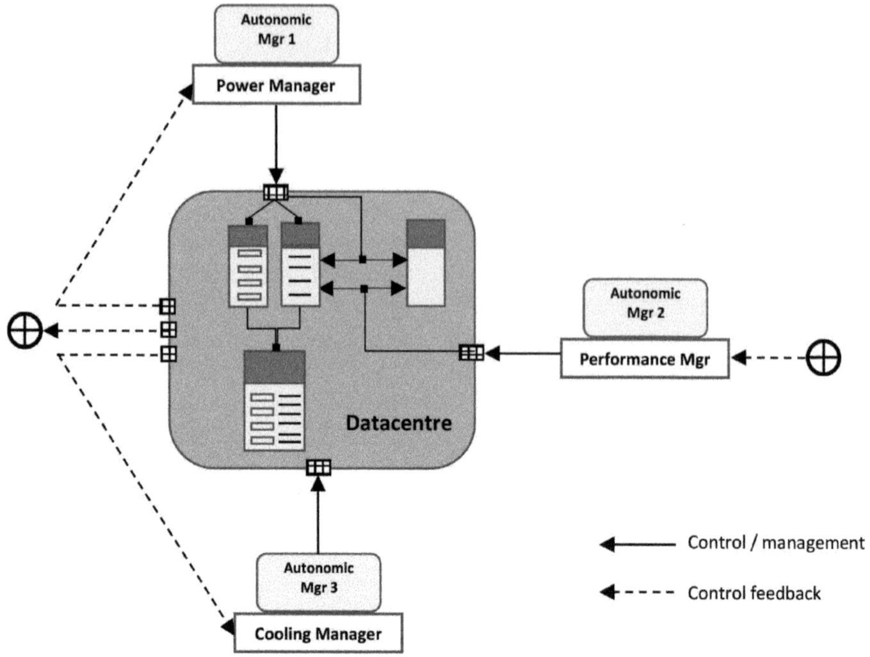

Figure 6.2 Illustration of a simple multi-manager datacentre. The power manager is responsible for optimising power usage while the performance manager is responsible for handling resource allocation, and the cooling manager is responsible for maintaining the desired room temperature

a. one manager seeks to shut down a server that another manager seeks to keep alive and
b. another manager seeks to maintain temperature, within a certain range, using power that another manager seeks to preserve.

The (in)activities of one autonomic manager affect the costs of provisioning (e.g., delay cost, scheduling cost, competition cost, etc.) for another autonomic manager in one way or the other. One way of mitigating this conflict is to have an external agent that can detect and diagnose the conflict. The problem with this is that it introduces more complexity (e.g., any additional autonomic manager will require rewiring of the other autonomic managers) as system is scaled up. This leads to adding more complexity in the process of solving a complexity problem which is not desirable. There are a couple of efforts in this direction. A trustworthy autonomic solution suitable for addressing this sort of scenario is demonstrated in section 6.4.

Kephart *et al.* [107] presented a clear demonstration of the need for interoperability mechanisms. In that work, two independently developed autonomic managers were implemented: the first dealt with application resource management (specifically central processing unit (CPU) usage optimisation) and the second, a power manager, dealt with modulating the operating frequency of the CPU to ensure that the power cap was not exceeded. It was shown that without a means to interact, both autonomic managers throttled and sped up the CPU without recourse to one another, thereby failing to achieve their intended optimisations and potentially destabilising the system. There is widespread repetition of this sort of problem requiring appropriate interoperability solution.

Anthony *et al.* [61] evaluated the nature and scope of the interoperability challenges for autonomic systems, identified a set of requirements for a universal solution and proposed a service-based approach to interoperability to handle both direct and indirect conflicts in a multi-manager scenario. In this approach, an *interoperability service* interacts with autonomic managers through a dedicated interface and is able to detect possible conflict of management interests. New autonomic managers register their capabilities and requirements (in terms of the kind of services they provide and what aspects of the system they intend to manage) with the interoperability service, which then grants management rights only if no other autonomic manager in its database is managing the same aspect of the system to which management right is requested. In this way, the interoperability service manages all interoperability activities by granting or withholding management rights to different autonomic managers as appropriate. One problem with this approach is that if a new autonomic manager is more capable of managing (e.g., in terms of efficiency) an aspect of the system that an existing autonomic manager is already managing, the new autonomic manager will be denied management right. Another challenge with the service-based approach is the complexity of reconfiguring the interoperability service each time a new autonomic manager is added whereas in the architecture-based solution presented in section 6.4, the autonomic managers seamlessly readjust their behaviour each time a new manager is added. Two types of conflicts in a multi-manager scenario are discussed in Reference 61: *direct conflicts* occur where autonomic managers attempt to manage the same explicit resource while *indirect conflicts* arise when autonomic managers control different resources, but the management effects of one have an undesirable impact on the management function of the other. This latter type of conflict is believed to be the most frequent and problematic, as there are such a wide variety of unpredictable ways in which such conflicts can occur.

Another form of interoperability that entails the collaboration of multiple managers in the form of information exchange to achieve an overall system objective is presented in Reference 157. In this arrangement, server machines are grouped into node groups, and a node group manager allocates server processes and requests to individual nodes using modelling and optimisation algorithms. The group manager also estimates the ability of each group to fulfil its service-level objectives based on the number of nodes available to it and then pushes the estimates to a provisioning manager which allocates server machines to the groups using the provided estimates. The exchange of information between these managers will require a form of interface for their communication, and this again brings us back to the issue of having to reconfigure interfaces each time a new autonomic manager is added. This approach only provides '*static interoperability*' solution and is somewhat scalability proof. The new solution proposed in this book is a '*dynamic interoperability*' approach in the sense that autonomic managers do not need recoding each time new managers are added. They autonomically retune (modulate) their behaviour as soon as they sense process conflicts.

There are also works that deal with homogenous competing autonomic managers. For example, in order to avoid jobs being starved of resources, Reference 48 implemented a two-level autonomic data management system. A global manager allocates physical resources to virtual servers while local managers manage the virtual servers, using fuzzy logic to infer the expected resource requirements of the applications that run on the virtual servers. Other works focus on bespoke interoperability solution [158], direct autonomic managers interactions at the level of autonomic elements to ensure that management obligations are met [159], hierarchical relationship to autonomic element interactions [160] and Monitor-Analyse-Plan-Execute (MAPE) architecture modification [105] where it is suggested to separate out the monitoring and analysis stages of the MAPE loop into distinct autonomic elements, with designed-in interactions between them.

The interoperability solutions discussed so far are some of the early efforts. They are more generic and provide solid foundation for addressing the interoperability issue. The recent solutions are more specific and application dependent. Several studies [36, 109, 111] have addressed the challenge of interoperability in many ways. Focus areas include interoperability within autonomous swarms of unmanned systems [108] and interference-aware load balancing [110]. Hadj *et al.* [109] focus on autonomic conflict management between coexisting applications while Ding *et al.* [36] look at interoperability in achieving service-level objectives, and Tsarev *et al.* [111] are interested in multi-agent interaction within supply scheduling.

The research community has made valuable progress towards autonomic manager interoperability but this progress has yet to lead to a standardised approach. Although the current state of research is a significant step, available solutions do not completely tackle the problem of unintended or unexpected interactions that can occur when independently developed autonomic managers coexist in a system. Furthermore from that, and more realistically, autonomic managers may not necessarily need to know about the existence of other managers – they are designed in isolation (probably by different vendors) and operate differently (for different goals) without recourse to one another. So, to have close-coupled interoperability (i.e., where specific actions in one autonomic manager react to, or complement those of another), the source code and detailed functional specifications of each autonomic manager must be available to all autonomic managers. This is near impossible and where it is possible, requires a rewiring (or recoding) of each autonomic manager whenever a new autonomic manager is added. That is why this book favours a solution that is tied to the autonomic architecture to provide a dynamic solution – hence, the architecture-based approach presented next. To avoid introducing further complexity through solving the interoperability problem, the autonomic architecture should envision (and provide for) interoperability support from scratch. That is to say, the autonomic architecture should be scalable and dynamic enough to accommodate expected and unexpected developments. This is one aspect of trustworthy autonomic computing – a trustworthy autonomic system should be designed with the capability to address unintended or unexpected complex (conflicting) interactions that can occur when independently developed autonomic managers coexist in a system.

6.4 The architecture-based interoperability

An efficient interoperability solution will need to be seamless and consider interoperability as an integral part of the system. This section presents a '*dynamic interoperability*' approach initially proposed in Reference 118. This approach uses stigmergy and is based on the TrAArch. The TrAArch (see Chapters 4 and 5), through its *DependabilityCheck* (DC) component can be extended to accommodate desired autonomic functionalities. In the proposed interoperability approach, a *TA* logic is implemented in the DC component to enable the autonomic manager to automatically detect conflicts, and using *dead-zone* (DZ) logic the autonomic manager is able to regulate its behaviour as appropriate. Datacentre case example experimentation is used to demonstrate this approach. The central idea here is that interoperability capability should be designed into the system from the beginning. This capability is achieved by utilising the stigmergic principle – the autonomic managers are designed to learn from the *signals* available in their operating environment and be able to adjust their behaviour to avoid potential conflicts.

6.4.1 Scheduling and resource allocation

Let us consider, in more detail (Figure 6.3), the multi-manager datacentre example presented earlier in section 6.3 (Figure 6.2): the datacentre comprises a pool of resources S_i (live servers), a pool of shutdown servers $\check{S}_i$ (ready to be powered and restored to S_i as need be), a list of applications A_j, a pool of services Ṳ (a combination of applications and their provisioning servers) and two autonomic managers A-M1 (performance manager (*PeM*)) and A-M2 (a *PoM*) that optimise the entire datacentre. A_j and S_i are, respectively, a collection of applications supported (as services) by the datacentre and a collection of servers available to the PeM for provisioning (or scheduling) available services according to requests. As service requests arrive, *PeM* dynamically populates Ṳ to service the requests (actual scheduling algorithm is presented in the experiment). Ṳ is defined by

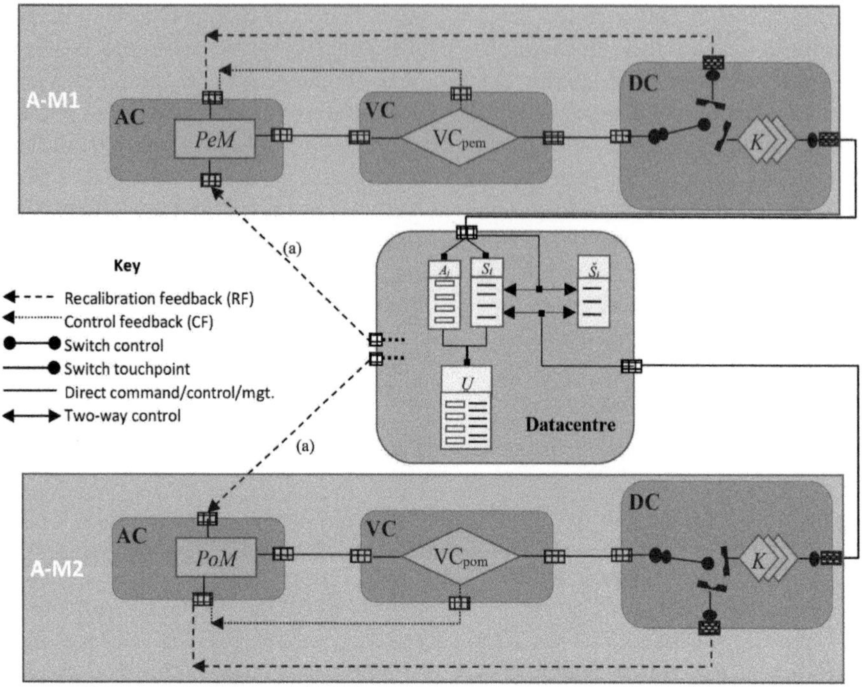

Figure 6.3 Architecture-based interoperability solution [118]. The DC component of TrAArch provides interoperability management. The two A-Ms are designed independently and operate independently as well.

$$\underset{\cdot\cdot}{U}=\begin{cases} A_1:(S_{11},\ S_{12},\ S_{13},\ \ldots,\ S_{1i}) \\ A_2:(S_{21},\ S_{22},\ S_{23},\ \ldots,\ S_{2i}) \\ \ldots\ \ldots\ \ldots\ \ldots\ \ldots\ \ldots \\ A_n:(S_{n1},\ S_{n2},\ S_{n3},\ \ldots,\ S_{ni}) \end{cases}$$

where $A_1:(S_{11},\ S_{12},\ S_{13},\ \ldots,\ S_{1i})$ means that $(S_{11},\ S_{12},\ S_{13},\ \ldots,\ S_{1i})$ servers are currently allocated to Application A_1, and A_n is the number of application entries into $\underset{\cdot\cdot}{U}$. This setting indicates that a server can be (re)deployed for different applications. All the servers in S_i are up and running (constantly available – or so desired by *PeM*) waiting for (re)deployment. The primary performance goal of *PeM* is to minimise oscillation and maximise stability (including just-in-time service delivery to meet SLA target) while the secondary performance goal is to maximise throughput. The goal of the PoM, on the other hand, is to optimise power consumption. This task is simply achieved, e.g., by shutting down any server that has been idle for time T_s.

To manage interoperability between *PeM* and *PoM* using TrAArch, Figure 6.3 shows the communications and control within the components of the TrAArch architecture. The autonomic managers take performance decisions, which are then validated by their respective *ValidationCheck* (VC) components (VC_{pom} and VC_{pem}) for correctness. A control feedback (CF) is generated if validation fails and with this feedback, the autonomic manager adjusts its decisions. The *DC* component takes a longer-term view of the autonomic managers' behaviour and either allows a manager to carry on with its actions (if check *passes*) or generates a recalibration feedback (RF) otherwise. DC contains other subcomponents (K), e.g., interoperability, stability, etc. The stability subcomponent is usually configured using DZ logic as shown in the experiments of Chapter 5. The interoperability subcomponent, in this case example, is configured using TA logic (which identifies patterns within streams of information supplied directly from different sources) with a combined effect of exponential smoothing technique (see Chapter 3). The details of the logic usage are explained in section 6.5.2. Note that the designer of the autonomic manager can define as many DC subcomponents as necessary.

Note: *It is important to first read Chapter 4, and possibly Chapter 5 as well, in order to understand how TrAArch works.*

Consider Figure 6.3. The interoperability component is implemented using knowledge-based technology. It learns and keeps track of the system's state following the historical decisions of the autonomic manager. If after a number of decision instances, the manager senses a conflict with its decisions (based on expected versus actual system state), another RF is generated to retune the manager's decisions. Take for instance, if after sometime *PoM* senses that the same set of servers it has shut down have constantly come back live without it powering them, there is only one conclusion: another operation (probably a human, another manager, etc.) is not '*happy*' with *PoM*'s decisions. So, *PoM*'s DC generates an RF with an appropriate tuning parameter value (β) to throttle the size of T_S as follows: ($T_s = T_s * \beta$). By sensing the effects of its actions and dynamically throttling T_S within an acceptable boundary, *PoM* is able to coexist with any other autonomic manager with conflicting actions. On the other hand, *PeM* can retune its behaviour, e.g., if it senses that the set of servers it tries to keep running are constantly switched off. However, there are boundaries within which each manager's *cleverness* is limited. For example, the size of T_S has a maximum limit.

Notice that the two autonomic managers do not need to know any details or even the existence of each other. In real life, this is typical of two staff that share an office space but work at different times. If each returns on their next respective shift and finds the office rearranged, they will each adjust in their arrangement of the office until an accepted compromise structure is reached. This can be achieved without both getting to meet. The DC component provides extra capacity for an autonomic manager to dynamically throttle its behaviour to suit the goal of the system. In actual sense this approach builds on the stigmergic phenomenon [161], which is a process of achieving indirect coordination between coexisting agents by means of indirect communication via the environment. That is, using their environment for indirect communication, the agents are able to sense and adjust their actions and this way they achieve efficient collaboration. So, the stigmergic interoperability solution provides indirect coordination between autonomic managers in a multi-manager scenario without the need for planning (or pre-knowledge of the existence of other autonomic managers), control or direct communications between coexisting autonomic managers. This provides efficient collaboration (as against competition) between coexisting autonomic managers.

There are costs associated with the operations of a datacentre. These costs are affected in one way or the other by the actions of the autonomic managers. These and many other metrics are used to analyse the proposed interoperability solution in the following experimentation.

6.5 Complex interactions in multi-manager scenario

This section presents experimental analysis of the proposed interoperability solution using a datacentre resource request and allocation management scenario. The datacentre scenario used is the same as the one used in Chapter 5 but in this case, there is an additional manager (*PoM*) that optimises the datacentre power consumption. The essence of this analysis is not to investigate datacentres but to examine the performance effects of the proposed interoperability solution in a multi-manager datacentre scenario using easy-to-assess examples. The analysis will investigate the performance of the datacentre with and without interoperability solution.

It is important, however, to point out that the proposed interoperability solution works well in a closed-world model but has some limitations in an open-world model and so may not be relied on to reach convergence. Convergence defines a point at which system is stable and has reached a steady state. In a closed system, there are a definite number of actors (in this case autonomic managers) that influence the environment and the individual actions of each autonomic manager can be tracked as a trend. In this way, it is possible for each manager to detect persistent actions that conflict with its actions and be able to readjust behaviour. However, in an open system, there are indefinite number of actors that can influence the environment. An actor in this model can be a third party that interferes with the system, and this interference could be a one-off instance or several instances from different actors. For example, the office share scenario discussed earlier in this section is a closed-world model but it becomes an open-world model if a third party

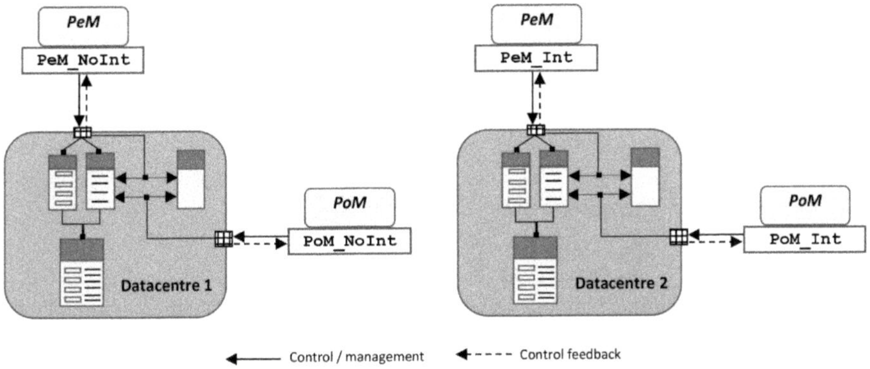

Figure 6.4 *Datacentre scenario with and without interoperability solution. Datacentre 1 implements no interoperability solution while Datacentre 2 does*

(say, different office cleaners) randomly contributes to the office (re)arrangement. So, the proposed solution can be relied on to reach convergence in a closed-world model but may require further readjustments to reach convergence in an open-world model.

6.5.1 Simulation design

The experiments here are designed and implemented using the TrAArch Simulator (discussed in section 5.2.1), which is a C#-based application specifically developed for simulating autonomic datacentre. Figure 6.4 is a pictorial illustration of the datacentre implementation scenarios used. The two implementations of the datacentre (Datacentre 1 and Datacentre 2) both have two autonomic managers as explained in section 6.4 – a *PeM* and a *PoM*, optimising resource allocation and power management, respectively. Each autonomic manager is *unaware* of the existence of the other. The scenarios are explained as follows:

- **Datacentre 1** – Both managers coexist without any form of interoperability solution. This means that both managers perform their tasks within the boundaries of their individual autonomic framework without recourse to one another. In this case, *PeM* and *PoM* are represented by *PeM_NoInt* and *PoM_NoInt,* respectively while the datacentre is represented by *NoInteroperability* in the simulation analysis.
- **Datacentre 2** – Both managers coexist with the proposed interoperability solution. This means that both managers, while performing their tasks within the boundaries of their individual autonomic framework, are sensitive to external interference. Here, external interference is defined as any action or effect that alters the manager's expected system state. In this case, *PeM* and *PoM* are

represented by *PeM_Int* and *PoM_Int,* respectively while the datacentre is represented by *Interoperability* in the simulation analysis.

Note that both managers are designed based on TrAArch framework (Figure 6.3), and the investigation herein focuses on Datacentre 1 (*NoInteroperability*) versus Datacentre 2 (*Interoperability*). So, this is performance analysis of a multi-manager datacentre with and without interoperability solution.

6.5.2 Autonomic manager logic

Manager logic describes the actual individual control logic employed by each of the autonomic managers in order to achieve the stated performance goal. This explains the logical composition of each manager. There are two instances of each manager, i.e., when the manager is designed without interoperability solution (*PeM_NoInt*) and when it is designed with interoperability solution (*PeM_Int*).

- **Performance Manager**

The PeM is directly responsible for resource request and allocation management. The manager receives requests and allocates resources according to the algorithm defined in section 6.4.1. The first instance of this manager (*PeM_NoInt*) has no inbuilt interoperability solution.

- PeM_NoInt

As requests arrive, the manager checks for resource availability and deploys server(s) according to the size of the request. When a server is deployed, it is queued for a certain amount of time (*ProvisioningTime*) simulating the time (delay) it takes to load or configure a server with necessary application. Servers are then 'provisioned' after spending *ProvisioningTime* in the queue. The provisioning pool is constantly populated as requests arrive. Additionally, the manager calculates a smoothing average (see Chapter 3) of the capacity of arriving requests:

*smoothedAvgCapacityPeM_NoInt = (smoothingConstant * avgAppCapacity) + ((1 − smoothingConstant) * oldMean)*

The *SmoothingConstant* used and the choice justification are presented later in the experimental analysis. The calculated smoothing average is a forecast of the next expected request MIPS – i.e., it is used to predict requests. (The size of application requests and the capacity of servers are defined in million instructions per second (MIPS).) With this forecast information, the manager constantly checks to ensure that the difference between the predicted MIPS and the available MIPS (idle server capacity ready for deployment) is not less than the equivalent of two servers. And if it is, the manager quickly checks and restores servers from the shutdown server pool ($\check{S}_i$). Procedure 6.1 is a basic algorithm explaining the server restoration process by the *PeM_NoInt* manager.

Procedure 6.1: Algorithm for checking and restoring servers

```
Calculate smoothedAvgCapacity
Calculate AvailableCapacity
Define a periodic Interval (PeM_NoIntTuningParam)
for every Interval
    value = (AvailableCapacity - smoothedAvgCapacity)
    if value < (ServerCapacity * 2)
        restore all servers
    else
       repeat check at next Interval
next
```

Note: *PeM_NoIntTuningParam is a parameter representing time interval at which the PeM_NoInt manager checks to decide whether or not to power and restore servers that are down. This parameter is measured in number of service requests.*

This check ensures that, where possible, the manager maintains at least the capacity equivalent of two servers readily available for deployment (i.e., enough resources for current request and the next expected request). Checks are carried out at an interval defined by a tuning parameter (*PeM_NoIntTuningParam*). This ensures that the manager does not wait until late, the critical point, before acting. So, at every interval, the manager checks and restores all servers on the $\check{S}_i$ pool.

- PeM_Int

The *PeM_Int* manager has an embedded interoperability solution based on the proposed interoperability solution (Figure 6.3). In addition to all the functionalities of *PeM_NoInt*, the *PeM_Int* manager performs further checks and retunes its behaviour. The manager tracks system state as it carries out the checks at the specified interval defined by *PeM_IntTuningParam*. Each check is calculated as '*one observation*' and if on a periodic third observation, the $\check{S}_i$ pool is not empty (signalling that the pool is being populated as it is being emptied by *PeM_Int*), the manager adjusts its checks interval (by increasing the tuning parameter) to reduce the rate at which it empties the $\check{S}_i$ pool (i.e., to be sympathetic to the other manager whose presence is implied, rather than to compete with it):

```
if ((serviceRequestCountPeM_Int - PeM_IntRefPoint) == PeM_IntTuningParam)
{
      PeM_IntObservationCount += 1;
      PeM_IntRefPoint = serviceRequestCountPeM_Int;

      if (PeM_IntObservationCount == 3)             // 3rd observation
      {
            PeM_IntObservationCount = 0;
            if (ShutServerCountInt != 0)            // if Š_i pool is not empty
            {
                  PeM_IntTuningParam += 4;
                  PeM_IntFurtherObservationCount += 1;

                  if (PeM_IntFurtherObservationCount == 4) // further observation
                  {
                        PeM_IntTuningParam += 5;
                        PeM_IntFurtherObservationCount = 0;
                  }
            }
      }
      ...
}
```

Note: *PeM_IntTuningParam is a parameter representing the initial time interval at which the PeM_Int manager checks to decide whether or not to power and restore servers that are down. Unlike PeM_NoIntTuningParam, the size of PeM_IntTuningParam parameter is dynamically adjusted by the PeM_Int manager. This parameter is measured in number of service requests.*

A further internal set of observation iterations, as shown above, are carried out. The tuning parameter is further adjusted if condition persists (i.e., persisted interference) after each fourth observation of the initial third interval of observations. So, what happens here is that the manager powers ON all servers (restores servers from $Š_i$) and keeps checking that there are enough reserves for prompt deployment. As, in this case, the *PoM_Int* manager continues to shut servers down, it causes instability in the system as both managers counter each other's actions. If the *PeM_Int* manager senses that the restored servers are constantly put out of service, it relaxes its rate of repowering the servers – this is because the whole essence is collaboration rather than competition. If after a certain time (defined by the new check interval) the interference continues, the manager further relaxes the rate of its actions. This process is repeated until a stable condition is reached. This is demonstrated in detail in section 6.5.4.

- **Power Manager**

The PoM is directly responsible for power usage optimisation in the datacentre. The power optimisation method implemented by the manager is in the form of power conservation in which idle servers are shut down to conserve power. Other researchers have used different forms of power management which optimises power consumption, e.g., by adjusting the processor speed of servers [162] and a power manager which is embedded in the firmware of a server and can use feedback control to precisely control the server's power consumption [163]. While these are processor-level power management, the *PoM* manager conserves power by shutting idle servers and repowering them as need arises. This is basic and sufficient to create conflicts with the *PeM* manager, which seeks to keep as many servers as possible running in order to have enough capacity reserve. This form of power management technique is also used in Reference 164 in which machines are turned ON/OFF to conserve power.

- PoM_NoInt

Here the manager checks and shuts down idle servers at a time interval defined by a tuning parameter (*PoM_NoIntTuningParam*). The idle servers are the same servers that *PeM_NoInt* considers as available resources. So, in essence, when servers are shut down, *AvailableCapacity* is depleted which in turn affects the performance of *PeM_NoInt*. So, *PoM_NoInt* continues to check and shut down servers within a certain boundary. Procedure 6.2 is a basic algorithm explaining how the *PoM_NoInt* manager checks and shuts down servers.

Procedure 6.2: Algorithm for checking and shutting down servers

```
int s = initial number of servers for the simulation
Define a periodic Interval (PoM_NoIntTuningParam)
for every Interval
  int d = number of available servers //Servers.Count
 if (d > (s/5)) //unsafe to shut servers below this point
  Shut Sever[d-1] //shut the last server on the S_i pool
  Add Server[d-1] To Š_i[] //add to shutdown server pool
next
```

So, what this means is that the *PoM_NoInt* manager will continue to shut idle servers as long as the number of servers in the S_i pool (available servers) is greater than one-fifth of the total servers. The DC component of *PoM_NoInt* is configured to stop shutting servers at $\left(\check{S}_i\ count\ =\ (server.sNumber\ /\ 5)\right)$ because if the manager continues shutting servers beyond this point it will drag the entire datacentre to the brink of unresponsiveness which ultimately leads to underprovisioning and inefficiency. This process continues regardless of the actions of the PeM. The *PeM_NoInt* manager may at this point be restoring the servers to increase *AvailableCapacity,* and this ultimately leads to high rate of server movement in the datacentre.

- PoM_Int

On the other hand, the embedded interoperability solution enables the manager to sense conflicts and then readjust its behaviour. The same method as in *PeM_Int* is used here. For example, the manager keeps count of servers in the $\check{S}_i$ pool (*listViewShutServer.Items.Count*) as it shuts and repowers servers and if on a periodic tenth check the server count does not match expected count (signifying an unknown interference), the manager adjusts the tuning parameter:

```
if ((serviceRequestCountPeM_Int - PoM_IntRefPoint) == PoM_IntTunningParam) //
        {
            PoM_IntObservationCount += 1;
            PoM_IntRefPoint = serviceRequestCountPeM_Int;

            if (PoM_IntObservationCount == 10)
            {
                PoM_IntObservationCount = 0;
                if (listViewShutServer.Items.Count < PoM_IntCheckPoint)
                {// if on a 10th observation S_i.Count doesn't match expected count
                    PoM_IntTunningParam += 1;       // adjusting tuning parameter
                }
            }

        // below is same as defined by the algorithm of Procedure 6.2
            int d = listViewServer.Items.Count;

            if (d > (server.sNumber / 5)) // a point unsafe to shut servers
            {
                listViewShutServer.Items.Add(listViewServer.Items[d - 1].Text);
                listViewServer.Items.Remove(listViewServer.Items[d - 1]);

                PoM_IntCheckPoint = listViewShutServer.Items.Count;
            }
        }
```

The manager keeps adjusting the tuning parameter (*PoM_IntTuningParam*) until it senses stability in the datacentre. Recall the conflict resolution example of the two staff sharing an office space discussed earlier. This is the fundamentals of the proposed stigmergic-inspired interoperability solution in this book.

6.5.3 Simulation scenarios and metrics

This simulation scenario is used to analyse the performance effects of the proposed stigmergic-inspired interoperability solution using the datacentre case example. The scenario and metrics used in the analysis are presented in Table 6.1. Further analysis can be done by downloading and running the TrAArch application (see section 5.2.1 in Chapter 5).

Scenario 1: In Scenario 1, all parameters are kept constant except those (e.g., DZConst) that may need dynamic tuning by the autonomic manager as need arises. This scenario gives a default view of the datacentre performance both when the two managers implement the proposed interoperability solution and when they do not. Under this scenario of normal conditions, all parameters are kept constant, and

Table 6.1 Interoperability simulation scenarios and metrics

Scenario	**Description**	**Metrics**
Scenario 1	Standard resource allocation management with uniform request rate and application size	Power consumption Power savings Instability SLA
Scenario 2	Varying application size with inconsistent request rate	

the two managers work independently without any physical or logical connections between them.

Scenario 2: This scenario is an exercise for the reader to complete, using the TrAArch Simulator. See full details at the end of the section (Challenge 6.2).

- **Workload and simulation parameters**

The result of every simulation analysis is relative to the set of workload or parameter set used. The parameter set used for the interoperability analysis is classified into internal and external variables. Most of these have been presented in Chapter 5 (section 5.2.2.2). The workload and simulation parameters specific to the interoperability analysis are:

- *PowerCoefficient*

Power coefficient represents the average server power consumption. That is, the average power a server consumes at any point in time for being active (switched on and running). This is measured in kilowatt (kw). According to References 151 and 152, on average, servers consume 3.195 MW/h worth of power. This value is scaled and *PowerCoefficient* is pegged at 0.887 kw/s in the simulations. This is just reflective and a guide as actual values can significantly vary owing to a lot of factors (e.g., cooling, processor, machine type, etc.). Interestingly, the TrAArch Simulator allows for the tailoring of all parameters according to user preferences. The usage of this variable is limited to investigating the impact of interoperability actions in terms of power consumption.

- *PeM_IntTuningParam*

Tuning parameter representing the initial time interval at which the *PeM_Int* manager checks to decide whether or not to power and restore servers that are down.

The manager dynamically adjusts the size of the parameter. This is measured in number of requests.

- *PeM_NoIntTuningParam*

Tuning parameter representing the time interval at which the *PeM_NoInt* manager checks to decide whether or not to power and restore servers that are down. The manager does not dynamically adjust the size of the parameter. This is measured in number of requests.

- *PoM_NoIntTuningParam*

Tuning parameter representing the time interval at which the *PoM_NoInt* manager checks to decide whether or not to shut down idle servers. Value is not dynamically adjusted and is measured in number of service requests.

- *PoM_IntTuningParam*

Tuning parameter representing the initial time interval at which the *PoM_Int* manager checks to decide whether or not to shut down idle servers. Value is dynamically adjusted by manager and is measured in number of service requests.

- **Metrics**

All metrics are mathematically defined to give the reader a clear picture of the definition and usage criteria for the metrics. The metrics are specifically chosen to reflect the impact of interoperability solution in a multi-manager datacentre.

Service level achievement: This has been discussed and defined in section 5.2.4.1 as:

$$\text{SLA} = \begin{cases} \dfrac{ProvisionedCapacity}{RequestedCapacity} & (i) \\[2ex] \dfrac{AvailableCapacity}{RunningCapacity} & (ii) \end{cases}$$

PowerConsumption: This metric represents the aggregated power consumption per unit time for all idle servers, i.e., servers that are running but not yet deployed. It is important to consider these servers as they can as well be switched OFF and powered ON only when needed. Although this could have a slight effect on SLA, the trade-off in power savings may be worthwhile. So, if we assume that each server, on average, consumes *PowerCoefficient* kilo watts worth of power per second, then PowerConsumption is calculated as:

$$\text{PowerConsumption} = PowerCoefficient * \#IdleServers$$

PowerConsumption is calculated at every time interval defined by request rate. Individual manager power consumption is different from the normal or general power consumption. For general power consumption, number of idle servers will be the total of server count in S_i and $\check{S}_i$ pools while for individual manager power consumption (with or without interoperability) number of idle servers will be the total of server count in S_i pool:

$$PowerConsumption = PowerCoefficient * (Server.Count + ShutServer.Count)$$

$$PowerConsumptionInt = PowerCoefficient * Server.Count$$

$$PowerConsumptionNoInt = PowerCoefficient * Server.Count$$

*Note that as a result of individual operations of the managers, server.count for Datacentre 1 will usually be different from that of Datacentre 2 (*Figure 6.4*).*

PowerSavings: PowerSavings is calculated as the difference between general power consumption and individual power consumption:

$$PowerSavings = GeneralPC - IndividualPC$$

So, e.g., the PowerSavings for Datacentre 1 will be calculated as

$$PowerSavingsNoInt = PowerConsumption - PowerConsumptionNoInt$$

and the PowerSavings for Datacentre 2 as

$$PowerSavingsInt = PowerConsumption - PowerConsumptionInt$$

As *PoM* intends to optimise power usage, which also entails saving power, the PowerSavings metric will be useful to analyse the impact of the manager's power management capability.

Instability: Instability measures the rate at which servers are moved around the datacentre. It is inefficient to move servers around frequently. The cost effect can be enormous in terms of cooling, power, scheduling costs, etc.

$$Instability = \#ServersMoved/Time$$

Instability in terms of irregular and high rate of server movement from one pool to another is a costly, unsafe and undesirable occurrence in datacentres. This is a potential situation when you have two managers optimising the same datacentre as in the case example here.

Table 6.2 Scenario 1 simulation parameters

Parameter		Value
Number of servers		1 000
Number of applications		4
Request rate		1 req/s
Application capacity (MIPS)		20 000
Server capacity (MIPS)		40 000
Internal variables	RetrieveRate	5×
	RequestRateParam	10
	RetrieveRequestParam	0.2
	PowerCoefficient	0.887 kw/s
	SmoothingConstant	0.05
	ServerProvisioningTime	3 (1.5 s)
Autonomic managers (PeMs and PoMs)		*PeM_NoInt* *PeM_Int PoM_NoInt* *PoM_Int*
DZConst		1.5

6.5.4 Results analysis

This section presents the analysis of the experimental results. Results are presented and analysed according to simulation scenarios and in doing this the metrics listed in Table 6.1 will be used. Each simulation will analyse the performances of Datacentre 1 (*NoInteroperability*) and Datacentre 2 (*Interoperability*) under the same conditions. Presented results are based on average of ten simulation runs per scenario. For more accurate analysis, consider performances between 201s and 1801s – reflecting when the simulation is settled.

Scenario 1: Resource request and allocation management with uniform request rate and application size

Table 6.2 is a collection of the major parameters used in this scenario. For precise results, the average of ten simulation results is presented. For each of the ten simulations, the same parameter set as in Table 6.2 is used. However, the number of requests and the distribution of those requests among the four applications will differ as they are dynamically generated and unpredictable. This does not distort the results as analysis is based on system-wide performance and not on individual application performance.

With 10 000 servers of 40 000 MIPS each, it means that there is a total of initial 40 000 000 MIPS available to share between four applications (App1, App2, App3 and App4). Reclaimed servers are subsequently added to this available capacity. Table 6.3 shows a distribution of requests and services for ten simulation runs of Scenario 1.

Table 6.3 High-level performance analysis over ten simulation runs of Scenario 1

	Unused server		Serviced request		Dropped/Queued request		Deployed server	
Sim.	**Int**	**NoInt**	**Int**	**NoInt**	**Int**	**NoInt**	**Int**	**NoInt**
1	6	0	2 166	2 166	118	118	1 012	1 023
2	0	0	2 196	2 196	101	101	1 016	1 013
3	13	0	2 170	2 180	129	119	1 000	1 011
4	18	0	2 139	2 152	110	97	996	1 008
5	0	0	2 208	2 226	116	98	1 014	1 010
6	11	0	2 177	2 182	114	109	1 007	1 022
7	0	0	2 197	2 207	140	130	1 022	1 017
8	29	0	2 155	2 161	121	115	985	1 015
9	6	0	2 150	2 170	117	97	1 008	1 011
10	0	0	2 187	2 188	107	106	1 019	1 020
Avg	**8.3**	**0**	**2174.5**	**2182.8**	**117.3**	**109**	**1007.9**	**1015**

From Table 6.3, there is no substantial performance difference between when interoperability solution is implemented (*Int*) and when it is not (*NoInt*) in terms of requests and services distribution. Although results slightly favour *Int*, the resource per service efficiency of (1007.9/2174.5) is to (1015/2182.8) that is (0.4635:0.4650), is negligible. This is shown in the SLA performance of both datacentres (Figure 6.5). However, of most importance is the cost of achieving both levels of performance which is explored later. Also, the *Int* scenario has more outstanding (*unused*) server capacity (8.3 * 40 000 = 332 000) and could service about 332 000/20 000 = 17 more application requests.

For SLA, Figure 6.5 shows that both datacentres performed optimally in terms of efficiently utilising available resources and meeting expected service level. This is indicated by the proximity of both SLAs to value 1, which is the mark of optimal performance. However, analyses of other results reveal that Datacentre 1 (*NoInteroperability*) was quite unstable and would cost more to maintain.

Figure 6.6 is the analysis of behaviour patterns (*ActionTrend*) in both datacentres. The level 0.5 is irrelevant as it is just used to indicate behaviour patterns (in terms of tuning and retuning actions) of autonomic managers in both datacentres in the face of conflict. Each line indicates a server move. Datacentre 1 (represented by _NoInt) shows no dynamic retuning of behaviour pattern. Because managers were designed without any embedded interoperability solution, they maintained their behaviour (persisted actions) despite any conflict (interference) or instability in the datacentre. On the other hand, there is a level of autonomic retuning of behaviour patterns in Datacentre 2 (represented by _Int). At 101s, the autonomic managers sense a conflict (resulting in high level of server movement) and readjust their tuning parameter (explained in section 6.5.2) which reduced the conflict. Further dynamic

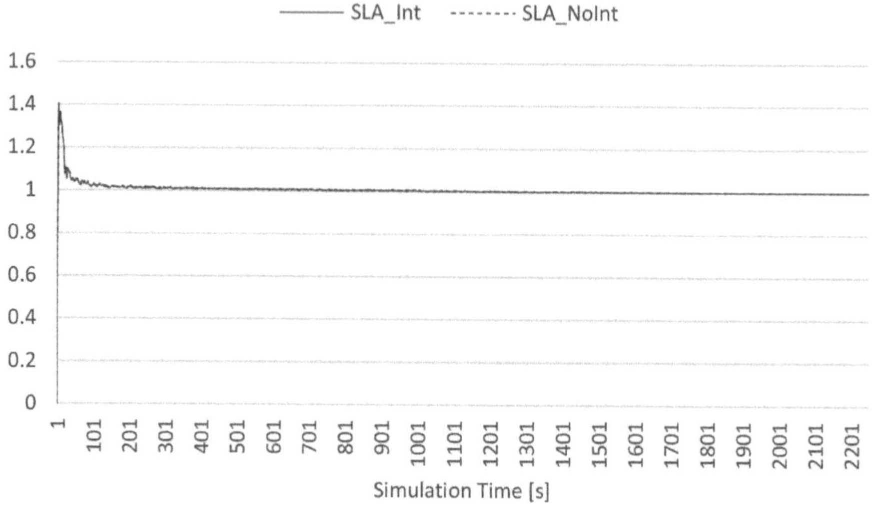

Figure 6.5 SLA analysis for both datacentres

readjustments are performed (e.g., at 201s, 401s) until an acceptable (stable) behaviour level is achieved at point 1001s. Both datacentres settle towards the end of the simulation.

Figure 6.7 shows how many servers were moved (from one pool to another) per time. Datacentre 1 shows high level of instability, and this is as a result of high frequency of server movement. The coexistence of *PeM_NoInt* and *PoM_NoInt* managers without any form of interoperability solution meant that more servers were frequently moved about. In isolation, both autonomic managers would adequately move servers about without causing instability in the datacentre while their coexistence led to conflicts which saw servers erratically moved between pools. Recall that while the *PeM_NoInt* seeks to keep servers running as reserves, *PoM_NoInt*

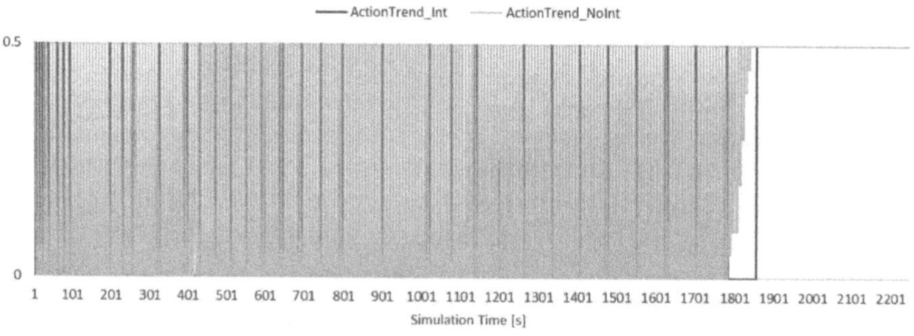

Figure 6.6 ActionTrend analysis for both datacentres

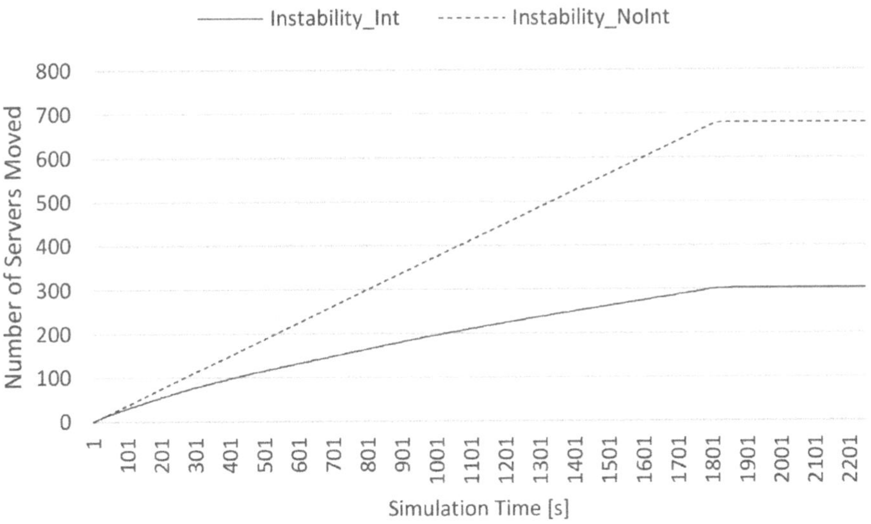

Figure 6.7 Instability analysis for both datacentres

seeks to shut servers that are idle and this leads to conflicts. This is not the case with Datacentre 2, which implements a dynamic interoperability solution that seamlessly resolves the conflicts experienced by Datacentre 1. This is achieved by both managers dynamically retuning their behaviour (section 6.5.2) whenever instability is sensed.

The movement of servers around the datacentre has some power cost implications. In this study, conflicts are specifically as a result of a PeM countering the actions of a PoM and to further understand the impact of the interoperability solution the analyses will hinge on power performance. The PoM in isolation can achieve huge reductions in power consumption. However, this achievement is significantly reduced when there are conflicts. Figure 6.8 shows the level of power consumption in both datacentres.

In Datacentre 1 (*NoInteroperability*), there is no noticeable drop in power consumption because the servers that are shut down to save power are constantly repowered by the PeM. So, the power consumption is almost as expected. There is, however, a tiny drop in power consumption in Datacentre 2. This is because the embedded interoperability solution allows the autonomic managers to relax their actions in the face of conflicts leading to more servers remaining shut down a longer time before being repowered. This may not be significant; however, these results depend on the scenario and set of parameters used. Figure 6.9 shows the power savings (i.e., difference between the actual and expected power consumptions) in both datacentres.

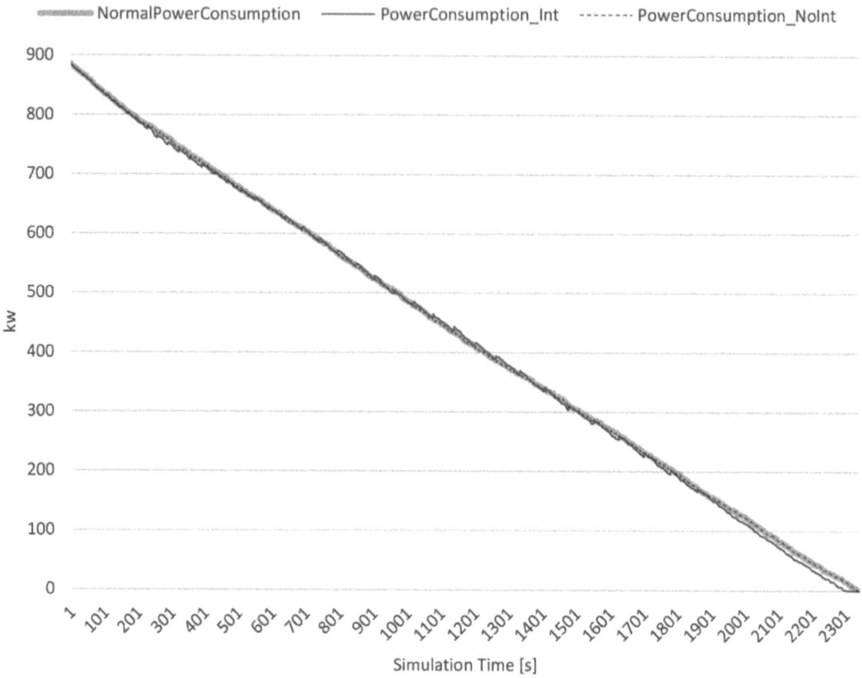

Figure 6.8 Power consumption analysis for both datacentres. 'NormalPowerConsumption' is the expected level of power consumption in the datacentre without a PoM

The power savings metric gives a clearer view of the datacentres' performances in terms of power optimisation and the impact of the interoperability solution. There is a consistent (uniform) power savings of about 1.8 kw/s for Datacentre 1 in the duration of the simulation. This is because both managers (*PeM_NoInt* and *PoM_NoInt*) operate within fixed autonomic boundaries – i.e., they persisted their actions despite any conflicts as long as such actions fall within their separate legal autonomic boundaries. So, we have a situation of almost equal action and reaction (server power down and server power up) on the same system which basically leaves the system on the same spot. Although there is occasional savings drop in the negative in Datacentre 2, there is significant overall improvement in power savings. The occasional drop in savings can be attributed to the time lag between when a manager detects a situation that warrants retuning of its behaviour and when it actually retunes itself to maintain stability. The interoperability solution is dynamically sensitive to interferences to manager actions. For more accurate analysis, consider performances between 201s and 1801s – reflecting when the simulation is settled.

In the analysed datacentre scenario, there are requirements for performance optimisation (in terms of resource request and allocation management) and power

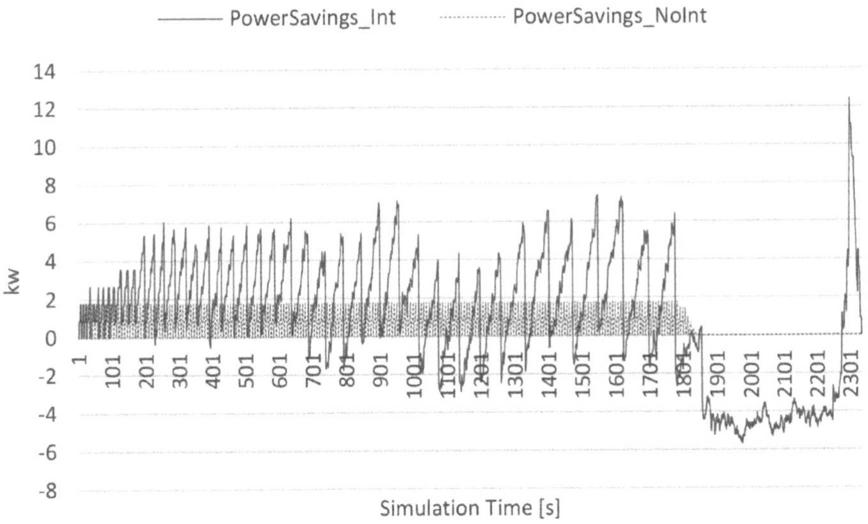

Figure 6.9 Power savings analysis for both datacentres

optimisation (in terms of power management), and these optimisations are handled by two conflicting managers. Results have shown that while performance optimisation is not significantly affected (Figure 6.5 and Table 6.3) by the conflict in both studied datacentres, power optimisation is significantly affected (Figures 6.8 and 6.9). In both datacentres, there is almost optimal resource provisioning with high level of efficiency and insignificant difference in level of performance. This is partly because the actions of the PeM have enormous impact on the PoM whereas the PeM has a way of mitigating the effects of the PoM's actions. Where impacts exist on the later the managers rely on the robustness of their underlying architecture (TrAArch) to stabilise the system. In Datacentre 1, with no interoperability solution, power optimisation is heavily affected because of the conflicts between the managers. These conflicts are dynamically addressed in Datacentre 2 by the interoperability solution. So, we can conclude, based on the presented results, that the proposed interoperability solution is capable of adequately handling complex interactions in multi-manager system scenarios. This is another step towards trustworthy autonomic computing. This assertion can be further tested – consider the following exercise.

Note: The performance analysis results of Scenario 1, between Datacentre 1 and Datacentre 2, do not show significant difference apart from the Instability metric. This is because simulation Scenario 1 is a basic setup. This is somewhat expected as the operating conditions are moderate. Significant performance differences have been observed in the results of more complex scenarios. For example, the setup in Scenario 2 (Challenge 6.2) represents a more complex operating condition in which significant performance differences are expected.

Table 6.4 Scenario 2 simulation parameters

Parameter		Value
Number of servers		400
Number of applications		2
App capacity (MIPS)	App1	30 000
	App2	15 000
Request rate (initial)		1 req/s
Server capacity (MIPS)		40 000
Internal variables	RetrieveRate	5×
	RequestRateParam	10
	RetrieveRequestParam	0.2
	BurstSize	2 500 ms
	ServerProvisioningTime	3 (1.5 s)
Managers (for *NoInt* and *Int*)		PeM and PoM
DZConst (initial)		1.5

Challenge 6.2
Table 6.4 presents a second simulation scenario, 'Scenario 2' – with varying application size and inconsistent request rate. This is a more complex scenario with resource contention and burst injection. This scenario creates a situation where there is resource contention (as a result of hugely varied request sizes) and the possibility of abrupt and inefficient server deployment as a result of inconsistent request rate. This condition is perfect for testing the robustness of the stigmergy-inspired interoperability solution. The effect of resource contention and irregular (sometimes erratic) request rate is usually rapid and frequent movement of servers around the datacentre. This is made worse when there is conflict between the two managers, with one restoring servers and another powering them down, which leads to more server movement. The robustness of the interoperability solution is tested by its level of sensitivity to this situation.

Conduct a new experiment using the parameters in Table 6.4 for Scenario 2. Analyse as many metrics as possible and discuss your findings about the stigmergic interoperability solution. You can access the TrAArch Simulator from Downloadable material. Once you export the simulation result to Microsoft Excel, you can analyse as many metrics as possible. Read section 5.2.1 in Chapter 5 for details on how to use the simulator.

6.6 Conclusion

This chapter has presented an overview of multi-agent systems coordination and the challenges of interoperability between autonomic managers in multi-manager scenarios. The very success of autonomic computing has inevitably led to situations where multiple autonomic managers need to coexist and/or interact directly or indirectly within the same system. Potentially, problems can arise due to conflict of interest when these managers (components) coexist. This is partly as a result of increasing scale and complexity of newer systems. Interoperability challenges stem from the fact that these components could be multi-vendor supplied, upgrades in one component could trigger compatibility issues, increasing scale can introduce bottlenecks, one component may be unaware of the existence of another and components, though tested and perfected in isolation, may not have been wired at design to coexist with other components.

An overview of a few interoperability solutions has been presented. These solutions are based on different established mechanisms. An architecture-based interoperability solution that addresses complex interactions between coexisting autonomic managers has also been presented. The interoperability solution, which is based on the TrAArch architecture, builds on the Stigmergy mechanism – this mechanism allows for indirect coordination, through the operating environment, between coexisting autonomic managers. In this approach, autonomic managers are designed to sense their environment and dynamically (re)adjust (retune) their behaviour as soon as they notice process conflicts. Experimental analyses have been presented to evaluate the performance of the stigmergy-inspired interoperability solution. The importance of considering interoperability capability as an integral part of the autonomic manager design has also been proposed. This is another step towards trustworthy autonomic computing.

Chapter 7

Level of autonomicity

This book has so far covered some grounds on the pillars of trustworthy autonomic systems which ensure, amongst other things, fit-for-purpose results (dependability/reliability, continuous evaluation of control actions) and validation. Another important aspect is the support for the definition of autonomic systems in universal language. This needs to be at both system design (for understanding the system and its requirements) and post system design (for system classification and evaluation).

In this chapter, the concept of measuring the level of autonomicity (LoA) for autonomic systems is introduced. A review of some of the existing approaches for measuring level of autonomicity is presented. Finally, a quantitative technique for measuring *LoA* along several dimensions of autonomic system self-* functionalities is discussed.

In this chapter you will:

- Understand the concept and importance of measuring LoA
- Be able to classify autonomic systems

7.1 Introduction to level of autonomicity

The rapid advancement in the study of autonomic computing is not without challenges. One of these challenges is the wide range of views, within the autonomic computing community, on meaning, architecture, methodology and implementations. This proliferation of views is majorly fuelled by the lack of universal standards for the technology itself and its development. Anyone can design a system and call it autonomic – but how does one really come to that conclusion? Chapter 1 has attempted to address the issue of definitions. However, moving from that, the criticality of understanding extent of autonomicity in defining autonomic computing systems has necessitated the need for evaluating these systems. Defining the LoA of autonomic systems is one of the building blocks of trustworthy autonomic computing. Also, as identified before in section 1.2, another building block is an appropriate testing methodology that seeks to validate the autonomic system decision-making process. But to know what validation is appropriate requires knowledge of the system in terms of its extent of autonomicity (either required or exhibited).

Understanding how and being able to measure level of autonomicity make it possible to compare autonomic systems and also facilitate a proper understanding of such systems. The majority of research in this area has been qualitative and application domain specific. Existing techniques have mainly qualitatively classified autonomic systems according to some defined levels with no reference to the building blocks (core autonomic functionalities) of the systems. There is lack of quantitative approach for assessing autonomic systems. However, there have been efforts towards classifying autonomic systems according to extent of autonomicity but these efforts have not successfully met the need for assessing autonomic systems. This chapter reviews some of the early approaches and presents a generic technique for measuring LoA along several dimensions of autonomic system self-* functionalities. Recall from Chapter 1 that while self-CHOP refers to the traditional four autonomic functionalities (the self-configuring, self-healing, self-optimising, and self-protecting functionalities) self-* refers to generic autonomic functionalities, which comprises of both the self-CHOP functionalities and any other possible or application-dependent functionalities (e.g., self-stabilising, self-aware, self-regulating). This is important for the LoA solution presented in this chapter.

Designers of autonomic systems need to answer the 'How autonomic should a system be?' question. This is important because autonomic specification is a critical part of the whole system requirements definition. It helps in determining the level of autonomy required for a specific system. For this, a level of autonomy assessment tool would be required. To address post system design phase, system designers and users need to answer the 'How autonomic is a system and how is this determined?' question. This question is in two parts. On one hand is the need to define systems according to a measure of autonomicity and on the other is the method and nature of the measure. Addressing this issue is the main thrust of this chapter. Another significant aspect addressed here is the need for a standard way for assessing, comparing and evaluating different autonomic systems (with flexibility across many domains) and also in terms of their individual functionalities. Not only do we measure autonomicity but also look at how systems can be evaluated and compared in terms of their autonomic compositions.

The 'How autonomic should a system be?' question has mainly been answered with scales that describe and analyse autonomy in systems. These scales provide fundamental understanding of system autonomy by categorising autonomy according to the level of human-machine involvement in decision-making and execution. One issue with this approach is that low human involvement does not always necessarily translate to high autonomicity and vice versa. Also, these methods do not assess autonomic systems based on demonstrated functionalities but on perceived or observed outcomes (performance). Efforts in this area include scale-based approaches, which define a number of autonomy scales for ranking system autonomy. For example, Proud *et al.* [165] designed an 8-level autonomy scale to rank human-machine involvement in decision-making, Clough [166] proposed a 10-level scale for determining unmanned aerial vehicles' autonomy, and IBM's white paper [23] describes 5 levels of automation for IT and business processes. These scales only characterise autonomy levels qualitatively and offer no quantitative means of measuring level (extent) of autonomicity. So, they are more suitable for proposing an appropriate level of autonomy during the design of a new system.

The ISO/IEC 9126-1 standard decomposes overall software product quality into characteristics, sub-characteristics (attributes) and associated measures. This means that the quality of a software can be effectively determined by evaluating how it meets or demonstrates the expected attributes and sub-attributes for that particular software – assuming that there is a standardised (or at least, a generally accepted) set of domain-specific attributes. This approach can be adapted in defining a framework for measuring LoA based on the autonomic system self-* functionalities. Systems are well-defined by their set of functional capabilities and a measure of these capabilities will form a better representation of the systems. These functional capabilities may be extended to mean, in other systems, characteristics (or attributes) and sub-characteristics (or sub-attributes). The technique presented here applies to both specific scenarios of core autonomic functionalities, the self-CHOP functionalities, and general scenarios of all possible essential functionalities, the self-* functionalities. This extends the scope of deployment of the technique thereby making it generic. Specific metrics for each of the functionalities are identified and the cumulative measure of these metrics defines a LoA. This technique is robust as it is based on the functionalities of systems making it possible to be tailored to suit the needs of any application domain. Also, it can be used for both autonomic and non-autonomic systems – all that is required is to identify system characteristics (autonomic functionalities in the case of autonomic systems) and define metrics for each characteristic or functionality. However, this book focuses on autonomic systems. The novelty of the technique is in the fact that it offers a quantitative measure of LoA in terms of system's functionalities-based description and can be flexibly applied across different application instances. This approach is originally published in Reference [167].

7.2 Measuring LoA

This section starts with a brief overview of existing techniques for classifying autonomic systems. This is followed by an introduction to autonomic measuring metrics, which are used in the proposed LoA measuring technique presented next.

One major existing proposal for classifying autonomic systems according to the extent of autonomicity (or measuring LoA) is the scale-based approach. This approach, based on the level of human-machine involvement in decision-making and execution, uses a scale of (1 – max) to define a system's LoA where '1' is the lowest autonomic level, usually describing a state of least machine involvement in decision-making and 'max' is the highest autonomic level describing a state of least human involvement (which can be different for different functionalities).

Examples in this category include References [165, 166, 168 and 169. Clough [166] proposes a scale of (1–10) for determining unmanned aerial vehicles' (UAV's) autonomy. Level 1 'remotely piloted vehicle' describes the traditional remotely piloted aircraft, while level 10 'fully autonomous' describes the ultimate goal of complete autonomy for UAVs. Clough populates the levels between by defining metrics for UAVs. Clough's work, although specific to UAVs, is useful for the technique presented here as it gives an example of how metrics can be used to define a system's operational characteristics.

Sheridan [168] also proposes a 10-level scale of autonomic degrees. Unlike Clough's scale, Sheridan's levels 2–4 centre on who makes the decisions (human or machine), while levels 5–9 centre on how to execute decisions. Proud *et al.* [165], in a study to determine the level of autonomy of a particular autonomic system decision-making function, developed an 8-level autonomy assessment tool (Table 7.1). The tool ranks each of the OODA (observe, orient, decide and act) loop functions across Sheridan's proposed scale of autonomy [168]. OODA is a decision-making loop architecture for autonomic systems. The scale's bounds (1 and 8) correspond to complete human and complete machine responsibilities, respectively.

The authors of that work [165] first identified the tasks encompassed by each of the functions and then tailored each level of the scale to fit appropriate tasks. The challenge here is ensuring relative consistency in magnitude of change between levels across the functions. The levels are broken into three sections. Levels 1–2 (human is primary, computer is secondary), levels 3–5 (computer and human have similar levels of responsibility) and levels 6–8 (computer is independent of human). To determine the level of autonomy needed to design into a spaceflight vehicle, Proud *et al.* [165] needed a way to map particular functions onto the scale and determine how autonomous each function should be. They designed a questionnaire and sent it to system designers, programmers and operators. The questionnaire considered what they call 'factors for determining level of autonomy', which include level of autonomy trust limit and cost/benefit ratio limit. This implies that a particular level of autonomy for a function is favoured when a balance is struck between trust and cost/benefit ratio limits. Ultimately, the pertinent question is 'How autonomous should future spaceflight vehicles be?.' This is a brilliant technique towards answering the first identified question ('How autonomic should a system be?').

IBM's five levels of automation [23] describes the extent of automation of the IT and business processes. However, these levels are too narrowly defined and the differentiation between levels is too vague to describe the diversity of self-management in autonomic systems.

One major concern with the scale-based approach is that a system is not necessarily less autonomic when a human interferes with its operations and vice versa. Another is the complexity of applying the approach across different application instances – this is in terms of populating the levels in-between the scales: the differentiation between levels is complex (and subjective and thus can vary significantly depending on who is using the approach) to determine appropriate magnitude for each level. In general, the autonomy scale approach is qualitative and does not discriminate between behaviour types. A more appropriate approach should comprise both qualitative and quantitative (as a way of assigning magnitude or value to the description and classification of systems) measures. These concerns are considered and addressed in the approach presented in this book.

Huang *et al.* [169] describe a government's front for addressing the challenge of classifying the pervasive Unmanned Systems (UMS) according to their levels of autonomy. They allude that UMS' autonomy cannot be rightly evaluated quantitatively without thorough technical basis and that the development of autonomy levels for unmanned systems must consider factors like task complexity, human interaction and environmental difficulty. The product in Reference [169] is autonomy

Table 7.1 Level of autonomy assessment scale by Proud et al. [165]. An example of a scale-based autonomy classification approach.

Level	Observe	Orient	Decide	Act
8	The computer gathers, filters and prioritizes data without displaying any information to the human.	The computer predicts, interprets and integrates data into a result which is not displayed to the human.	The computer performs ranking tasks. The computer performs final ranking, but does not display results to the human.	Computer executes automatically and does not allow any human interaction.
7	The computer gathers, filters and prioritizes data without displaying any information to the human. Though, a program functioning flag is displayed.	The computer anlayses, predicts, interprets and integrates data into a result which is only displayed to the human if result fits programmed context (context dependant summaries).	The computer performs ranking tasks. The computer performs final ranking and displays a reduced set of ranked options without displaying 'why' decisions were made to the human.	Computer executes automatically and only informs the human if required by context. It allows for override ability after execution. Human is shadow for contingencies.
6	The computer gathers, filters and prioritizes information displayed to the human.	The computer overlays predictions with analysis and interprets the data. The human is shown all results.	The computer performs ranking tasks and displays a reduced set of ranked options while displaying 'why'decisions were made to the human.	Computer executes automatically, informs the human, and allows for override ability after execution. Human is shadow for contingencies.

(Continues)

Table 7.1 Continued

Level	Observe	Orient	Decide	Act
5	The computer is responsible for gathering the information for the human, but it only displays non-prioritised, filtered information.	The computer overlays predictions with analysis and interprets the data. The human shadows the interpretation for contingencies.	The computer performs ranking tasks. All results, including 'why' decisions were made, are displayed to the human.	Computer allows the human a context-dependant restricted time to veto before execution. Human is shadow for contingencies.
4	The computer is responsible for gathering the information for the human and for displaying all information, but it highlights the non-prioritised, relevant information for the user.	The computer analyses the data and makes predictions, though the human is responsible for interpretation of the data.	Both human and computer perform ranking tasks, the results from the computer are considered prime.	Computer allows the human a preprogrammed restricted time to veto before execution. Human is shadow for contingencies.
3	The computer is responsible for gathering and displaying unfiltered, unprioritised information for the human. The human still is the prime monitor for all information.	Computer is the prime source of analysis and predictions, with human shadow for contingencies. The human is responsible for interpretation of the data.	Both human and computer perform ranking tasks, the results from the human are considered prime.	Computer executes decision after human approval. Human is shadow for contingencies.
2	Human is the prime source for gathering and monitoring all data, with computer shadow for emergencies.	Human is the prime source of analysis and predictions, with computer shadow for contingencies. The human is responsible for interpretation of the data.	The human performs all ranking tasks, but the computer can be used as a tool for assistance.	Human is the prime source of execution, with computer shadow for contingencies.
1	Human is the only source for gathering and monitoring (defined as filtering, prioritising and understanding) all data.	Human is responsible for analysing all data, making predictions, and interpretation of the data.	The computer does not assist in or perform ranking tasks. Human must do it all.	Human alone can execute decision.

levels for unmanned systems (ALFUS) framework which, more specifically, provides the terminology for prescribing and evaluating the level of autonomy that an unmanned system can achieve. The framework, in which the levels of autonomy can be described, addresses the technical aspects of UMS and includes terms and definitions (set of standard terms and definitions that support the autonomy level metrics), detailed model for autonomy levels, summary model for autonomy levels and guidelines, processes and use cases. While it is accepted that autonomicity cannot be correctly evaluated without thorough technical basis, the approach in this book further considers key functionalities of autonomic systems rather than individual breakdown of technical operations and operational conditions – a major difference with this work. The work in Reference [169] has been updated in Reference [170] to focus more on standardised categorisation of UMS.

In evaluating the autonomy of software agents, Alonso *et al.* [171] believe that a measure of autonomy (or any other agent feature) can be determined as a function of well-defined characteristics. First, they identify the agent autonomy attributes (as self-control, functional independence and evolution capability) and then define a set of measures for each of the identified attributes. By normalising the results of the defined measures using a set of functions, the agent's LoA is defined. This method considers autonomicity measure with reference to system's characteristics and attributes. But these 'characteristics' are a broad range of attributes that describe a system, which also include features outside the system's core functionalities. This approach differs to the approach proposed in this book in terms of the constitution of system attributes (or functionalities), but the important aspect to note is the idea of defining a system with respect to its attributes and characteristics. This approach has been adapted for the solution presented in this book but with reference to [core] autonomic self-* functionalities.

7.2.1 Autonomic measuring metrics

This section introduces the core four autonomic functionalities and suggests how to define metrics for each of them. Though metrics are application domain dependent, the ideas presented in this section are generic and serve as examples only. Autonomic functionalities are emergent and these vary (or are defined) according to application instances. The point is that, for any system (whether autonomic or not), there are required functionalities which can be measurable by some identifiable metrics. For any system, it is left to the designer and/or user to identify appropriate functionalities and define corresponding metrics. This work suggests how to define at least one metric for each of the functionalities (using the self-CHOP functionalities as example). This is part of a wide and separate research focus. This section only suggests examples of how autonomic metrics can be generated. How metrics values can be normalised is presented in section 7.2.2. We will start with a definition of each CHOP functionality, as presented in Reference [167]. (For more on these definitions see [6, 7].)

Self-configuring: A system is self-configuring when it is able to automate its own installation and setup according to high-level goals. For example, when a new component is introduced into an autonomic system, it registers itself so that other components can easily interact with it. The extent of this co-existence is a measure of self-configuration, measured as ratio of the actual number of components successfully interacting with the new component (after configuration) to the number of components expected to interact with the new component. This measures the extent to which a system is distorted by an upgrade. A system is self-configuring to the extent of its ability to curb this distortion.

Self-healing: A system is self-healing when it is able to detect errors or symptoms of potential errors by monitoring its own platform and automatically initiate remediation [8]. Fault tolerance is a typical example of self-healing. It allows the system to continue its operation possibly at a reduced level instead of stopping completely as a result of a part failure. One critical factor here is latency, i.e., the amount of time the system takes to detect a problem and then react to it. Reaction time is defined as a metric for self-healing capability. This is crucial to the reliability of a system. If a change occurs at time t_a and the system is able to detect and work out a new configuration and is ready to adapt at time t_b, then the difference between t_b and t_a defines the reaction time. Where variations of reaction time are possible, average may be taken instead. A case scenario is a stock trading system where time is of paramount importance. The system needs to track changes (e.g., in trade volumes, price, rates) in real time in order to make profitable trading decisions.

Self-optimising: A system is self-optimising when it is capable of adapting to meet current requirements and also of taking necessary actions to self-adjust to better its performance. Resource management (e.g., load balancing) is a typical example of self-optimisation. An autonomic system is then required to be able to learn how to adapt its state to meet the new challenges. Also needed is consistent updating of the system's knowledge of how to modify its state. State is defined by a set of variables such as current load distribution, CPU utilisation, resource usage, etc. The values of these variables are influenced by certain event occurrences like new requirements (e.g., process fluctuations or disruptions). By changing the values of these variables, the event also changes the state of the system. The status of these variables is then updated by a set of executable statements (policies) to meet any new requirement. A typical example would be an autonomic job scheduling system. At first, the job scheduler could assign equal processing time quanta to all systems requiring processing time. The size of the time quantum becomes the current state and as events occur (e.g., fluctuations in processing time requirement, disruptions of any kind), the scheduler is able to adjust the processing time allocation according to priorities specified as policies. In this way the state of the system is updated. But this may lead to erratic tuning (as a result of over or under compensation) causing instability in the system.

Stability is defined as a measure of self-optimisation. If an event leads to erratic behaviour, incoherent results or system is not able to retrace its working state beyond a certain safe margin – a margin within which instability is tolerated, then the system is not effectively self-optimising. Note that where metrics are an affirmation of a capability, such as in this case, this can be normalised into a value as discussed in section 7.2.2.

Self-protecting: A system is self-protecting when it is able to detect and protect itself from attacks by automatically configuring and tuning itself to achieve security. It may also be capable of proactively preventing a security breach through its knowledge based on previous occurrences. While self-healing is reactive, self-protecting is proactive. A proactive system, e.g., would maintain a log of trends (or signatures) leading to security threats and breaches and a list of solutions to resolve them – a list of problems and corresponding solutions only applies to self-healing. One major metric here is the ability of the system to prevent security issues based on its experience of past occurrences. For example, let us assume $p \in \{P_{ij}\}$ to be true if i^{th} trend leads to j^{th} problem where p_{ij} is a log of all identified trends and corresponding problems. p is a particular instance of trend-problem combination. A self-protecting manager will avoid a situation of same trend leading to the same problem again by blocking the problem, addressing it or preventatively shutting down part of the system. Ability to detect repeat events E is defined as a self-protecting metric. E is a Boolean value (*True* indicates that the manager is able to stop a repeating problem while *False* indicates otherwise). If we choose two samples of $\{P_{ij}\}$ at different times (t_1 and t_2), then $E = True \quad \forall_{ij} \text{if} \{P_{ij}\} t_1 \cap \{P_{ij}\} t_2 = \varnothing$. Different trends may lead to the same problem but a repeated trend-problem combination indicates a failure of the system to prevent a reoccurrence.

7.2.2 *Normalisation and scaling of autonomic metrics dimensions*

There is still a point though that needs to be addressed. When computing LoA, we are normalising values that are products of aggregated metric values of different units and dimensions. Depending on the application domain, metrics could be scalar (of different measures) or non-scalar values (e.g., observing a capability, Boolean based decisions). So, despite what measure or form these metrics take, there needs to be a way of scaling the metric values of all contributing metrics to a centric unit of autonomic metric contribution within a certain normalised range. But, because the range of values and metrics can vary significantly, each choice of how these are scaled can influence very differently the final LoA. A possible solution is to define scaling factors for all contributing metrics within the normalised range of [0, 1] in this case. In this way, the metrics' values, irrespective of units of measure, are normalised into real numbers that are summed to give LoA. One challenge here, though, is defining the scaling factors. Two simple methods for normalisation are suggested:

1. By ranking values according to high, medium, and low. The meaning of this ranking is metric-dependent and is based on a defined margin. For example, if a maximum expected value is 6, a value of 0–2 will likely be ranked low, while

3–4 will be ranked medium and 5–6 high. A medium value would contribute 50 per cent of the metric's autonomic value contribution in the range of [0, 1], while the two extremes would contribute 0 and 100 per cent — these may differ depending on choice of usage. This can be used for scalar metrics like the co-existence and reaction time metrics discussed in section 7.2.1 earlier.

2. By having a Boolean kind of contribution where two values can suggest two extremes – either affirming a capability or not. For example, if a 'True' outcome affirms a capability then it contributes 100 per cent of the autonomic value contribution, while a 'False' outcome contributes zero. Another example in this category is where an instance of an event either does or does not confirm a capability (e.g., the stability metric for self-optimising functionality). Other specific methods, like the Mahalanobis distance discussed and used in Reference 172, have been proposed. In scaling the different dimensions of distance between points (measured in different distance measurement units), Huebscher and McCann [172] used a simplified form of the Mahalanobis distance, where for each dimension, they compute the standard deviation over all available values and then express the components of the distances between points as multiples of the standard deviation for each component.

For this work, autonomic contributions across functionalities should be normalised within the range ($0.0 \leq a_{ij} \leq 1.0$) so that the total autonomic contribution of each functionality is a maximum of the number of metrics for that functionality according to the normalisation rule in section 7.3.2. Scaling and normalisation should be used uniformly to enable the evaluation and comparison of different systems. As noted earlier, autonomics measuring metrics is a new research area and also not a main focus of this book. What is provided here, in terms of metrics, normalisation, and scaling, serve as examples and can be improved upon.

7.3 Methodology for measuring LoA

This section presents a quantitative technique for measuring LoA. This technique is based on the self-* functionalities and is presented in two formats – for specific and generic considerations. The approach is to define LoA for an autonomic system in terms of its extent of achieving the self-* functionalities [8]. Note that 'self-*' is generic and covers all the self-CHOP functionalities as well as any identified functionalities, relevant for a particular autonomic system. So, a system must demonstrate at least a certain level of one of the self-* functionalities in order to be considered autonomic. It also follows that, for a particular autonomic system, a set of autonomic functionalities may be identified as required for that particular system. If the system demonstrates all of the required functionalities that system is said to have achieved 'full' autonomicity. The methods here are defined mathematically.

Each autonomic functionality is defined by one or more metrics, which are combined together to give a level of autonomic value for that functionality. This means that each autonomic metric contributes a proportion of the autonomic value for the relevant autonomic functionality. Metrics and functionalities may be weighted to reflect relevance or importance. The cumulative normalisation of the measure of all metrics (for all functionalities) defines a LoA. The normalisation of values makes it possible and easy to compare different autonomic systems. As there is no standardised list of functionalities that defines an autonomic system, the proposed approach is generic to accommodate evolving functionalities as may be defined by the user. Figure 7.1 illustrates the proposed approach. An autonomic system is expressed along the dimensions of its functionalities and corresponding functionality metrics.

Note that the number of autonomic metrics may vary for the same functionality across different autonomic systems. For example, self-healing for autonomic system 1 may have different number of metrics compared to self-healing for autonomic system 2. Normalisation is performed to ensure that the resultant LoA values are always between 0 and 1 regardless of the number of metrics or the weight of individual metrics. Given that any autonomic system is defined by a number of self-* autonomic functionalities, say *n*, the following mathematical expression represents the possible combinations of the functionalities:

$$\sum_{r=1}^{n} nC_r \tag{7.1}$$

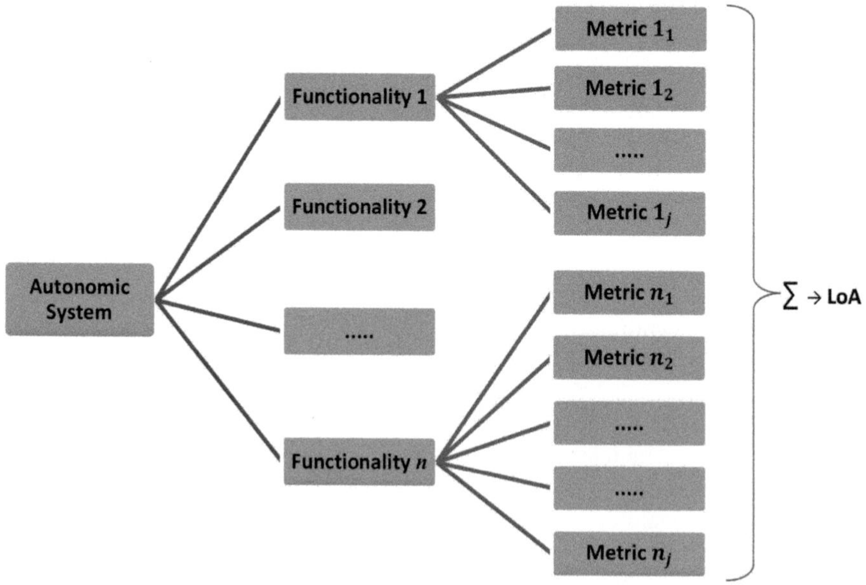

Figure 7.1 Illustration of how LoA is achieved by summing the metric autonomic value contributions of all metrics defining all functionalities of a particular autonomic system [167]

The above expression (7.1) indicates the possible functionality compositions of a system where n is the number of functionalities (the self-*) and r is a category of the possibilities – a specific implementation combination of the functionalities. For example, if $n = 4$ (in the case of the self-CHOP functionalities), then $r \leq 4$. With $r = 4$, the expression computes to 15 which indicates the number of possible functionality combinations – (see Figure 7.2). Note that the 16th category is non-autonomic. The functionalities may not be of equal importance to an application domain, so categories indicate which functionality is important to an application domain. Also, depending on choice of usage, this may be defined as required functionalities (in which case $r = n$) or demonstrated functionalities (in which case $r \leq n$). Required functionalities are those functionalities that are not optional for a particular system while demonstrated functionalities are a combination of required and optional ('nice to have') functionalities demonstrated by the autonomic manager. For example, self-optimisation is a required functionality in a load balancing system while self-protection may be optional. So, if a load balancing autonomic manager self-optimises as well as self-protects, then it can be said that in terms of required

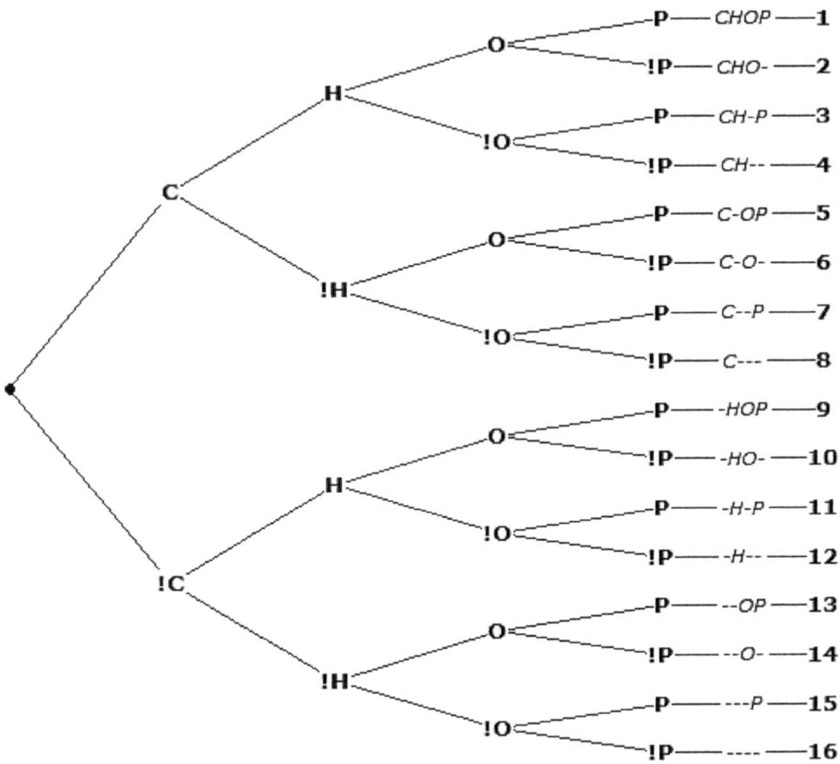

Figure 7.2 Combination of autonomic functionalities (for self-CHOP systems with n=4 and r=4). This is a representative example as n could potentially be more than 4 as in self- based systems [167].*

functionality $r = 1$ while in terms of demonstrated functionalities $r = 2$. The importance of each functionality is indicated by the weight assigned to it as discussed later.

We understand that autonomic functionalities may overlap as they are not necessarily orthogonal. The generic case methodology addresses situations where some algorithms may influence several autonomic functionalities by applying weighting. By implication, if an algorithm influences more than one functionality, the level of influence is taken care of by the weights applied. We also understand that systems, and by extension, functionalities, are not always linear as all functional adjustments may not uniformly affect the achieved LoA. The case of non-linearity can also be catered for by weighting and normalisation. Weights are applied to reflect impact. For example, the level of one functionality can be indirectly proportional to another and this is dependent on importance or relevance which is reflected by the weights. In general, dealing with (non-)orthogonality and (non-)linearity are open challenges that need further addressing. However, the proposed LoA methodology is flexible and can be applied to both cases.

Two LoA methodologies, addressing specific and generic cases, are presented. For the specific case, the autonomic functionalities are known and fixed while for the generic case, the autonomic functionalities can be any number. Table 7.2 presents a

Table 7.2 LoA notations [167]

Key	Description
a_{ij}	Autonomic value contribution for individual metric j of functionality i
k_i	Autonomic value contribution for individual functionality i
LoA	Total LoA measure for all n_i and m_{ij}
M_i	Number of metrics for functionality i
M_c , M_h , M_o, and M_p	Number of metrics for each of the self-CHOP functionalities, respectively
j	Individual metrics
n	Number of functionalities
i	Individual functionalities
r	Category of functionalities possible combinations
R_i	Rank of a functionality i in the autonomic composition of a system
v_i	Weighting for functionality i
w_{ij}	Weighting for metric j of functionality i
c_i, h_i, o_i and p_i	Autonomic metric contributions of the functionalities for a CHOP-based system

All indices (i and j) begin at 1

list of notations used in the mathematical algorithms that define the methodologies. To measure the LoA of a system, we require the following:

- The *number of functionalities* present or required in a particular system – i.e., a specific implementation combination of the functionalities.
- The *number of metrics* identified for the respective functionalities.
- The *weighting* assigned to functionalities and metrics according to priority or importance.

7.3.1 A specific case method

This method works well in cases where autonomic functionalities are orthogonal and for specific systems of limited (known) number of functionalities. Now, following on from the initial expression 7.1) for the possible combination of all autonomic functionalities, and taking a specific system in isolation (e.g., a system with only four functionalities, say, a self-CHOP-based system), this will give 15 possible combinations (Figure 7.2). Note that $n = 4$, while $r = 1, 2, 3$ *and* 4 – zero value is a special case so it is excluded and not considered further as it means the system demonstrates no autonomic functionality. The self-CHOP functionalities may not be of equal importance to an application domain so categories indicate what CHOP functionality is important to an application domain. Category 2, $r = 2$, means that only two functionalities are of importance to the system's domain – so e.g., {C, H, Not O, Not P} is a specific category representing a system indicated by System 4 (CH--) in Figure 7.2 . Note that the numbers [1–16] on the right of Figure 7.2 are just labels identifying individual systems and not categories.

According to Figure 7.2, an autonomic system, within the boundaries of the self-CHOP autonomic functionalities, can be described in one of fifteen ways. Each trace of line (1–16) from start to finish represents an autonomic system except line 16. If we can define autonomic metrics for each of the functionalities, the LoA for that particular system is calculated by the sum total of the autonomicity in each of the constituent functionalities for that systems (7.1). For example, the LoA of autonomic system 6 in Figure 7.2 will be the summation of the autonomic metrics defining the self-configuring and self-optimising functionalities.

$$LoA = \sum_{i=1}^{M_C} [c_i] + \sum_{i=1}^{M_h} [h_i] + \sum_{i=1}^{M_O} [o_i] + \sum_{i=1}^{M_p} [p_i] \qquad (7.2)$$

where, M_c, M_h, M_o and M_p are the numbers of identified metrics for the respective functionalities. c_i, h_i, o_i and p_i are the autonomic metric contributions of the functionalities. These may have values of different measures which can be normalised, as explained in section 7.2.2. It is important to note that the specific case method is limited to addressing systems of discrete functionalities. There is need to cater for systems of indiscrete functionalities as well.

7.3.2 A generic case method

This section presents a generic method for calculating LoA for autonomic systems of unknown number of functionalities. This LoA approach is suited for application across different scenario instances. This is achieved by introducing weighting to the specific case approach. This is because autonomic functionalities are not necessarily orthogonal – a single behaviour could enhance the contribution of more than one metric and this could be across more than one functionality. This is important because the measurement approach has to work in situations where the functionalities either are or are not orthogonal. In cases of non-orthogonality, the weighting is applied to tune sensitivity of contributing behaviours. For flexibility, all values are normalised within the same interval range (0, 1):

$$\text{Normalisation interval}=\begin{cases} 0.0 \le LoA \le 1.0 \\ 0.0 \le a_{ij} \le 1.0 \\ 0.0 \le w_{ij} \le 1.0 \\ 0.0 \le v_i \le 1.0 \end{cases} \tag{7.3}$$

The need for normalisation is to be able to compare different systems and address varying circumstances. The way we measure the system should not on its own change the outcome, e.g., higher number of metrics should not result in higher LoA value and as well does not translate to being 'more autonomic'. So, in all cases, and for normalisation purposes, the following rules must apply:

$$\text{Normalisation rule}\begin{cases} \sum_{i=1}^{M_i} w_{ij} = 1.0 \rightarrow \text{the sum of the weights for all} \\ \text{metrics for a given} \\ \text{functionality must be 1.0} \\ \sum_{i=1}^{n} v_i = 1.0 \rightarrow \text{the sum of the weights for all} \\ \text{functionalities must be 1.0} \\ \sum_{i=1}^{M_i} a_{ij} \le M_i \rightarrow \text{the sum of all metric autonomic} \\ \text{contribution for a giving functionality is} \\ \text{a maximum ofthenumberofmetrics for} \\ \text{that functionality as } 0 \le \text{a}_{\text{ij}} \le 1.0 \end{cases} \tag{7.4}$$

where w_{ij} and a_{ij} are both with reference to individual functionalities and so are bound to the number of metrics for those functionalities (M_i) while v_i is with reference to the system itself and so is bound to the total number of functionalities (n) for the system. This enables the total individual autonomic value contribution ($\sum \boldsymbol{k_i}$) to go up to n (i.e., not be limited to the four self-CHOP functionalities) – see (7.5) .

If we ignore, for now, all indices and have a top-level view of the proposed LoA calculation, for a single functionality, then:

$$k = (a \times w) \leq 1.0$$
$$\sum k \leq n \tag{7.5}$$

That is to say, if individual functionality autonomic contribution is bound to maximum of '1', then the total autonomic contribution of all functionalities will be a maximum number of functionalities, n. So, the overall achieved LoA will be the sum of the product of total autonomic contribution and weighting:

$$LoA = \sum (k \times v)$$
$$\rightarrow \sum [(a \times w) \times v] \qquad \forall\, a, w, v \leq 1.0 \tag{7.6}$$

Decomposing (7.5) and (7.6) above, and for total autonomic value contribution of all functionalities n_i:

$$k_i = \sum_{j=1}^{M_i} (a_{ij} \times w_{ij}) \;\; \forall\, i \; and \, j \tag{7.7}$$

where, j represents individual metrics and M_i represents the number of metrics. Applying the functionality weighting to the individual autonomic value contribution (k_i):

$$LoA_i = v_i \times \left(\sum_{j=1}^{M_i} (a_{ij} \times w_{ij}) \right) \qquad \forall\, i \; and \, j \tag{7.8}$$

So, the overall achieved autonomicity level LoA is then given by summing (7.8) for all values of i and j:

$$LoA = \sum_{i=1}^{n} \left(v_i \times \left(\sum_{j=1}^{M_i} (a_{ij} \times w_{ij}) \right) \right) \tag{7.9}$$

In the case of orthogonality or where weighting is not required, the LoA is given by the basic expression:

Table 7.3 Autonomic contributing values for a n = 3 system

Functionality (n)	**Weight** (v_i)	**Metric** (M_i)	**Metric weight** (w_{ij})	**Metric contribution** (a_{ij})
Self-optimisation	0.60	Stability	0.25	30
		Trend analysis	0.50	20
		Switching	0.25	50
Self-healing	0.30	Sensitivity	0.40	50
		Robust	0.60	50
Self-configuration	0.10	Unsupervised	0.25	25
		Continuous	0.25	50
		Awareness	0.50	25

$$LoA = \sum_{i=1}^{n} \sum_{j=1}^{M_i} (a_{ij}) \tag{7.10}$$

Equation (7.10) is equivalent to (7.2). Procedure 7.1 is a basic algorithm of the implementation of the proposed measure of autonomicity.

Procedure 7.1: Algorithm for implementing LoA

```
Input (main) variables: n and M_i
i = 1, 2, …, n and j = 1, 2, …, M_i
        if at n_1, M_1 = y, then j = 1, 2, ..., y
      k_1 = (w_11 × a_11) + (w_12 × a_12) + (w_13 × a_13)
k(1) = 0 //initialising k array
for i = 1 to n
  for j = 1 to M_(i)
    sum(j) = w(ij) × a(ij)
    k(i) = k(i) + sum(j)
  next j
next i
  LoA = (k_1 × v_1) + … + (k_n × v_n)
```

LoA example:

To illustrate this system of measurement, consider a very basic example to explain the implementation of the technique. Table 7.3 shows relevant values for a particular self-optimising, self-healing and self-configuring (i.e., three functionalities) system. The LoA of the system can be calculated as follows:

$$n = 3$$

For $n_1 : M_1 = 3$, $v_1 = 0.60$, $w_{11} = 0.25$, $w_{12} = 0.50$, $w_{13} = 0.25$, $a_{11} = 0.30$, $a_{12} = 0.20$ and $a_{13} = 0.50$

For $n_2 : M_2 = 2$, $v_2 = 0.30$, $w_{21} = 0.40$, $w_{22} = 0.60$, $a_{21} = 0.50$ and $a_{22} = 0.50$

For $n_3 : M_3 = 3$, $v_3 = 0.10$, $w_{31} = 0.25$, $w_{32} = 0.25$, $w_{33} = 0.50$, $a_{31} = 0.25$, $a_{32} = 0.50$ and $a_{33} = 0.25$

$k_1 = (a_{11} * w_{11}) + (a_{12} * w_{12}) + (a_{13} * w_{13}) = (0.30 * 0.25) + (0.20 * 0.50) + (0.50 * 0.25)$

$= (0.075) + (0.10) + (0.125) = 0.30$

$k_2 = (a_{21} * w_{21}) + (a_{22} * w_{22}) = (0.50 * 0.40) + (0.50 * 0.60)$

$= (0.20) + (0.30) = 0.50$

$k_3 = (a_{31} * w_{31}) + (a_{32} * w_{32}) + (a_{33} * w_{33}) = (0.25 * 0.25) + (0.50 * 0.25) + (0.25 * 0.50)$

$= (0.063) + (0.125) + (0.125) = 0.313$

then,

LoA $= (\boldsymbol{k_1} * \boldsymbol{v_1}) + (\boldsymbol{k_2} * \boldsymbol{v_2}) + (\boldsymbol{k_3} * \boldsymbol{v_3})$

$= (0.30 * 0.60) + (0.50 * 0.30) + (0.313 * 0.10)$

$0.18 + 0.15 + 0.0313 = 0.3613$

7.4 Evaluating autonomic systems

Evaluating autonomic systems using (7.2) or (7.9) gives their separate LoA values. – which are aggregated values. This, however, does not give a fine-grained picture of the systems' performances in terms of individual functionalities. Systems are classified according to categories (r). This is in terms of what self-* functionalities are required or demonstrated in their specific application domains. One thing remains to be clarified at this point: 'How do we rank each functionality in the autonomic composition of a system?' This can be in terms of importance or extent of functionality provided. We focus on the later – the extent of functionality provided as against what is needed. Take for instance, if two systems are of the same category we may wish to know which of them provides a greater degree of say self-healing (or any other self-*) functionality in any application domain. To address this, a function that measures agent's decision-making power in a multiagent autonomic system defined in Reference [173] is adapted. The rank of a functionality $\boldsymbol{R_i}$ in the autonomic composition of a system is defined by the ratio of its autonomic contribution ($(k_i \times v_i)$ or $\boldsymbol{a_{ij}}$) to the total autonomic contribution of all metrics defining the composite functionalities of that system:

$$R_i = \frac{(k_i \times v_i)}{LoA} \tag{7.11}$$

In the case of (7.10) weighting is considered. But in a case where weighting is not considered, $\boldsymbol{R_i}$ is given in:

$$R_i = \frac{\sum_{j=1}^{M_i} a_{ij}}{LoA} \tag{7.12}$$

Table 7.4 ***Challenge 7.1*** *This table is a representation of three systems – SysA, SysB and SysC. These are three progressive stages of the same system, showing different autonomic capabilities. This means that the systems are all in the same domain and are expected to have/demonstrate the same autonomic functionalities,* $n = 4$ *and* $r = 3$*. Calculate the LoA of all three systems.*

Characteristics (metrics)	Label	Contributing CHOP	SysA	SysB	SysC
Continuous	Knt	C	√	√	√
Unsupervised	Uns	C	√	√	√
Trends examination	TE	O	-	√	√
Stability	Stb	O	-	√	√
Dynamic (logic switching)	DS	O	-	-	√
Signal characteristics	SC	C	√	√	√
Signal differentiation	SD	C	√	√	√
Failure sensitivity (sensors)	FS	H	-	-	-
Robust (fault tolerance)	Rbs	H	-	-	√

where ($\boldsymbol{k_i}$ or $\boldsymbol{a_{ij}}$) is the autonomic contribution of the considered functionality which could be the summation $\boldsymbol{c_i}$, $\boldsymbol{h_i}$, $\boldsymbol{o_i}$ or $\boldsymbol{p_i}$ in (7.2) or the calculation of $\boldsymbol{k_i}$ in (7.7) or the summation of $\boldsymbol{a_{ij}}$ (e.g., the case in (7.10)). With (7.11) , (7.12) any composite functionality can be ranked in terms of their autonomic contribution.

7.5 Conclusion

This chapter has discussed the idea of measuring LoA and has presented a quantitative approach. The methodology presented here is a two-dimensional definition, supporting only two levels of description – a system on one hand and its characteristics (functionalities) on the other hand. To support higher dimensional definition – a system, its characteristics and sub-characteristics, a bit of adaptation is required.

Also note that while this approach can be used to quantitatively measure the LoA of an autonomic system, there are assumptions to consider when comparing LoA achievements of different systems. For example, using the proposed approach, the LoA of two autonomic systems can only be directly compared if both systems are of the same category (i.e., if the same number and level of autonomic functionalities are required for both systems). It is also assumed that all autonomic metric contributions would be normalised within the range of (0–1).

Chapter 8

Conclusions and future work

This chapter concludes the work and summarises the key points covered in this book. It also discusses the direction of future work.

Autonomic and self-managing systems are now increasingly pervasive across an ever-widening spectrum of application domains. The autonomic technology is advancing at a high rate, yet there are no universal standards for the technology itself, the design methods and the definitions used. On the positive side, this meant that researchers had (and still have) a very wide scope for potential ideas (for evaluating a wide range of techniques) and improvements into the technology. On the negative side, the lack of universal standards, definitions, design and implementation fuels the proliferation of views. This is in terms of the research community getting stuck and everyone pursuing their individual approaches as against a coherent and consistent standardised and widely accepted approach. In the end, this has led to a number of difficult challenges and has not made the autonomic research any easier. For example, there have been significant limitations to the way in which autonomic systems are validated, with heavy reliance on traditional design-time techniques, despite the highly dynamic behaviour of such systems in dealing with runtime configuration changes and environmental and context changes. These limitations ultimately undermine the trustability of autonomic systems and are barriers to eventual certification. This book has focused on autonomic trustworthiness, setting the groundwork for the introduction of standards for autonomic computing, and with a longer-term vision of contributing towards certification of autonomic systems, which entails providing behavioural guarantees for these dynamic adaptive systems despite exposure to changing environmental and operating contexts.

The background study (Chapter 2) shows that research efforts, in the beginning, predominantly concentrated on autonomic design and architecture with bespoke application of autonomic techniques to specific problems in isolation. This book has established the evolution of the autonomic computing paradigm, identifying what has been achieved in the first two decades of the introduction of autonomic computing and the remaining open challenges. There is a lack of concrete effort towards trustworthy autonomics, despite its significance to the goal of autonomic computing, and as a result attaining autonomic system certification still has a long way to go. It is proposed, in this book, that the first vital step in this chain is to introduce robust techniques by which the systems can be described in universal language, starting with a description of, and means to measure the extent of autonomicity exhibited by a particular system. Referred to as the level of autonomicity (LoA), this is covered in Chapter 7 of this book. Also, this book posits that trustworthy autonomic computing is essential to attaining autonomic system certification and that a robust solution would need to be thought through from design up support for trustworthiness should be designed in and integral at the architectural level, and not treated as add-on. The approach to this in this book is trustworthy autonomic architecture (TrAArch) and this is covered in Chapter 5.

8.1 A case for trustworthy autonomics

The importance of trustworthiness in computing, in general, has been echoed in the computing research association's 'four grand challenges in trustworthy computing' [174] and Microsoft's white paper on trustworthy computing [141]. The Committee on Information Systems Trustworthiness in Reference [142] defines a trustworthy system as one which does what people expect it to do—and nothing more—despite any form of disruption. Although this definition has been the driving force for achieving trustworthiness both in autonomic and non-autonomic systems, the peculiarity of context dynamism in autonomic computing places unique and different challenges on trustworthiness for autonomic systems. Validation, e.g., which is an essential requirement for trustworthiness, can be design-time based for non-autonomic systems but must be runtime based for autonomic systems. Despite the different challenges, it is generally accepted that trustworthiness is a non-negotiable priority for computing systems.

For autonomic systems, the primary concern is not how a system operates to achieve a result but how dependable that result is from the user's perspective. For complete reliance on autonomic computing systems, the human user will need a level of trust and confidence that these systems will satisfy specified requirements and will not fail. It is not sufficient that systems are performing within required boundaries; outputs must also be seen to be reliable and dependable. This is necessary for self-managing systems in order to mitigate the threat of losing control and confidence [175].

Chapter 1 makes a case for trustworthy autonomic computing and has shown the importance of trustworthiness along the progressive stages towards autonomic system certification. Trustworthiness is a prerequisite to certification. With the lack of standards and generally accepted definitions of terminologies in the autonomic computing domain, it is difficult to offer a generic meaning of trustworthiness in autonomic computing as it may itself be context dependent. For example, in some circumstances it may be appropriate to allow some level of changes, which under different circumstances may be considered destabilising, and also validation is always goal dependent. However, trustworthiness, in this book, means a quality that enables us to be confident that an autonomic system will remain correct in the face of any possible contexts and environmental inputs and sequences of these, and this is achieved through robust runtime decision self-validation, process conformity, etc.

8.2 The autonomic computing state of the art

The major theme in this book deals with identifying and developing techniques to make autonomic computing systems trustworthy. To achieve this, it is important to first understand the level of work that has already gone into the autonomic computing research and how that can be harnessed. A broad analysis of autonomics research, to show the trends in and direction of the autonomic computing research and where the work needs to be concentrated in order to achieve trustworthiness and certification, has been presented. This also includes a holistic view of the entire field of research in order to gain a clearer picture of the need for and lack of effort towards trustworthy autonomic computing.

Since its introduction, in 2001, the autonomic computing concept has received strong interest amongst the academic and industrial research communities. Although efforts in this research area have led to significant successes, there are still open and emerging challenges. An analysis-by-problem approach has been used to show the pattern, in terms of maturity stages, of how researchers have attempted addressing the autonomic computing challenge. This has been addressed in two broad periods —the first decade, covering years 2001 to 2011 and the second decade, covering studies and developments from the years 2012 to 2019.

A broad and general analysis of the autonomic computing research in terms of identifying trends in the research from 2004 to 2019 has also been presented. This gives a thorough review of the state-of-the-art in trustworthy autonomics. Results show that trustworthy autonomics, which is essential to the success of autonomic computing, has received very little attention compared to other focus areas. Only 9 per cent of over 1 000 reviewed research publications identify trustworthiness as a challenge, while only about 3 per cent propose actual methodologies targeting validation and trustworthiness, although majority of these methodologies are application dependent.

8.3 Techniques that power autonomic computing

Autonomic computing has been powered by a combination of many established and new techniques. These include different algorithms, logics, functions, mechanisms, routines, tools, etc., which are used to deliver desired autonomic functionalities. Each of the autonomic functionalities can be enabled by a single technique or a combination of different techniques. For example, self-healing can be achieved by implementing any fault-tolerant technique. Self-healing can also be achieved by specifying relevant behaviours as policies (or rules). Self-optimisation can be achieved by implementing any load balancing technique. Building autonomic systems requires imbedding these autonomic enabling techniques into the design of the systems.

Chapter 3 presents some of these techniques and shows examples of how they can be used to achieve relevant autonomic computing features. These autonomic enabling techniques can individually be adapted to achieve some level of autonomic functionalities and can also be combined to achieve greater autonomic functionality. These include:

- Simple exponential smoothing
- Dead-zone logic
- Stigmergy
- Policy autonomics
- Utility function
- Fuzzy logic
- Autonomic nervous system

8.4 Trustworthy autonomic architecture

The traditional monitor-analyse-plan-execute-(MAPE) based autonomic architecture, as originally presented in the autonomic computing blueprint [23], has been widely accepted and autonomic research efforts are predominantly based on this architecture's control loop. We must admit that a good research success has been achieved using the traditional autonomic architecture. However, this book supposes, like other studies, e.g., [11, 18], that this architecture is vague and thus cannot lead to the full goal of autonomic computing. For example, the MAPE-based architecture does not explicitly and integrally support runtime self-validation, which is a prerequisite for trustworthiness; a common practice is to treat validation and other needed capabilities as add-on and these cannot be reliably retro-fitted to systems. Thus, this architecture (and its variations) is not sophisticated enough to produce trustworthy autonomic systems. At a glance, the traditional autonomic efforts look like a 'race to the finish line' to achieve self-management. But the ultimate goal of autonomic computing is not just to achieve self-management but will include achieving consistency and reliability of results through self-management.

It is also important to note that validation alone does not always guarantee trustworthiness, as each individual decision could be correct (validated), but the overall system may be inconsistent or unstable and thus not dependable. For example, a window blind controller is validated as long as it automatically opens and closes the blind within the boundaries of set policies (which may be a function of the intensity of sun rays). But it could be undesirable and distractingly annoying to human users if the blind keeps operating every minute because of slight changes in sun intensity. In this case, the actions of the controller are validated but at the same time, lead to unstable and undesirable conditions. So, it is important to consider situations beyond the level of validation where logical processes/actions could sometimes lead to overall system instability. A situation where the autonomic manager erratically (though legally) changes its mind, thereby injecting oscillation into the system, is a major concern, especially in large-scale and sensitive systems. Consequently, a new approach is required in which validation and support for trustworthiness are not treated as add-on.

A new architecture for trustworthy autonomic systems is presented in Chapter 4. Different from the traditional autonomic solutions, this new architecture consists of inbuilt mechanisms and instrumentation to support runtime self-validation and trustworthiness. The new TrAArch guarantees self-monitoring over short-time and long-time frames. At the core of the architecture are three components: the *AutonomicController*, *ValidationCheck* and *DependabilityCheck*, which allow developers to specify controls and processes to improve system trustability. To demonstrate the feasibility and practicability of TrAArch, two empirical analysis case example scenarios have been presented in Chapter 5. The first case scenario demonstrates how the proposed architecture can maximise cost, improve trustability and efficient target-marketing in a company-centric

Autonomic Marketing System that has many dimensions of freedom and which is sensitive to a number of contextual volatility. The second case example scenario, which is an implementation of a datacentre resource request and allocation management, is a more complex experimental analysis designed to analyse the performance of the proposed TrAArch architecture over existing autonomic architectures.

8.5 Interoperability

The very success of autonomic computing has inevitably led to situations where multiple autonomic managers need to coexist and/or interact directly or indirectly within the same system. This is evident, e.g., in the increasing availability of large datacentres with heterogeneous managers that are independently designed. Potentially, problems can arise as a result of conflict of interest when these managers (components) coexist. Interoperability challenges stem from the following facts:

- Components (and indeed autonomic managers) could be multi-vendor supplied
- Upgrades in one autonomic manager could trigger unfamiliar events
- Increasing scale can introduce bottlenecks
- One autonomic manager may be unaware of the existence of another
- Although tested and perfected in isolation, autonomic managers may not have been wired at design to coexist with other autonomic managers.

There is a growing concern that the lack of support for interoperability will become a break issue for future systems.

Researchers, e.g. [61, 107, 155, 176], have made valuable progress towards autonomic manager interoperability but this progress is yet to lead to a standardised approach. Although these efforts are significant, they have not successfully tackled the problem of unintended or unexpected interactions that can occur when independently developed autonomic managers coexist in a system. Further from that, and more realistically, autonomic managers may not necessarily need to know about the existence of other managers —they are designed in isolation (probably by different vendors) and operate differently (for different goals) without recourse to one another. Thus, close-coupled interoperability (i.e., where specific actions in one autonomic manager react to, or complement those of another) cannot be a reliable solution as it will require the source code and detailed functional specifications of each autonomic manager to be available to all autonomic managers. This is near impossible and where it is possible, requires a rewiring (or recoding) of each autonomic manager whenever a new autonomic manager is added to the system. A robust solution that is insulated from the identified challenges is required and this book suggests that the autonomic architecture can provide us with such solution.

This book posits that the autonomic architecture should envision (and provide for) interoperability support from the scratch. This is to say that the autonomic architecture should be scalable and dynamic enough to accommodate expected and unexpected developments. So, a stigmergic interoperability approach based on TrAArch has been presented. The stigmergic interoperability solution provides indirect coordination between autonomic managers in a multi-manager scenario without the need for planning (or pre-knowledge of the existence of other autonomic managers), control or direct communications between coexisting autonomic managers. This provides efficient collaboration (as against competition) between coexisting autonomic managers. See Chapter 3 for detailed discussion on stigmergy.

The stigmergic, architecture-based interoperability solution is presented in Chapter 6. This approach is based on the TrAArch architecture, which includes mechanisms and instrumentation to explicitly support interoperability and trustworthiness. The interoperability support of the architecture builds on the stigmergic phenomenon. In the actual sense of this approach, autonomic managers are designed to sense their environment and dynamically adjust (retune) their behaviour as soon as they notice process conflicts. In real life, this is typical of two staff that share an office space but work at different times. If each returns to their next respective shift and finds the office rearranged, they will each adjust in their arrangement of the office until an accepted compromise structure is reached. This can be achieved without both staff ever meeting. It has been shown how the TrAArch architecture can enable the design of autonomic managers that support efficient collaborations with other managers without individual awareness or pre-knowledge of each other. The experimental analysis of a multi-manager datacentre scenario shows that the proposed interoperability solution achieves over 42 per cent performance improvement (in terms of stability) in a complex, conflict-prone, coexistence of autonomic managers.

8.6 Level of autonomicity (LoA)

Measuring Level of Autonomicity (LoA) is an ongoing challenge that is being addressed in the autonomic computing research community. Existing approaches include the scale-based approach [165, 168] and the metrics-based approach [166], etc. However, these approaches are qualitative (relying on interpretation of description of a system) and do not discriminate between behaviour types. It is proposed that a more appropriate approach should comprise both qualitative and quantitative (as a way of assigning magnitude or value to the description and classification of systems) measures. According to Hawthorne [177], such a method of measuring autonomicity would be hugely beneficial as new autonomic solutions could be quantifiably substantiated rather than as an abstract quality. According to the findings of the background study (see Chapter 2), there is a lack of a quantitative approach for assessing autonomic systems. Chapter 7 presents a novel quantitative technique for measuring LoA along several dimensions of autonomic system self-* functionalities. This technique is robust as it is based on the functionalities of systems, making it possible to be tailored to suit the needs of any application domain.

A system is better defined by its functionalities, and so measuring the LoA of autonomic systems without a reference to autonomic functionalities would be inaccurate. In the proposed functionality-based LoA measurement, a typical autonomic system is defined by some core autonomic functionalities and LoA is measured with respect to these functionalities. Each functionality is defined by a set of metrics. The metric values are normalised and aggregated to give the autonomic contribution of each functionality, which are then combined to yield a LoA value for an autonomic system.

The proposed approach is in two forms: the specific case approach and the generic case approach. The specific case approach works perfectly well in cases where functionalities are orthogonal and for specific systems of a limited (fixed) number of functionalities (e.g., the self-CHOP functionalities). The generic case approach is used to demonstrate a generic case instance where functionalities are not necessarily orthogonal and where systems are defined by *n* number of autonomic functionalities (e.g., the self-* functionalities). It has been shown, with examples, how this approach can flexibly adapt existing qualitative approaches (e.g., the scale-based approach) to enable qualitative interpretation of LoA results. This new approach is sufficiently more sophisticated than existing approaches in a number of ways:

- It is the only approach that ties down LoA to a numeric value;
- It takes into account individual weights for metrics and functionalities;
- It is generic and flexible in the sense that it is independent of the number of autonomic functionalities;
- It is also independent of the number of metrics used to measure each of the autonomic functionalities; and
- The numeric value is scaled always to a normalised value. If you do not normalise it, more dimensions of autonomicity will result in bigger scores which gives the wrong impression that the more metrics that are used, the higher the resulting autonomicity level. Normalisation provides the power to compare two different systems no matter the number of individual metrics.

The standardisation of a technique for the measurement of LoA will bring many quality-related benefits which include being able to compare alternative configurations of autonomic systems, and even to be able to compare alternate systems themselves and approaches to building autonomic systems, in terms of the LoA they offer. This in turn has the potential to improve the consistency of the entire lifecycle of autonomic systems and in particular links across the requirements analysis, design and acceptance testing stages.

8.7 Future work

It is important to note that while progress has been made in this work towards trustworthy autonomic systems, achieving the full goal of trustworthiness remains an open challenge that requires more research. A broad and general analysis of the autonomic computing research, in terms of identifying trends in the research, gives a thorough review of the state-of-the-art in trustworthy autonomics. Results show that trustworthy autonomics, which is essential to the success of autonomic computing, has received very little attention compared to other focus areas.

The identified challenges for future work include the study and standardisation of autonomic measuring metrics for different autonomic systems. The metrics definitions can be grouped or modularised (e.g., the standardised categorisation of unmanned systems in Reference [11]). This will involve looking at standardised ways of properly defining and generating autonomic metrics to strengthen the proposed LoA measurement approach. Another future challenge is to focus on improving the robustness of the proposed TrAArch. For TrAArch, this will include scaling the *DependabilityCheck* component to be able to provide mechanisms and instrumentations for emerging autonomics capabilities — ability to flexibly add more sub-components (e.g., predictive/learning sub-component). Also, of importance is verifying how results of this approach can vary in other contexts and seeing which factors could influence its adoption or not in practice. Another open challenge is interoperability, discussed in Chapter 6. The required effort here will include evaluating the nature and scope of the interoperability challenges for autonomic computing systems, identifying a set of requirements for a universal solution, and proposing a service-based interoperability approach to handle both direct and indirect conflicts in a multi-autonomic manager scenario.

These are only a few of the main open challenges. As technology evolves, leading to new complexities and issues, the trustworthy autonomic computing solutions will need to evolve too.

References

[1] Paul H. *Autonomic computing: IBM perspective on the state of information technology*. NY: IBM T.J. Watson Labs; 2001.

[2] Eze T., Anthony R., Walshaw C., Soper A. 'Autonomic computing in the first decade: trends and direction'. *The Eighth International Conference on Autonomic and Autonomous Systems: ICAS*; St. Maarten, The Netherlands Antilles, 2012.

[3] Truszkowski W., Hallock H., Rouff C, *et al.* '*Autonomous and autonomic systems: with applications to nasa intelligent spacecraft operations and exploration systems*'. London: Springer, XVII; 2010. p. 56.

[4] Schmidt A., Thews G. 'Autonomic nervous system' in Janig W. (ed.). *Human physiology*. 2 edn. New York, NY: Springer-Verlag; 1989. pp. 333–70.

[5] Tianfield H. 'Multi-agent based autonomic architecture for network management'. *Proceedings of IEEE International Conference on Industrial Informatics (INDIN)*; 2003. pp. 462–69.

[6] McCann J., Huebscher M. 'Evaluation issues in autonomic computing'. *Proceedings of Grid and Corporative Computing (GCC) Workshop, LNCS 3252*; Springer-Verlag, Birlin Heidelber, 2004. pp. 597–608.

[7] Kephart J.O., Chess D.M. 'The vision of autonomic computing'. *Computer*. 2003, vol. 36(1), pp. 41–50.

[8] Bantz D.F., Bisdikian C., Challener D., *et al.* 'Autonomic personal computing'. *IBM Systems Journal*. 2003, vol. 42(1), pp. 165–76.

[9] Hoi Chan, Segal A., Arnold B., Whalley I. 'How can we trust an autonomic system to make the best decision?'. *Second International Conference on Autonomic Computing (ICAC'05)*; Seattle, WA, USA, 2003.

[10] Hall J., Rapanotti L. 'Assurance-driven design in problem oriented engineering'. *International Journal On Advances in Intelligent Systems (IntSys)*. 2009, vol. 2, pp. 26–37.

[11] Shuaib H., Anthony R., Pelc M. 'A framework for certifying autonomic computing systems'. *Proceedings of the Seventh International Conference on Autonomic and Autonomous Systems: (ICAS)*; Venice, Italy, 2011.

[12] Kikuchi S., Tsuchiya S., Adachi M., Katsuyama T. 'Constraint verification for concurrent system management workflows sharing resources'. *Third International Conference on Autonomic and Autonomous Systems (ICAS'07)*; Athens, Greece, 2006.

[13] Yang L.T., Jin H., Ma J., Ungerer T. '*Autonomic and trusted computing*'. Berlin, Heidelberg; 2006. pp. 143–52.

[14] Anderson S., Hartswood M., Procter R., *et al.* 'Making autonomic computing systems accountable'. *Proceedings of the fourteenth International Workshop on Database and Expert Systems Applications (DEXA)*; 2003.

[15] Heo J., Abdelzaher T. 'AdaptGuard: guarding adaptive systems from instability'. *Proceedings of the sixth International Conference on Autonomic Computing (ICAC)*; Barcelona, Spain, 2009.

[16] Hawthorne J., Anthony R., Petridis M. 'Improving the development process for teleo-reactive programming through advanced composition'. *Proceedings of the Seventh International Conference on Autonomic and Autonomous Systems (ICAS*); Venice, Italy, 2011.

[17] Hawthorne J., Anthony R. 'A reconfigurable component model using reflection'. *Proceedings of the 2008 RISE/EFTS Joint International Workshop on Software Engineering for Resilient Systems*; Newcastle, ACM, 2008. pp. 95–100.

[18] Diniz A., Torres V., José C. 'A self-adaptive process that incorporates A self-test activity'. *Monografias em Ciência da Computação, number 32/09*; Rio – Brazil, 2009.

[19] Richards D., Taylor M., Busch P. 'Expertise recommendation: A triangulated approach'. *International Journal On Advances in Intelligent Systems (IntSys*). 2009, vol. 2, pp. 12–25.

[20] Anthony R.J. 'Policy-based autonomic computing with integral support for self-stabilisation'. *International Journal of Autonomic Computing*. 2009, vol. 1(1), p. 1.

[21] DySCAS Project 'Dynamically self-configuring automotive systems' in *Part of the portfolio of the embedded systems unit – G3 directorate general information society & media*;

[22] King T.M., Ramirez A.E., Cruz R., Clarke P.J. 'An integrated self-testing framework for autonomic computing systems'. *Journal of Computers*. 2007, vol. 2(9), pp. 37–49.

[23] IBM Autonomic Computing White Paper '*An architectural blueprint for autonomic computing*'. 2005.

[24] Salehie M., Tahvildari L. 'Autonomic computing: emerging trends and open problems' in *Workshop on the design and evolution of autonomic application software (DEAS*). St Louis Missouri USA; 2005.

[25] Kephart J. 'Autonomic computing: the first decade'. *Keynote at the 8th International Conference on Autonomic Computing (ICAC)*; Germany, 2011.

[26] Eze T., Anthony T., Walshaw C., Soper A. 'The challenge of validation for autonomic and self-managing systems'. *The 7th International Conference on Autonomic and Autonomous Systems (ICAS)*; Venice, Italy, 2011.

[27] Krupitzer C., Roth F.M., Pfannemuller M., Becker C. 'Comparison of approaches for self-improvement in self-adaptive systems'. *2016 IEEE International Conference on Autonomic Computing (ICAC)*; Wurzburg, 2016.
[28] Maggio M., Hoffmann H. 'Decision making in autonomic computing systems: comparison of approaches and techniques'. *8th International Conference on Autonomic Computing (ICAC)*; Karlsruhe, Germany, 2011.
[29] Alhaisoni M., Liotta A., Ghanbari M. 'An assessment of self-managed P2P streaming'. *5th International Conference on Autonomic Computing (ICAC), 2009*; Washington DC, USA, 2009.
[30] Mohamed M., Romdhani M., Ghedira K. 'MOF-EMF alignment'. *Third International Conference on Autonomic and Autonomous Systems (ICAS'07)*; Athens, Greece, 2007.
[31] Gjørven E., Eliassen F., Aagedal J. 'Quality of adaptation'. *The 2nd International Conference on Autonomic and Autonomous Systems (ICAS)*; CA, USA, 2006.
[32] Nami M.R., Bertels K. 'A survey of autonomic computing systems'. *Third International Conference on Autonomic and Autonomous Systems (ICAS'07)*; Athens, Greece, 2007.
[33] Klein C., Schmid R., Leuxner C., Sitou W., Spanfelner B. 'A survey of context adaptation in autonomic computing'. *The 4th International Conference on Autonomic and Autonomous Systems (ICAS)*; Gosier, Guadeloupe, 2008.
[34] Khalid A., Haye M.A., Khan M.J., Shamail S. 'Survey of frameworks, architectures and techniques in autonomic computing'. *The 5th International Conference on Autonomic and Autonomous Systems (ICAS)*; Karlsruhe, Germany, 2009.
[35] Higgins F., Tomlinson A., Martin K.M. 'Survey on security challenges for swarm robotics'. *The 5th International Conference on Autonomic and Autonomous Systems (ICAS)*; Karlsruhe, Germany, 2009.
[36] Ding J., Cao R., Saravanan I., Morris N., Stewart C. 'Characterizing service level objectives for cloud services: realities and myths'. *2019 IEEE International Conference on Autonomic Computing (ICAC)*; Umea, Sweden, 2019.
[37] Musunoori S., Horn G., Eliassen F., Mourad A. 'On the challenge of allocating service based applications in a grid environment'. *Proceedings of the second International Conference on Autonomic and Autonomous Systems (ICAS)*; California, USA, 2006.
[38] Ranganathan A., Campbell R. 'Self-optimization of task execution in pervasive computing environments'. *Proceedings of the second International Conference on Autonomic Computing (ICAC)*; Seattle, USA, 2005.
[39] Bonino D., Bosca A., Corno F. 'An agent based autonomic semantic platform'. *Proceedings of the first International Conference on Autonomic Computing (ICAC)*; New York, USA, 2004.

[40] Menasc′e D., Bennani M. 'Autonomic virtualized environments'. *Proceedings of the second International Conference on Autonomic and Autonomous Systems (ICAS)*; California, USA, 2006.

[41] Bennani M., Menasc′e D.I. 'Resource allocation for autonomic data centers using analytic performance models'. *Proceeding of the second International Conference on Autonomic Computing (ICAC)*; Seattle, USA, 2005.

[42] Lee C., Kim H. 'A part release considering tool scheduling and dynamic tool allocation in flexible manufacturing systems'. *Proceedings of the second International Conference on Autonomic and Autonomous Systems (ICAS)*; California, USA, 2006.

[4] Anthony R.J. 'Policy-centric integration and dynamic composition of autonomic computing techniques'. *Proceedings of the fourth International Conference on Autonomic Computing (ICAC)*; Florida, USA, 2007.

[5] Bahati R.M., Bauer M.A., Vieira E.M. 'Adaptation strategies in policy-driven autonomic management'. *Third International Conference on Autonomic and Autonomous Systems (ICAS'07)*; Athens, Greece, 2007.

[45] Stehle E., Shevertalov M., deGrandis P., Mancoridis S., Kam M. 'Perception of utility in autonomic voip systems'. *International Journal On Advances in Intelligent Systems (IntSys)*. 2009, vol. 2, pp. 92–106.

[46] Perez J., Germain-Renaud C., Loomis C. 'Utility-based reinforcement learning for reactive grids'. *Proceedings of the fifth International Conference on Autonomic Computing (ICAC)*; Illinois, USA, 2008.

[47] Yu T.-J., Lai K.R., Lin M.-W., Kao B.-R. 'A fuzzy constraint-directed autonomous learning to support agent negotiation'. *Third International Conference on Autonomic and Autonomous Systems (ICAS'07)*; Athens, Greece, 2007.

[48] Xu J., Zhao M., Fortes J., Carpenter R., Yousif M. 'On the use of fuzzy modeling in virtualized data center management'. *Proceedings of the fourth International Conference on Autonomic Computing (ICAC)*; Florida, USA, 2007.

[49] Eze T., Anthony R. 'Dead-zone logic in autonomic systems'. *2014 IEEE Conference on Evolving and Adaptive Intelligent Systems (EAIS)*; Linz, Austria, 2014.

[50] Benoit D.G. 'Performance diagnosis for changing workloads'. *Third International Conference on Autonomic and Autonomous Systems (ICAS'07)*; Athens, Greece, 2007.

[51] Calinescu R. 'Implementation of a generic autonomic framework'. *Proceedings of the fourth International Conference on Autonomic and Autonomous Systems (ICAS)*; Gosier, Guadeloupe, 2008.

[52] Ghanbari S., Soundararajan G., Chen J., Amza C. 'Adaptive learning of metric correlations for temperature-aware database provisioning'. *Proceedings of the fourth International Conference on Autonomic Computing (ICAC)*; Florida, USA, 2007.

[53] Kusic D., Kephart J.O., Hanson J.E., Kandasamy N., Jiang G. 'Power and performance management of virtualized computing environments via

lookahead control'. *Proceedings of the fifth International Conference on Autonomic Computing (ICAC)*; Illinois, USA, 2008.

[54] Moore J., Chase J.S., Ranganathan P. 'Weatherman: automated, online and predictive thermal mapping and management for data centers'. *Proceeding of the Third International Conference on Autonomic Computing (ICAC)*; Dublin, Ireland, 2006.

[55] Toure M., Stolf P., Hagimont D., Broto L. 'Large scale deployment'. *Proceedings of the sixth International Conference on Autonomic and Autonomous Systems (ICAS)*; Cancun, Mexico, 2010.

[56] Wang C., Schwan K., Talwar V., Eisenhauer G., Hu L., Wolf M. 'A flexible architecture integrating monitoring and analytics for managing large-scale data centers'. *Proceedings of the eighth International Conference on Autonomic Computing (ICAC)*; Karlsruhe, Germany, 2011.

[57] Zhang H., Jiang G., Yoshihira K., Chen H., Saxena A. 'Resilient workload manager: taming bursty workload of scaling internet applications'. *Proceedings of the sixth International Conference on Autonomic Computing (ICAC)*; Barcelona, Spain, 2009.

[58] Nou R., Torres J. 'Heterogeneous qos resource manager with prediction'. *Proceedings of the Fifth International Conference on Autonomic and Autonomous Systems (ICAS)*; Karlsruhe, Germany, 2009.

[59] Ramachandran V., Gupta M., Sethi M., Chowdhury S.R. 'Determining configuration parameter dependencies via analysis of configuration data from multi-tiered enterprise applications'. *Proceedings of the sixth International Conference on Autonomic Computing (ICAC)*; Barcelona, Spain, 2011.

[60] Zheng Z., Yu L., Lan Z., Jones T. '3-dimensional root cause diagnosis via co-analysis'. *Proceedings of the ninth International Conference on Autonomic Computing (ICAC)*; California,USA, 2011.

[61] Anthony R., Pelc M., Shauib H. 'The interoperability challenge for autonomic computing'. *Proceedings of the third International Conference on EMERGING Network Intelligence (EMERGING)*; Lisbon, Portugal, 2011.

[62] Beran B., Valentine D., Zaslavsky I., Jonathan S., Cox D., McGee J. 'Web services solutions for hydrologic data access and cross-domain interoperability'. *International Journal On Advances in Intelligent Systems (IntSys)*. 2009, vol. 2, pp. 317–24.

[63] Huang S., Liang S., Fu S., Shi W., Tiwari D., Chen H. 'Characterizing disk health degradation and proactively protecting against disk failures for reliable storage systems'. *The 16th International Conference on Autonomic Computing (ICAC)*; Umea, Sweden, 2019.

[64] Trotter M., Wood T., Hwang J. 'Forecasting a storm: divining optimal configurations using genetic algorithms and supervised learning'. *The 16th International Conference on AutonomicComputing (ICAC)*; Umea, Sweden, 2019.

[65] Sun H., Birke R., Binder W., Bjorkqvist M., Chen L.Y. 'AccStream: accuracy-aware overload management for stream processing systems'. *The*

14th International Conference on AutonomicComputing (ICAC); Columbus, OH, USA, 2017.

[66] Poghosyan A.V., Harutyunyan A.N., Grigoryan N.M. 'Compression for time series databases using independent and principal component analysis'. *The 14th International Conference on Autonomic Computing (ICAC)*; Columbus, OH, USA, 2017.

[67] Lee G.J., Fortes J.A.B. 'Hierarchical self-tuning of concurrency and resource units in data-analytics frameworks'. *The 14th International Conference on Autonomic Computing (ICAC)*; Columbus, OH, USA, 2017.

[68] Balasubramanian S., Ghosal D., Balasubramanian Sharath K.N, *et al.* 'Autotuned publisher in a pub/sub system: design and performance evaluation'. *The 15th International Conference on Autonomic Computing (ICAC)*; Trento, 2018.

[69] Mehta A., Elmroth E. 'Distributed cost-optimized placement for latency-critical applications in heterogeneous environments'. *The 15th International Conference on Autonomic Computing (ICAC)*; Trento, Italy, 2018.

[70] Riley I., Gamble R. 'Using system profiling for effective degradation detection'. *The 15th International Conference on Autonomic Computing (ICAC)*; Trento, Italy, 2018.

[71] Larsson L., Tarneberg W., Klein C., Elmroth E. 'Quality-elasticity: improved resource utilization, throughput, and response times via adjusting output quality to current operating conditions'. *The 16th International Conference on Autonomic Computing (ICAC)*; Umea, Sweden, 2019.

[72] Adiththan A., Ravindran K., Ramesh S. 'Management of qos-oriented adaptation in automobile cruise control systems'. *The 14th International Conference on Autonomic Computing (ICAC)*; Columbus, Ohio-USA, 2017.

[73] Sliem M., Salmi N., Ioualalen M. 'Using performance modelling for autonomic resource allocation strategies analysis'. *The 10th International Conference on Autonomic and Autonomous Systems (ICAS)*; Chamonix, France, 2014.

[74] Hadded L., Tata S. 'Efficient resource allocation for autonomic service-based applications in the cloud'. *The 15th International Conference on Autonomic Computing (ICAC)*; Trento, Italy, 2018.

[75] Barlaskar E., Dichev K., Kilpatrick P., Spence I., Nikolopoulos D.S. 'Supporting cloud iaas users in detecting performance-based violation for streaming applications'. *The 15th International Conference on Autonomic Computing (ICAC)*; Trento, Italy, 2018.

[76] Baylov K., Petrova-Antonova D., Dimov A. 'Platform for autonomous service composition'. *The 11th International Conference on Autonomic and Autonomous Systems (ICAS)*; Rome, Italy, 2015.

[77] Orleans L., Zimbrao da Silva G. 'QoS-aware scale up on iaas clouds'. *The 12th International Conference on Autonomic and Autonomous Systems (ICAS)*; Lisbon, Portugal, 2016.

[78] Maroulis S., Zacheilas N., Kalogeraki V. 'ExpREsS: energy efficient scheduling of mixed stream and batch processing workloads'. *The 14th International Conference on Autonomic Computing (ICAC)*; Columbus, Ohio-USA, 2017.

[79] Krzywda J., Ali-Eldin A., Wadbro E., Ostberg P.-O., Elmroth E. 'ALPACA: application performance aware server power capping'. *The 15th International Conference on Autonomic Computing (ICAC)*; Trento, Italy, 2018.

[80] Malla S., Christensen K. 'Reducing power use and enabling oversubscription in multi-tenant data centers using local price'. *The 14th International Conference on Autonomic Computing (ICAC)*; Columbus, Ohio-USA, 2017.

[81] Schmitt N., Ifflander L., Bauer A., Kounev S. 'Online power consumption estimation for functions in cloud applications'. *The 16th International Conference on Autonomic Computing (ICAC)*; Umea, Sweden, 2019.

[82] Imes C., Zhang H., Zhao K., Hoffmann H. 'CoPPer: soft real-time application performance using hardware power capping'. *The 16th International Conference on Autonomic Computing (ICAC)*; Umea, Sweden, 2019.

[83] Safieddine I., de Palma N. 'Efficient management of cooling systems in green datacenters'. *The 11th International Conference on Autonomic and Autonomous Systems (ICAS)*; Rome, Italy, 2015.

[84] Srivastava B., Bigus J., Schlosnagle D. 'Bringing planning to autonomic applications with ABLE'. *The 1st International Conference on Autonomic Computing (ICAC)*; New York, USA, 2004.

[85] Topalova I., Radoyska P. 'Adaptive control of traffic congestion with neuro-fuzzy based weighted random early detection'. *The 15th International Conference on Autonomic and Autonomous Systems (ICAS)*; Athens, Greece, 2019.

[86] Tesauro G., Das R., Walsh W., Kephart J. 'Utility-function-driven resource allocation in autonomic systems'. *The 2nd International Conference on Autonomic Computing (ICAC)*; Seattle, USA, 2005.

[87] Walsh W., Tesauro G., Kephart J., Das R. 'Utility functions in autonomic systems'. *The 1st International Conference on Autonomic Computing (ICAC)*; New York, USA, 2004.

[88] Arellanes D., Lau K.-K. 'Workflow variability for autonomic IoT systems'. *The 16th International Conference on Autonomic Computing (ICAC)*; Umea, Sweden, 2019.

[89] Boubin J., Chumley J., Stewart C., Khanal S. 'Autonomic computing challenges in fully autonomous precision agriculture'. *The 16th International Conference on Autonomic Computing (ICAC)*; Umea, Sweden, 2019.

[90] Mahabhashyam S., Gautam N. 'Dynamic resource allocation of shared data centers supporting multiclass requests'. *The 1st International Conference on Autonomic Computing (ICAC)*; New York, USA, 2004.

[91] David V., Nikolai I. 'A reinforcement learning framework for dynamic resource allocation: first results'. *The 2nd International Conference on Autonomic Computing (ICAC)*; Seattle, USA, 2005.

[92] Das R., Kephart J., Whalley I., Vytas P. 'Towards commercialization of utility-based resource allocation'. *The 3rd International Conference on Autonomic Computing (ICAC)*; Dublin, Ireland, 2006.
[93] Bu X., Rao J., Xu C.-Z. 'CoTuner: A framework for coordinated auto-configuration of virtualized resources and appliances'. *The 7th International Conference on Autonomic Computing (ICAC)*; Washington, USA, 2010.
[94] Anthony R.J., Pelc M., Byrski W. 'Context-aware reconfiguration of autonomic managers in real-time control applications'. *The 7th International Conference on Autonomic Computing (ICAC)*; Washington, USA, 2010.
[95] Gaudin B., Vassev E.I., Nixon P., Hinchey M. 'A control theory based approach for self-healing of un-handled runtime exceptions'. *The 8th International Conference on Autonomic Computing (ICAC)*; Germany, 2011.
[96] Hachemi Bendahmane E., Dillenseger B., Moreaux P. 'Introduction of self optimization features in a selfbenchmarking architecture'. *The 7th International Conference on Autonomic and Autonomous Systems (ICAS)*; Venice, Italy, 2011.
[97] He R., Lacoste M., Leneutre J. 'A policy management framework for self-protection of pervasive systems'. *The 6th International Conference on Autonomic and Autonomous Systems (ICAS)*; Cancun, Mexico, 2010.
[98] Gupta A., Kalé L.V. 'Optimizing VM placement for HPC in the cloud'. *The 9th International Conference on Autonomic Computing (ICAC)*; San Jose, USA, 2012.
[99] Hu L., Schwan K., Gulati A., Zhang J., Wang C. 'Net-cohort: detecting and managing VM ensembles in virtualized data centers'. *The 9th International Conference on Autonomic Computing (ICAC)*; San Jose, USA, 2012.
[100] Campello D., Crespo C., Verma A., Rangaswami R., Jayachandran P. 'Coriolis: scalable VM clustering in clouds'. *The 10th International Conference on Autonomic Computing (ICAC)*; San Jose, USA, 2013.
[101] Delimitrou C., Bambos N., Kozyrakis C. 'QoS-aware admission control in heterogeneous datacenters'. *The 10th International Conference on Autonomic Computing (ICAC)*; San Jose, USA, 2013.
[102] Ayadi I., Simoni N., Diaz G. 'QoS-aware component for cloud computing'. *The 9th International Conference on Autonomic and Autonomous Systems (ICAS)*; Lisbon, Portugal, 2013.
[103] Gadafi A., Broto L., Sayah A., Hagimont D., Depalma N. 'Autonomic energy management in a replicated server system'. *The 6th International Conference on Autonomic and Autonomous Systems (ICAS)*; Cancun, Mexico, 2010.
[104] Eze T., Anthony R., Soper A., Walshaw C. 'A technique for measuring the level of autonomicity of self-managing systems'. *The 8th International Conference on Autonomic and Autonomous Systems (ICAS)*; Maarten, Netherlands Antilles, 2012.

[105] Kutare M., Eisenhauer G., Wang C., Schwan K., Talwar V., Wolf M. 'Monalytics: online monitoring and analytics for managing large scale data centers'. *Proceedings of the seventh International Conference on Autonomic Computing (ICAC)*; Washington DC, USA, 2010.

[106] Jones D., Keeney J., Lewis D., O'Sullivan D. 'Knowledge delivery mechanism for autonomic overlay network management'. *The 6th International Conference on Autonomic Computing (ICAC)*; Barcelona, Spain, 2009.

[107] Kephart J.O., Chan H., Das R., *et al.* 'Coordinating multiple autonomic managers to achieve specified power-performance tradeoffs'. *Proceedings of the fourth International Conference on Autonomic Computing (ICAC)*; Florida, USA, 2007.

[108] Autefage V., Chaumette S., Magoni D. 'A mission-oriented service discovery mechanism for highly dynamic autonomous swarms of unmanned systems'. *The 12th International Conference on Autonomic Computing (ICAC)*; Grenoble, France, 2015.

[109] Hadj R.B., Chollet S., Lalanda P., Hamon C. 'Sharing devices between applications with autonomic conflict management'. *The 13th International Conference on Autonomic Computing (ICAC)*; Würzburg, Germany, 2016.

[110] Javadi S.A., Gandhi A. 'DIAL: reducing tail latencies for cloud applications via dynamic interference-aware load balancing'. *The 14th International Conference on Autonomic Computing (ICAC)*; Columbus, Ohio-USA, 2017.

[111] Tsarev A., Skobelev P., Ochkov D. 'Effective interaction in asynchronous multi-agent environments for supply scheduling in real-time'. *The 11th International Conference on Autonomic and Autonomous Systems (ICAS)*; Rome, Italy, 2015.

[112] Naidoo N., Bright G. 'Support vector machine learning in multi-robot teams'. *The 11th International Conference on Autonomic and Autonomous Systems (ICAS)*; Rome, Italy, 2015.

[113] Mishra N., Lafferty J.D., Hoffmann H. 'ESP: A machine learning approach to predicting application interference'. *The 14th International Conference on Autonomic Computing (ICAC)*; Columbus, Ohio-USA, 2017.

[114] Page V., Webster M., Fisher M., Jump M. 'Towards a methodology to test uavs in hazardous environments'. *The 15th International Conference on Autonomic and Autonomous Systems (ICAS)*; Athens, Greece, 2019.

[115] Kikuchi S., Tsuchiya S., Adachi M., Katsuyama T. 'Policy verification and validation framework based on model checking approach'. *The 4th International Conference on Autonomic Computing (ICAC)*; Florida, USA, 2007.

[116] Landauer C., Bellman K.L. 'An architecture for self-awareness experiments'. *The 14th International Conference on Autonomic Computing (ICAC)*; Columbus, Ohio-USA, 2017.

[117] Kantert J., Tomforde S., von Zengen G., Weber S., Wolf L., Muller-Schloer C. 'Improving reliability and reducing overhead in low-power sensor networks using trust and forgiveness'. *The 13th International Conference on Autonomic Computing (ICAC)*; Würzburg, Germany, 2016.

[118] Eze T., Anthony R. 'Stigmergic interoperability for autonomic systems: managing complex interactions in multi-manager scenarios'. *IEEE SAI Computing Conference (SAI)*; London, UK, 2016.

[119] Brown R. *Exponential smoothing for predicting demand.* Arthur D Little Inc; 1956.

[120] Hyndman R., Athanasopoulos G. 'Forecasting: principles and practice' in *OTexts*. 2nd edition; 2018.

[121] Shmueli G., Lichtendahl K. *Practical time series forecasting with R: A hands-on guide*. 2nd edition. Axelrod Schnall Publishers; 2016.

[122] Ravinder H.V. 'Determining the optimal values of exponential smoothing constants – does solver really work?'. *American Journal of Business Education (AJBE)*. 2019, vol. 9(1), pp. 1–14.

[123] Ravinder H.V. 'Forecasting with exponential smoothing whats the right smoothing constant?'. *Review of Business Information Systems (RBIS)*. 2019, vol. 17(3), pp. 117–26.

[124] Prestwich S.D. 'Tuning forecasting algorithms for black swans'. *IFAC-PapersOnLine*. 2019, vol. 52(13), pp. 1496–501.

[125] Karmaker C. 'Determination of optimum smoothing constant of single exponential smoothing method: A case study'. *International Journal of Research in Industrial Engineering*. 2017.

[126] Dhali M.N., Barman N., Hasan M.B. 'Determination of optimal smoothing constants for holt - winter's multiplicative method'. *Dhaka University Journal of Science*. 2016, vol. 67(2), pp. 99–104.

[127] Theraulaz G., Bonabeau E. 'A brief history of stigmergy'. *Artificial Life*. 1999, vol. 5(2), pp. 97–116.

[128] Heylighen F. 'Stigmergy as a universal coordination mechanism: components, varieties andapplications' in *Cognitive systems research - human-human stigmergy*. Vol. 38. Elsevier; 2016. pp. 1–13.

[129] Lewis T.G., Marsh L. 'Human stigmergy: theoretical developments and new applications'. *Cognitive Systems Research*. 2016, vol. 38, pp. 1–3.

[130] Rubenstein M., Cornejo A., Nagpal R. 'Robotics. programmable self-assembly in a thousand-robot swarm'. Science. 2014, vol. 345(6198), pp. 795–99.

[131] Berlinger F., Gauci M., Nagpal R. 'Implicit coordination for 3D underwater collective behaviors in a fish-inspired robot swarm'. *Science Robotics*. 2021, vol. 6(50), eabd8668.

[132] O'Reilly G., Ehlers E. 'Synthesizing stigmergy for multi agent systems' in *Lecture notes in computer science (LNCS)*. Vol. 4088. Springer; 2006. pp. 34–45.

[133] Hadeli K., Valckenaers P., Kollingbaum M., Brussel H. 'Multi-agent coordination and control using stigmergy' in *Lecture notes in computer science (LNCS)*. Vol. 2977. Springer; 2004. pp. 105–23.
[134] Ronen O., Allen R. 'Autonomic policy creation with singlestep unity'. *Proceedings of the second International Conference on Autonomic Computing (ICAC)*; Seattle, USA, 2005.
[135] Zuefle M., Bauer A., Lesch V., *et al*. 'Autonomic forecasting method selection: examination and ways ahead'. *The 16th International Conference on Autonomic Computing (ICAC)*; Umea, Sweden, 2019.
[136] Shopov V., Markova V. 'Deep learning with evolutionary strategies for building autonomous agents behaviour'. *The 15th International Conference on Autonomic and Autonomous Systems (ICAS)*; 2019.
[137] Ramirez Y.M., Podolskiy V., Gerndt M. 'Capacity-driven scaling schedules derivation for coordinated elasticity of containers and virtual machines'. *The 16th International Conference on Autonomic Computing (ICAC)*; Umea, Sweden, 2019.
[138] Tantawi A.N., Steinder M. 'Autonomic cloud placement of mixed workload: an adaptive bin packing algorithm'. *The 16th International Conference on Autonomic Computing (ICAC)*; Umea, Sweden, 2019.
[139] Khan M.J., Shamail S., Awais M.M. 'Decision making in autonomic managers using fuzzy inference system'. *Proceedings of the Fifth International Conference on Autonomic and Autonomous Systems (ICAS)*; Karlsruhe, Germany, 2009.
[140] Ashby W.R. *Design for a brain*. Dordrecht: Chapman & Hall Ltd; 1960.
[141] Mundie J.J., Eichna D.M., DeLima M.D. 'Orientation outcomes in 2000 and beyond: an educational and financial partnership'. *Journal for Nurses in Staff Development*. 2002, vol. 18(5), pp. 241–47.
[142] Schneider F. 'Trust in cyberspace' in *Committee on information systems trustworthiness*. Washington, D.C: National Academy Press; 1998.
[143] Hamdi S., Bouzeghoub A., Gancarski A.L., Yahia S.B. 'Trust inference computation for online social networks'. *Proceedings of the twelfth IEEE International Conference on Trust, Security and Privacy in Computing and Communications (TrustCom)*; Melbourne, VIC Australia, 2013. pp. 210–17.
[144] Li H., Venugopal S. 'Using reinforcement learning for controlling an elastic web application hosting platform'. *Proceedings of the eighth International Conference on Autonomic Computing (ICAC)*; Karlsruhe, Germany, 2011.
[145] Brooks R. 'A robust layered control system for A mobile robot'. *IEEE Journal on Robotics and Automation*. 2011, vol. 2(1), pp. 14–23.
[146] Ashby W.R. *Design for a brain*. Dordrecht: Chapman & Hall Ltd; 1960.
[147] Parashar M., Hariri S. 'Autonomic computing: an overview' in *Lecture notes in computer science (LNCS)*. Vol. 3566. Springer; 2005. pp. 257–69.
[148] Das R., Kephart J.O., Lenchner J., Hamann H. 'Utility-function-driven energy-efficient cooling in data centers'. *Proceeding of the Seventh*

International Conference on Autonomic Computing (ICAC); Washington, DC, USA, 2005.

[149] Goiri I., Fito J.O., Julia F., *et al.* 'Multifaceted resource management for dealing with heterogeneous workloads in virtualized data centers'. *Proceedings of Eleventh IEEE/ACM International Conference on GRID Computing (GRID)*; Brussels, Belgium, 2010.

[150] Chase J.S., Anderson D.C., Thakar P.N., Vahdat A.M., Doyle R.P. 'Managing energy and server resources in hosting centers'. *ACM SIGOPS Operating Systems Review*. 2005, vol. 35(5), pp. 103–16.

[151] Berral J., Gavalda R., Torres J. '"Living in barcelona" li-BCN workload 2010' in *Technical report libcn10*. Barcelona, Spain: Barcelona Supercomputing Centre; 2010.

[152] Pretorius M., Ghassemian M., Ierotheou C. 'An investigation into energy efficiency of data centre virtualisation'. *Proceedings of International Conference on P2P, Parallel, Grid, Cloud and Internet Computing*; Fukuoka, Japan, 2010.

[153] Pretorius M., Ghassemian M., Ierotheou C. 'Virtualisation –securing a greener tomorrow with yesteryear's technology'. *Proceeding of the Twelfth IFIP/IEEE International Symposium on Integrated Network Management (IM 2011)*; Dublin, Ireland, 2011.

[154] Stone P., Veloso M. 'Multiagent systems: A survey from A machine learning perspective' in *Autonomous robots*. Vol. 8. Springer; 2000. pp. 345–83.

[155] Liu H., Iba H. 'Multi-agent learning of heterogeneous robots by evolutionary subsumption' in *Lecture notes in computer science (LNCS)*. Vol. 2724. Springer; 2003. pp. 1715–28.

[156] Hadeli K., Valckenaers P., Zamfirescu C, *et al.* 'Self-organising in multi-agent coordination and control using stigmergy' in *Lecture notes in computer science (LNCS)*. Vol. 2977. Springer; 2004. pp. 105–23.

[157] Chess D., Pacifici G., Spreitzer M., Steinder M., Tantawi A., Whalley I. 'Experience with collaborating managers: node group manager and provisioning manager'. *Proceedings of the second International Conference on Autonomic Computing (ICAC)*; Seattle, USA, 2005.

[158] Wang M., Kandasamyt N., Guezl A., Kam M. 'Adaptive performance control of computing systems via distributed cooperative control: application to power management in computing clusters'. *Proceedings of the third International Conference on Autonomic Computing (ICAC)*; Dublin, Ireland, 2006.

[159] Zhao M., Xu J., Figueiredo J. 'Towards autonomic grid data management with virtualized distributed file systems'. *Proceedings of the third International Conference on Autonomic Computing (ICAC)*; Dublin, Ireland, 2006.

[160] Khargharia B., Hariri S., Yousif M.S. 'Autonomic power and performance management for computing systems'. *Proceedings of the third International Conference on Autonomic Computing(ICAC)*; Dublin, Ireland, 2004.

[161] Dorigo M., Bonabeau E., Theraulaz G. 'Ant algorithms and stigmergy'. *Future Generation Computer Systems*. 2000, vol. 16(8), pp. 851–71.

[162] Durani V. *'IBM bladecenter systems up to 30 percent more energy efficient than comparable HP blades.'* IBM Press Release; 2006.

[163] Wang X., Lefurgy C., Ware M. 'Managing peak system-level power with feedback control' in *Research report RC23835*. IBM; 2005.

[164] Berral J.Ll., Goiri Í., Nou R., *et al.* 'Towards energy-aware scheduling in data centers using machine learning'. *Proceeding of the 1st International Conference on Energy-Efficient Computing and Networking (e-Energy)*; New York, USA, 2010.

[165] Proud R., Hart J., Mrozinski R. 'Methods for determining the level of autonomy to design into A human spaceflight vehicle: A function specific approach'. *Proceedings of the 2003 Performance Metrics for Intelligent Systems (PerMIS'03) Workshop*; Gaithersburg, MD, 2003.

[166] Clough B. 'Metrics, schmetrics! how the heck do you determine A UAV's autonomy anyway?'. *Proceedings of the 2003 Performance Metrics for Intelligent Systems (PerMIS'03) Workshop*; Gaithersburg, MD, 2003.

[167] Eze T., Anthony R., Walshaw C., Soper A. 'A generic approach towards measuring level of autonomicity in adaptive systems'. *International Journal on Advances in Intelligent Systems*. 2012, vol. 5, pp. 553–66.

[168] Sheridan T. *Telerobotics, automation, and human supervisory control*. Cambridge, MA, USA: The MIT Press; 1992.

[169] Huang H., Albus J., Messina E., Wade R., English W. 'Specifying autonomy levels for unmanned systems: interim report'. *Proceedings of SPIE Defense and Security Symposium, Conference 5422*; Orlando, Florida, USA, 2004.

[170] Huang H.-M., Gerhart G.R., Shoemaker C.M., *et al.* 'Autonomy levels for unmanned systems (ALFUS) framework: an update'. *Defense and Security*; Orlando, Florida, USA, 2005.

[171] Alonso F., Fuertes J.L., Martinez L., Soza H. 'Towards a set of measures for evaluating software agent autonomy'. *Proceedings of the eighth Mexican International Conference on Artificial Intelligence (MICAI)*; Guanajuato, Mexico, 2009.

[172] Huebscher M.C., McCann J.A. 'An adaptive middleware framework for context-aware applications'. *Personal and Ubiquitous Computing*. 2006, vol. 10(1), pp. 12–20.

[173] Barber K., Martin C. 'Agent autonomy: specification, measurement, and dynamic adjustment'. *Proceedings of the Autonomy Control Software Workshop at Autonomous Agents (Agents'99)*; Seattle, USA, 1999.

[174] Computing Research Association 'Four grand challenges in trustworthy computing'. *Proceedings of Second Conferences on Grand Research Challenges in Computer Science and Engineering, November 16–19*; 2003.

[175] Yang L., Ma J. *Introduction to the Journal of autonomic and trusted computing*. American Scientific Publishers; Available from www.aspbs.com/joatc.html 26/08/13

[176] White S., Hanson J., Whalley I., Chess M., Kephart J. 'An architectural approach to autonomic computing'. *Proceedings of the first International Conference on Autonomic Computing (ICAC)*; New York, USA, 2004.

[177] Hawthorne J. 2013. 'Investigation of a Teleo-Reactive Approach for the Development of Autonomic Manager Systems'. [PhD thesis in computing and mathematical sciences]. University of Greenwich

Index